C000132690

Eleanor Parker is Lecturer in Medieval English Literature at Brasenose College, Oxford. Dr Parker writes an acclaimed blog in her guise as 'A Clerk of Oxford', which was likened by Christopher Howse in the *Daily Telegraph* to 'orchards of golden apples'. In 2015 her blog won the Longman–*History Today* Award for Digital History, and she now writes a regular column for *History Today*.

'*Dragon Lords* offers an absorbing and authoritative account of the survival of Scandinavian legends and history in post-Conquest England. From dragon-ships to bears' sons, and sinners to saints, Eleanor Parker's nuanced readings of English, French, Old Norse and Latin sources unpack a wealth of unfamiliar and exciting stories. This beautifully written book succeeds in casting Viking invaders and settlers in an unexpected new light.'

– **Carolyne Larrington, Professor of Medieval European Literature, University of Oxford, author of *The Land of the Green Man: A Journey Through the Supernatural Landscapes of the British Isles* (I.B.Tauris, 2015)**

'*Dragon Lords* tells the fascinating and hitherto unknown story of how the Viking invasions of England were turned into myth and legend by those whom the Scandinavians raided and later ruled. Eleanor Parker vividly retells and contextualises this material (with its dragons, raven banners and unturning tides) while demonstrating at the same time a truly impressive command of Anglo-Scandinavian history and literature.'

– **Heather O'Donoghue, Professor of Old Norse, University of Oxford, author of *From Asgard to Valhalla: The Remarkable History of the Norse Myths* (I.B.Tauris, 2007)**

'In this welcome new book, Eleanor Parker sketches the fascinating and varied ways in which the people of medieval England reflected upon their Viking past – both real and imagined. Part literary study, part historical investigation and part folkloric inquiry, it makes a riveting and rewarding read.'

– **Levi Roach, Lecturer in Medieval History, University of Exeter, author of *Æthelred: The Unready***

DRAGON LORDS

THE HISTORY AND LEGENDS OF
VIKING ENGLAND

Eleanor Parker

BLOOMSBURY ACADEMIC
LONDON · NEW YORK · OXFORD · NEW DELHI · SYDNEY

BLOOMSBURY ACADEMIC
Bloomsbury Publishing Plc
50 Bedford Square, London, WC1B 3DP, UK
1385 Broadway, New York, NY 10018, USA
29 Earlsfort Terrace, Dublin 2, Ireland

BLOOMSBURY, BLOOMSBURY ACADEMIC and the Diana
logo are trademarks of Bloomsbury Publishing Plc

First published in Great Britain by I. B. Tauris & Co. Ltd in 2018
This edition published in Great Britain by Bloomsbury Academic in 2021
Reprinted 2021

Copyright main text © 2018 Eleanor Parker

Eleanor Parker has asserted her right under the Copyright,
Designs and Patents Act, 1988, to be identified as Author of this work.

For legal purposes the Acknowledgements on p. xiii constitute
an extension of this copyright page.

Cover image:
Carved dragon head post from the ship burial at Oseberg, c.850 AD
(Photo by Werner Forman/Universal Images Group/Getty Images)

All rights reserved. No part of this publication may be reproduced or
transmitted in any form or by any means, electronic or mechanical,
including photocopying, recording, or any information storage or retrieval
system, without prior permission in writing from the publishers.

Bloomsbury Publishing Plc does not have any control over, or responsibility for,
any third-party websites referred to or in this book. All internet addresses given
in this book were correct at the time of going to press. The author and publisher
regret any inconvenience caused if addresses have changed or sites have
ceased to exist, but can accept no responsibility for any such changes.

Every effort has been made to trace copyright holders and to obtain their permissions for the
use of copyright material. The publisher apologizes for any errors or omissions and would be
grateful if notified of any corrections that should be incorporated in future
reprints or editions of this book.

A catalogue record for this book is available from the British Library.

A catalog record for this book is available from the Library of Congress.

ISBN: PB: 978-1-3501-6535-9
ePDF: 978-0-8577-2447-2
eBook: 978-0-8577-3703-8

Typeset by Riverside Publishing Solutions, Salisbury, UK
Printed and bound in Great Britain

To find out more about our authors and books visit
www.bloomsbury.com and sign up for our newsletters.

CONTENTS

LIST OF ILLUSTRATIONS

Images are the author's own, unless stated otherwise.

TIMELINE OF KEY TEXTS
AND EVENTS

793	Viking attack on Lindisfarne
866–7	A Viking army captures York; Osberht and Ælla, kings of Northumbria, are both killed
869	Edmund, king of East Anglia, is killed by a Viking army
937	Æthelstan, king of Wessex, defeats an alliance of Norse and Scottish armies at the Battle of Brunanburh
941	Oda, son of a Danish settler, becomes Archbishop of Canterbury
c.985–7	Abbo of Fleury, *Passio Sancti Eadmundi*
1013	Svein Forkbeard, king of Denmark, invades England, but dies the following year
1016	Cnut becomes king of England
c.1040–2	*Encomium Emmae Reginae*
1055	Death of Siward, earl of Northumbria, Huntingdon and Northampton
1066	Harold Godwineson becomes king of England and is killed in battle at Hastings. Beginning of Norman rule over England
1076	Execution of Waltheof
1080s	Osbern of Canterbury, *Vita* and *Translatio* of St Ælfheah
1090s	Completion of Herman's *Miracula Sancti Eadmundi*

ACKNOWLEDGEMENTS

At the beginning of a book full of origin-myths and ancestry legends, it is a pleasure to thank those who have helped to make this book what it is. The research on which it is based was carried out at the University of Oxford, made possible by support from the Arts and Humanities Research Council and the Mellon Foundation. At every stage it has benefited immeasurably from the wisdom and generosity of Heather O'Donoghue; I owe the first idea for this project to her, among countless other things. Special thanks are due to Carolyne Larrington, Matthew Townend, Levi Roach, Laura Ashe, Alex Wright, and my colleagues, students and friends at Brasenose College, Oxford. This book is dedicated to my family, because I could not have written it without them. From Winchester to Wallingford, Crowland to Cuckhamsley, they have been with me every step of the way.

A NOTE ON NAMES

The Old Norse names of the people discussed in this book appear in various forms in the medieval texts, so to avoid confusion I have adopted standard anglicisations as far as possible: Cnut, Ivar, Olaf, in place of Knútr, Ívarr, Óláfr, and so on, except in some quotations. Medieval English writers were very far from being consistent in their treatment of Norse names; I have attempted to be so, but some inconsistencies will doubtless remain. Readers unfamiliar with Anglo-Saxon and Norse names may find it helpful to know that the letters ð and þ both represent 'th'.

INTRODUCTION

Why did the Vikings come to England? The causes which lay behind what we now call the Viking Age – the movement of peoples from Scandinavia to other parts of Europe between the eighth and the eleventh centuries – are still a subject of debate for modern historians, and medieval writers found the question no less challenging to answer. Today we look to economic, political or sociological explanations for this phenomenon, but medieval historians interpreted it very differently. The Anglo-Norman chronicler Henry of Huntingdon, looking back at the Viking Age from the perspective of the early twelfth century, believed that the defining characteristic of the Scandinavian invaders – the key difference between the Vikings and other conquerors of England, including the Romans, the Saxons and the Normans – was that they came to destroy, not to rule: 'the Danes swooped and rushed upon the land from all directions very frequently over a long period,' he says, 'not aiming to possess it but rather to plunder it, and desiring not to govern but rather to destroy everything.'[1] Like many medieval historians, Henry argued that the Vikings were permitted to do this as a divine punishment for the sins of the English, sent by God to chastise and purify a nation which had gone astray.

However, even medieval writers proposing such a view knew that Scandinavians in the Anglo-Saxon period did not only come to raid and destroy. Many settled in England, too, founding towns, holding lands, and ruling kingdoms in the north. Legends and stories recorded in a range of medieval sources from the eleventh and twelfth centuries onwards explore different interpretations of the Vikings (or 'the Danes', as they were usually called in medieval England). These narratives imagine why the Vikings came to settle in England, what they did there, and what effect they might have had on English society. Although many writers followed the common view of Viking invasion expressed by Henry of Huntingdon – that the Vikings were indiscriminate raiders, motivated by love of violence and greedy desire for plunder – there were also strong and enduring popular traditions running alongside this which told more complex stories about why Scandinavian invaders and settlers decided to come to England. In these narratives the Vikings come not just to raid but to resolve personal feuds, to intervene in English politics, to search for adventure, or to find a safe and peaceful home. Rather than simply plundering England and returning to Scandinavia with their spoils, the Vikings in these stories leave a lasting impact on the areas where they settle down, and the legends describe how their legacy can be traced in the landscape, in place-names, and in local history.

These stories seem to reflect a diversity of regional traditions about the Vikings existing in medieval England, especially in the north, the East Midlands and East Anglia. These parts of England had all been areas of Scandinavian settlement in the Anglo-Saxon period, and some narratives attempt to explore the role of Viking invasion in the history of these regions, to understand its causes and describe its effects. Although they generally have little historical basis, they can tell us fascinating things about how the Vikings were viewed in medieval England, especially by those who may have believed themselves to be in some sense their descendants. In this book we will trace the paths of these narratives, exploring how they imagine and interpret England's Viking history and the contribution of the Vikings to the culture and identity of different regions of England.

1. A group of warriors on a carved stone from Lindisfarne,
the island monastery attacked by the Vikings in 793

RAIDERS AND SETTLERS: THE FIRST VIKING AGE

It will be helpful to begin with a brief account of the historical
events – as far as we know them – which in time gave rise to
such a large and varied body of narrative, legend and myth. In
its entry for the year 787, the *Anglo-Saxon Chronicle* records
an event which it interprets as the beginning of a new phase
in English history: three ships from Scandinavia arrived at
Portland, on the coast of Dorset, and when the king's reeve
came out to meet them, they killed him. 'These were the first
ships of Danes which sought out the land of the English', the
chronicler observes, writing some time later and interpreting
this apparently isolated incident, with the benefit of hindsight,
as the start of something new and dangerous.[2] In 793 came an
attack on the island monastery of Lindisfarne, an event marked,
according to the *Anglo-Saxon Chronicle*, by the appearance of
ominous fiery dragons in the sky – a grave portent of disaster
to come.[3] These may not in fact have been the first Viking raids
in England, but in retrospect they seemed to the chroniclers to
mark the first signs of a new kind of threat. Intermittent waves
of Viking attacks followed over the next few decades.[4]

To begin with, these bands of raiders may have been fairly small, but in time they grew larger and more threatening. The situation began to escalate around the middle of the ninth century, and in 865 what the *Anglo-Saxon Chronicle* calls a 'great heathen raiding-army' descended on the country and swept through the kingdoms of Anglo-Saxon England one by one.[5] They conquered the region north of the Humber, captured the city of York amid much slaughter, and killed the Northumbrian kings Osberht and Ælla. In 869 they moved south to East Anglia, where they put King Edmund to a grisly death which led to him being venerated as a saint and martyr. The leaders of this fearsome army included several men who would later be grouped together as the sons of the semi-legendary Viking warrior Ragnar Lothbrok, and these men and their triumphs over Osberht, Ælla and Edmund feature very prominently in later medieval narratives about the Danes in England. Although there were many battles and many other notable leaders on both sides, the later English sources return again and again to the capture of York and the death of Edmund of East Anglia.

The ninth-century invasions were a sustained and almost overwhelming wave of attacks, and they had long-lasting consequences. These Viking kings never succeeded in ruling the whole of England; Alfred the Great managed to retain command of Wessex and defended it from the repeated attacks of a number of Viking armies. However, in the following decades large parts of the north and east of England remained under Scandinavian control, and members of these armies settled in England – they 'began to plough and support themselves', as the *Anglo-Saxon Chronicle* puts it.[6] They settled in what later became known as the Danelaw, a region stretching at its height from Essex in the south to the northern borders of Northumbria, and for a period in the early tenth century the north formed part of a Viking kingdom extending across the Irish Sea, with strongholds in Dublin and York.[7]

2. The Oseberg ship (Larry Lamsa)

The impact of this Scandinavian settlement in the north and east of England has long been recognised as an important factor in the early history of those regions, and there are many forms of evidence which reveal its lasting effects. The written sources provide few details, so historians have frequently disagreed about the size, dating and character of the settlement, but there is no question that it left a deep and permanent impression.[8] The distinctive place-names of northern England are perhaps the most obvious lasting legacy of these Scandinavian settlers: the classic examples include names ending in the Old Norse elements -by and -thorpe (Whitby, Derby, Scunthorpe) or incorporating Norse words, personal names or pronunciation (Skegness, Ormskirk, Skipton, etc.).[9] They left an impact too on the English language throughout the country, not only in northern dialects but in some of the most commonly used English words.[10] Material evidence casts light on the culture of the Scandinavian settlers and their descendants, revealing a complex picture of assimilation, cultural interaction, and religious and social change in the

3. A carving from Viking York: Sigurðr the Völsung
fights the dragon Fafnir

years after the settlement.[11] The pagan settlers rapidly adopted
Christianity, but they seem to have brought with them beliefs,
stories and traditions which correspond to those found in later
collections of Norse myth and heroic legend. In this period,
poetry in Old Norse was being composed and performed in
England, including skaldic verse, the intricate court poetry
of Scandinavian kings, and possibly also some of the poems
about Norse gods and heroes preserved in the *Poetic Edda*.[12]
Perhaps the most vivid evidence for the culture of Anglo-
Scandinavian England is the depiction of scenes from Norse
myth on sculpture from the north of England, mostly dating
to the ninth and tenth centuries: on these stones, Thor can
be seen fishing for the World-Serpent; Loki, bound, awaits
Ragnarök; Sigurðr, the greatest dragon-slayer of Norse legend,
fights the serpent Fafnir.[13]

It is possible – though ultimately unprovable – that oral
legends introduced from Scandinavia to England at this date
were the origins of some of the much later narratives about

Viking history that we will be looking at in this book.[14] The real story is, however, likely to be richer and more varied than this. The Scandinavian settlers who came to live in England brought with them a culture and a language closely related to those of the people among whom they settled, and interactions between the two groups must have been influenced by a range of factors, more complex than the available evidence allows us to reconstruct. Recent studies of Scandinavian settlement in England have increasingly emphasised the importance of avoiding overly simplistic assumptions about the construction of ethnic and cultural identity in this period, attempting to move away from the two opposing models which were previously the focus of critical debate: that the Scandinavian settlers either retained a distinctive ethnic identity for some time after settling in England, or quickly assimilated into the native population.[15] The evidence suggests that it is instead more accurate to speak of the development of an Anglo-Scandinavian society, a fusion and intermingling of the two cultures which is reflected in the linguistic, artistic and archaeological record. As Katherine Holman puts it:

Just as the law of the Danelaw was neither Scandinavian or English, so the stone sculptures produced there in the tenth and eleventh centuries, the artefacts found in archaeological excavations and the personal names used by the settlers all testify to something that was different from what had gone before but also, crucially, from what was found back in Scandinavia [...] The ethnicity in question is not Scandinavian, it is Anglo-Scandinavian.[16]

This is an important reminder of the complex issues of identity involved, not only in the first generations after the settlement but for later centuries too. Some medieval writers who talk about 'the Danes' in England view identity in binary and deterministic ways: a person is either Danish or English, and that origin influences how he or she behaves. However, many

of the narratives we will be examining in this book have a more
nuanced understanding of the factors which might influence
how individuals identify their own or their family's origins:
shifting political allegiances, intermarriage, and linguistic and
cultural fashion all affect what it meant to be Danish, or to call
someone Danish, in medieval England.

1016 AND 1066

In the first half of the tenth century, successive kings of Wessex
fought to extend their power over areas of England under
Scandinavian rule, and in the process paved the way for a united
kingdom of England, subsuming the formerly independent
kingdoms of Northumbria, Mercia and East Anglia. The political landscape, however, remained complex: the command of
northern England was contested by Norwegian, Scottish and
Anglo-Saxon kings, as well as the Norse kings of Dublin and
York.[17] When the West Saxon king Æthelstan won a famous

4. The Cuerdale hoard, one of the largest hoards of Viking silver
ever found (©Jorge Royan, CC BY-SA 3.0)

victory at Brunanburh in 937 – a battle which, as we shall see, became the subject of many later legends – his opponents were an alliance of Norse and Scottish armies led by Constantine of Scotland and Olaf Guthfrithson, Viking king of Dublin.[18] While these leaders fought over Northumbria and York, the Danish settlers of the Midlands seem to have increasingly become an accepted part of the English kingdom, culturally and legally distinct, yet under the rule of the kings of Wessex: in 942, a poem in the *Anglo-Saxon Chronicle* could praise Æthelstan's brother Edmund for recovering the 'Five Boroughs' of the Danelaw – Derby, Nottingham, Lincoln, Leicester and Stamford – and rescuing the Danes of those regions from the 'captive fetters' of the heathen Norsemen.[19]

At the end of the tenth century, Viking invasion once again became a pressing threat in the south of England. During the reign of Æthelred II ('the Unready'), England began once more to be raided by Scandinavian armies, under the control of leaders including the kings of Denmark and Norway and the Viking warlord Thorkell the Tall.[20] It is in this period that we begin to see a growing interest in exploring the earlier history of Danish invasion and settlement in England, with attempts to trace its patterns and understand cause and effect. Some examples of this interest, from both the Danish and English sides, will be discussed in Chapter 1; the triumphs of earlier Viking invaders, and the fates of the English kings they fought, had suddenly become intensely topical. In 1013, after two decades of raids, the Danish king Svein Forkbeard, accompanied by his son Cnut, finally embarked on a full-scale invasion of England. Within a few months they had driven Æthelred into exile, and Svein became the first Viking king to rule the whole of England. The 1013 conquest was the final stage of a long campaign of attrition, and it exposed something very interesting about the political situation of late Anglo-Saxon – or rather, Anglo-Scandinavian – England. At this date England had only been a unified country for a few generations, and when the Danes returned under Svein the kingdom fractured along old borders.

Immediately on arrival in 1013, Svein came to Gainsborough in Lincolnshire and met with the leaders of Northumbria and the Midlands, who submitted to his rule without a fight, and he accepted the submission of all the people north of Watling Street – the ancient road which formed the traditional boundary between northern and southern England, and in this case, it would seem, between 'Danish' and 'English' England. Svein seems to have recognised and exploited this political faultline: the *Anglo-Saxon Chronicle* says his army did not raid in the north, but only began to cause damage once they had crossed the border of Watling Street into Wessex and the south of England.[21] This seems to give us a glimpse into the Danes' perception of English territory, and perhaps also into the allegiances of the men who came to meet Svein and accepted him as king. No doubt opposition to Æthelred, as well as sheer expediency, played some role in their decision to submit to the Danes; but many of them might well have had Scandinavian ancestry, some generations back, and they probably knew that the Danes had ruled in northern England before. For various reasons, Anglo-Saxon written sources tend to privilege the perspective of Wessex and the south, and we can only catch occasional glimpses of how the situation may have been viewed from other parts of England, but in 1013 it seems possible that there may have been many people in the north who did not object to the return of the Danes.

After Svein's death early in 1014, his son Cnut had to fight for two years to recover his father's kingdom, which was defended by Æthelred and his son, Edmund Ironside. By the end of 1016, however, with Æthelred and Edmund both dead, Cnut had established himself as king of England. He went on to rule, apparently without much opposition, for nearly 20 years, and England became part of a Scandinavian empire ruled by a Danish king. This was a situation rich in potential for mutual cultural exchange, when England and the Scandinavian world were more closely entwined than ever before or since. Many of Cnut's Danish and Norwegian followers made their homes in

England, marrying into English families and holding lands all over the country, and in these years a Scandinavian presence can be traced not only in the former Danelaw, but throughout England, from Wessex to Northumbria.[22]

Cnut's two sons both died young, and his dynasty in England died with them. Æthelred's son Edward ('the Confessor') returned from exile in Normandy to restore the line of the West Saxon kings, and the period of Danish rule in England proved to be short-lived. It was not quickly forgotten: men and women from Anglo-Danish families continued to hold positions of influence during Edward's reign, and even for a short time after the Norman Conquest. However, the events of 1066, the year which saw one of the last serious attempts at a Viking invasion of England, led by the Norwegian king Harald Hardrada, also brought about a fundamental and irreversible change in England's relationship with Scandinavia. England's focus shifted towards the continent, and by the twelfth century the time of significant Anglo-Scandinavian interaction was increasingly a thing of the past. There are some exceptions: for a few years after the Conquest, Scandinavian involvement in English affairs remained a politically sensitive issue, as the Danes came to the aid of anti-Norman rebels, and Scandinavia became a place of refuge for English aristocrats displaced by the Conquest.[23] Some parts of England continued to have ongoing ties with Scandinavia through commerce and trade, and it is important to remember that in the later medieval period, especially in the north, contact with Scandinavia was not only the stuff of distant history and legend – we cannot understand the texts which deal with England's Viking past without taking into account the continuing links between the lands around the North Sea, and Iceland too.[24] As well as trade, there were also enduring connections between the English and Scandinavian churches; in the Anglo-Saxon period the English church had played an important role in establishing Christianity in Scandinavia, and those ecclesiastical networks continued throughout the Middle Ages.[25]

History becomes legend:
remembering the Vikings

The centuries following the Norman Conquest saw an explosion in interest in narratives about England's pre-Conquest history, in romance, historical writing and hagiography.[26] In many cases, writing about the history of Anglo-Saxon England necessarily involved attempts to interpret England's Viking Age past, and to understand the role that Scandinavian conquest and settlement played in national and regional history. It is these narratives about the Vikings in England – interpreting and reimagining the past from the perspective of decades and centuries later – which are the subject of this book. Although the history of Viking contact with England, briefly sketched in this introduction, spans more than three centuries at the most conservative dating – between the first Viking raids on northern England, conventionally dated to the end of the eighth century, and the end of the eleventh century – two periods in that lengthy history take on special prominence in post-Conquest English narratives: the invasions led by the (supposed) sons of Ragnar Lothbrok in the ninth century and by Svein Forkbeard and Cnut in the eleventh. As a result, there are huge swathes of Viking history which are hardly touched upon in this body of material. The narratives we will be considering deal primarily with England, only rarely mentioning the activities of the Vikings in Ireland, Scotland and other parts of Europe; they also tend to refer to all Scandinavians as 'Danes', whether or not they originated in Denmark. As 'Danes' is the term most commonly used in the English medieval sources, it will frequently be used in this book, and in many cases it will be best understood as not referring strictly to people from Denmark (or their descendants), but reflecting a later, Anglo-centric perception of Viking Age raiders and settlers from Scandinavia.[27]

It is important to note, too, that this retrospective interest in England's Viking Age history was by no means one-way. There are many medieval histories and sagas from Norway, Iceland,

Denmark and other parts of Scandinavia, mostly dating from the twelfth century and afterwards, which explore the activities of the Vikings in England, as well as in the rest of northern Europe and further afield.[28] Just as in England, medieval historians in Scandinavia and Iceland were well aware that the Viking Age had been a period of very close ties between England and the Scandinavian world, when invasion, trade and settlement provided many contexts for cultural interaction – particularly during the eleventh century, when England was part of Cnut's great North Sea empire. In discussing this period, Old Norse sagas sometimes include England as part of the region they call *Norðrlönd*, 'the northern lands', more commonly a term for Scandinavia.[29] Later writers also knew that this close political and cultural relationship had been fundamentally altered in the second half of the eleventh century, chiefly as a result of the Norman Conquest and the events of 1066 – a year which had momentous consequences for Scandinavia too, because of the death of the Norwegian king Harald Hardrada on an English battlefield. A famous passage from *Gunnlaugs saga*, written in Iceland in the thirteenth century but set several centuries earlier, describes this closeness in the time of Æthelred II, around the year 1000:

> Ein var þá tunga á Englandi sem í Nóregi ok í Danmǫrku. En þá skiptusk tungur í Englandi, er Vilhjálmr bastarðr vann England; gekk þaðan af í Englandi valska, er hann var þaðan ættaðr.[30]

> (At that time there was the same language in England as in Norway and Denmark. But the language in England was changed when William the Bastard conquered the country; French prevailed in England from that time forth, since he himself was French by birth.)

It is fascinating to see the author of this saga so conscious of the changes in the English language which had taken place between the late Anglo-Saxon period and his own day. In the saga, this detail of linguistic history is introduced in order to set the scene for a literary interaction – a story of an Icelandic poet composing a poem, in Old Norse, for an English king. It is one of numerous Norse sagas which imagine contact between Iceland, Scandinavia and Anglo-Saxon England, describing Scandinavian characters participating in English politics and fighting battles in England (often on behalf of Anglo-Saxon kings, as well as against them). These stories have varying amounts of historical plausibility, but they reflect a continuing interest in the relationship between England and Scandinavia; at times they also seem to be drawing on English oral or written sources about this period of history, providing details or perspectives which no longer survive from England, and so from time to time we will have cause to refer to these Norse sources as a comparison for the English material.

Almost as soon as the Vikings began to make an impact on England, legends and stories about them began to spread. The narratives we will look at may in some cases have originated as early as the ninth century, even if they were not written down until long after the Norman Conquest. We will begin, however, at the end of the tenth century, on the eve of Svein Forkbeard's conquest of England. This starting point has been chosen for two reasons. Firstly, this was a moment when past examples of Viking invasion and settlement were of the utmost contemporary relevance – when to write about the history of the Danes in England was a politically sensitive act, an intervention in a fraught and contentious debate about how to respond to Viking invasion. Secondly, it is intended to underline the significance of the Danish conquest, so often overshadowed by the events of 50 years later; the purpose is to emphasise the potential for continuity as well as change across the traditional boundary of the Norman Conquest, the complex processes of assimilation and accommodation which were at work in both Anglo-Scandinavian and Anglo-Norman England, and the extent to which literature in the second half of the eleventh century and afterwards drew on texts and traditions from before the Norman Conquest.[31]

For many of the medieval writers we will be looking at in this book, England's pre-Conquest history – including the history of the Scandinavian invasions – was a formative period in national and regional identity, which had shaped and influenced the country they knew. Beginning in the late Anglo-Saxon period, then, when Viking attacks were still a potent threat, we will see how the earliest waves of Viking invasion first became the subject of legend, and then how the questions of integration and cultural exchange which these stories dramatise again became pressing in the aftermath of another conquest by a foreign power in 1066. After this we will turn to the most capacious and widely circulated body of legend about the Danes in England: stories about the sons of Ragnar Lothbrok, which give various interpretations for their invasion of England, exploring their motives, their characters, and their different fates. We will then look at some narratives about the adventures of the Danish warrior Siward, earl of Northumbria, and the heroes Waldef and Hereward the Wake, and we will see how a long-standing belief among some medieval writers that the Danes had a legitimate claim to rule England became linked to one of the most popular heroes of medieval romance, the dragon-slayer, pilgrim and pious Norman knight Guy of Warwick. Then we will turn to stories about Havelok, the Danish king beloved in medieval Lincolnshire, and his foster-father Grim, the founder of Grimsby. Finally, we will explore how the Danes were remembered in English folklore, long after the end of the medieval period.

CHAPTER 1

'FROM THE NORTH COMES ALL THAT IS EVIL': VIKINGS, KINGS AND SAINTS, C.985–1100

The last decades of the tenth century saw an intensification of Viking activity in England, after a period of relative calm. From the 980s onwards England was again being raided by a number of Scandinavian armies at once, working separately or together, in search of plunder and, eventually, of conquest. The poem which has most often been used to exemplify literary representations of the Vikings in this tense period is *The Battle of Maldon*, which memorialises a battle fought between an English army and a force of Vikings on the coast of Essex in 991.[1] Although the English were defeated, the poem casts their loss in a heroic light: the conflict is framed as a national struggle against an army of Vikings, who are described as *wælwulfas* (96), 'slaughter-wolves' and *hæðene scealcas* (181), 'heathen warriors'.[2] They are a nameless, faceless band: the poem provides us with a great deal of information about the names, families and homes of many of the English warriors, from the high-ranking leaders of the army to the most humble foot-soldier, but not a single member of the Viking force is given a name. Since the leaders of the Viking army may well have included some prominent men, among them Svein Forkbeard, king of Denmark, this seems like deliberate and wilful ignorance – a poetic choice, a conscious decision to deny the Danes any kind of differentiating or individualising details.[3]

In this poem the leader of the English army, Byrhtnoth, famously returns a fiercely defiant answer to the Viking messenger who comes to demand money in exchange for peace: he offers the Danes spears instead of tribute, a rhetorical flourish we will encounter again. As he stands on the Essex shore, he calls the Vikings *brimmen* (49), 'seamen', creatures of the waters, and talks about defending *eþel þysne* (52), 'this homeland', linking the land on which the Vikings are encroaching to the very name of the English king – this *eþel*, his wordplay implies, cannot be anything other than *Æthelred's* land. The picture is

5. A modern statue of Byrhtnoth, killed fighting against the Vikings in 991, at Maldon in Essex

of a strong, united England standing behind Byrhtnoth, ready to repel the raiders who have come from the sea. His rhetoric is powerful, but even within the poem it proves to be futile: despite his threats, it is Byrhtnoth himself who falls in battle, the consequence of having allowed the Vikings too far onto the land. In later medieval narratives of this period, the poem's play on Æthelred's name was to be overtaken by another and less flattering pun: the king has gone down in history as the 'unready', since in Old English *Æthelræd* means 'noble counsel', and *unræd* is the opposite, 'bad counsel, lack of wisdom'. Modern historians have increasingly been kinder in their assessment of Æthelred's reign than their medieval counterparts,[4] but it is true that Æthelred and his counsellors were unwise or unlucky in most of their attempts to mount an effective response to the Viking threat. In the aftermath of the battle at Maldon, they decided to pay tribute to the Danes in the hope of encouraging them to stay away – the very policy scorned by Byrhtnoth in the poem. Nonetheless, attacks continued on and off for the next two decades.

The entries in the *Anglo-Saxon Chronicle* for these years record a catalogue of destruction, listing towns and manors throughout the country which were plundered and burned by the Danes.[5] But not all the devastation of these years was caused by the Vikings. In 1002, Æthelred gave an order that 'all the Danes who were among the English people' should be killed, apparently because he was afraid they were plotting against his life.[6] The order was to be carried out on St Brice's Day, 13 November, and

6. The gatehouse of Ramsey Abbey, all that remains of the medieval abbey where the first works on St Edmund were written in the tenth century

we know from a contemporary source what happened in one southern town: in Oxford, a group of Danes were pursued by the townspeople and took refuge in St Frideswide's church, on the site of what is now Christ Church Cathedral. Their pursuers set fire to the church, and it was consumed by the flames. As we will see, later medieval narratives of the period give prominence to St Brice's Day as a crucial moment in Æthelred's downfall and the rallying of the Danes.

In these years the history of earlier Viking invasions was now a matter of pressing relevance, and a growing interest in this history can be traced in various sources from the end of the tenth century. This was a period of flourishing in the cult of St Edmund of East Anglia, the most famous victim of the ninth-century Danish conquest, and in the closing decades of the tenth century the earliest important works on St Edmund were produced. In 985–7, while staying at Ramsey Abbey, the monk and scholar Abbo of Fleury wrote a *Passio Sancti Eadmundi*, providing the first authoritative account of Edmund's death at the hands of the Danes.[7] Within a decade or so Abbo's text was translated into English by the prolific homilist Ælfric, who explains the chain of transmission on which his account draws:

> Sum swyðe gelæred munuc com suþan ofer sæ fram sancte Benedictes stowe on Æþelredes cynincges dæge to Dunstane ærce-bisceope, þrim gearum ær he forðferde, and se munuc hatte Abbo. Þa wurdon hi æt spræce oþþæt Dunstan rehte be sancte Eadmunde, swa swa Eadmundes swurd-bora hit rehte Æþelstane cynincge þa þa Dunstan iung man wæs, and se swurd-bora wæs forealdod man. Þa gesette se munuc ealle þa gereccednysse on anre bec, and eft ða þa seo boc com to us binnan feawum gearum þa awende we hit on englisc, swa swa hit her-æfter stent.[8]

(In the days of King Æthelred, a very learned monk came from the south across the sea from St Benedict's monastery [Fleury], to Archbishop Dunstan, three years before he died; and the monk was called Abbo. They talked together until

Dunstan told the story of St Edmund, just as Edmund's
sword-bearer told it to King Æthelstan in the days when
Dunstan was a young man and the sword-bearer was a very
old man. Then the monk set down all the story in a book,
and afterwards when the book came to us a few years later
we turned it into English, as follows hereafter.)

This is a summary of Abbo's own preface, in which he describes
Dunstan telling the story of Edmund's death in his presence,
with tears flowing from his eyes, recounting what had been told
to him by Edmund's aged sword-bearer. Abbo's *Passio*, which
is dedicated to Dunstan, does not explain what prompted the
archbishop to recall this story, and only says that he decided
to write it down to prevent Dunstan's memories from being
forgotten. The association with Dunstan, the dynamic and influential Archbishop of Canterbury, and with Æthelstan, one of the
most glorious of Anglo-Saxon kings, gives Abbo's narrative an
authenticating pedigree. If it is accurate, it also provides a striking example of how information might be transmitted in oral
tradition across the course of more than a century,[9] and seems to
reveal a surge of interest in Edmund's story at two key moments
in the years between his death in 869 and the time of writing,
985–7: first at Æthelstan's court in the 930s, where Dunstan
supposedly heard the story from Edmund's sword-bearer, and
again, half a century later, in the reign of Æthelred. Both were
moments when the history of Viking invasion in England may
have seemed of particular contemporary relevance: Æthelstan
was celebrated for his victories over the Vikings, especially the
battle of Brunanburh,[10] while in the 980s Dunstan had good
reason to be interested in the resumption of Viking attacks.
Dunstan died in 988, and it was soon being said that he had
prophesied the return of the Vikings: the belief that he had
prophetic foreknowledge of the Danes' return is first mentioned in a series of lections for St Dunstan's feast composed
by Adelard of Ghent between 1006 and 1012.[11] Abbo's reference
to Dunstan recalling his memory of St Edmund's story suggests

7a. St Edmund's death depicted in a fourteenth-century Psalter
(British Library, Royal MS. 2 B VII, f. 277)

that Dunstan may indeed have taken an interest in this question
towards the end of his life.

The view of the Danes in Abbo's *Passio Sancti Eadmundi*
presents what was to become a very familiar picture – to some
degree, it is the canonical interpretation, to which many of the
later narratives we will look at are responding. Abbo tells how
the saintly King Edmund, virtuous, generous and just, attracts
the hatred of the devil, who sends agents to destroy him. These
are the Danes Ivar and Ubbe, later identified in English and
Scandinavian tradition as the sons of Ragnar Lothbrok. Abbo
attributes the evil inclinations of these villains to their northern
origins:

> [...] conatus est in exterminium adducere totius fines
> Britanniæ. Nec mirum, cum venerint indurati frigore suæ
> malitiæ ab illo terræ vertice, quo sedem suam posuit [...]
> [C]onstat, juxta prophetæ vaticinium, quod ab aquilone
> venit omne malum, sicut plus æquo didicere perperam passi
> adversos jactus cadentis tesseræ, qui aquilonalium gentium
> experti sunt sævitiam.

([they attempted] to reduce to destruction the whole
confines of Britain. And no wonder! seeing that they came
hardened with the stiff frost of their own wickedness from
that roof of the world where [Satan] had fixed his abode [...]
[I]t is proverbial, according to the prediction of the prophet,
that from the north comes all that is evil, as those have had
too good cause to know, who through the spite of fortune
and the fall of the die have experienced the barbarity of the
races of the north.)[12]

The peoples of the north are pagans, pirates, even cannibals,
Abbo explains, and nothing but evil can be expected from them;
they are the instrument of God's punishment against the wicked,
and a tool of the devil. He has biblical authority for this, alluding
to the words of the prophet Jeremiah: 'from the north shall an
evil break forth upon all the inhabitants of the land', a passage
often linked by early medieval writers to the Vikings.[13]

Abbo goes on to tell how Ivar and Ubbe descend on the
English coast with fire and destruction, and their terrible
crimes – pillage, rape, the murder of children – are committed
'from sheer love of cruelty'.[14] When the Danes reach East Anglia,

7b. St Edmund's death, from a fourteenth-century Book of Hours
(British Library, Yates Thompson MS. 13, f. 192)

7c. A fifteenth-century carving of Edmund, above the door of St Edmund's Church, Kessingland, Suffolk

7d. St Edmund's death, from a window in St Mary's Church, Bury St Edmunds

7e. A statue of St Edmund by Elisabeth Frink, near the site of the
abbey of Bury St Edmunds

Ivar demands that Edmund pay him tribute and become his
under-king, but Edmund scornfully refuses. He is seized by the
Danes and brutally murdered, shot through with arrows and
finally beheaded. The Danes hide his head in a wood – an act
Abbo ascribes to their pagan hatred for Christian burial – but
it is carefully guarded by a wolf until it is found by Edmund's
followers and rejoined to his body. These elements of the

story – Edmund's body covered with arrows, the severed head miraculously calling out to its rescuers, the protective wolf – became hugely popular aspects of the saint's iconography, widely depicted and repeated for many centuries to come.[15]

Abbo's text was an influential one, establishing the key features of the cult of a martyr who was to become one of the most celebrated English saints, as well as a prevalent interpretation of the actions and motivations of the Vikings. It casts the Danes as enemies of Christianity and as instruments of the devil, framing Viking attacks on England as a moral conflict between good and evil. The response to such a threat can never be political accommodation, or an acknowledgement that the Danes might have played any role in East Anglian history other than that of foreign enemy; they are fundamentally inimical to English Christian society, and so the resumption of Viking raids is to be interpreted, from the perspective of the late tenth century, as a continuation of this evil – rather than, for instance, an attempt to reconquer territory once under Danish rule.[16] In his English version of Abbo's *Passio*, Ælfric makes the relevance of this saint's death to his own time explicit, switching into the present tense when describing how 'þa deniscan leode ferdon mid scip-here hergiende and sleande wide geond land swa swa heora gewuna is' ('the Danish people came with a ship-army, raiding and slaying throughout the country, as is their wont').[17] Ælfric's grim aside underlines a strong perception of continuity between the ninth-century Danish invasion and his own time, more than a century after Edmund's death: this is the Danes' usual custom, their unpleasant but apparently innate habit. Ælfric does not repeat Abbo's comments on the iniquity of everything that comes from the north – this bitter remark serves as sufficient explanation for the Danes' behaviour.

Even in this tense period, however, the history of the Danes in England was also recognised to be a complex subject, which over the years had involved settlement and integration as well as violence. Fifteen years or so after Abbo produced his *Passio Sancti Eadmundi* while staying at Ramsey Abbey, the scholar

Byrhtferth, a monk of Ramsey who had been Abbo's pupil, wrote an account of St Oswald, the founder of the monastery.[18] Oswald was a major figure in the tenth-century English church: he was Archbishop of York and Bishop of Worcester until his death in 992, and he owed his high position in part to the patronage of his uncle Oda, who had been Archbishop of Canterbury between 941 and 958. Oswald and Oda were of Danish descent, and Byrhtferth begins his *Vita S. Oswaldi* by describing their ancestry. These two prominent churchmen, he says, were descended from a member of the same army which had killed St Edmund: 'Certain people say that [Oda's] father was one of the Danes who came with the ship-army of Ubbe and Ívarr: for that reason his father did not wholly seek to serve Christ'.[19] Byrhtferth goes on to tell how the young Oda, despite his pagan father's fierce opposition, begins to frequent Christian churches and seeks the protection of an English nobleman named Æthelhelm. Æthelhelm arranges for him to be baptised and educated, and in time Oda becomes a priest. His connection with Æthelhelm brings him into contact with the royal court, where King Æthelstan is impressed by his devotion to his patron and his holiness of life; he is made a bishop and then, in 941, Archbishop of Canterbury. In his turn, Oda supports the education of his young nephew Oswald, whose life is the main subject of Byrhtferth's *Vita*.

Although Byrhtferth tells us very little about the Danish family from which Oda and Oswald came, what he does say is important. His statement about their ancestry appears to be essentially correct: Oda's name is of Danish origin (Old Norse *Oddr*), as are the names of two of his probable kinsmen, Oscytel, Archbishop of York between 958/9 and 971, and Thurcytel, abbot of Bedford Abbey. The family had close links to East Anglia, where they were substantial landowners, and Oda seems to have taken a particular interest in the renewal and reorganisation of the church in the southern Danelaw.[20] The Danish origins of Oda and his family provide a suggestive glimpse – all too tantalising in its lack of detail – at the conversion of the ninth-century settlers to Christianity, a process which seems to have been remarkably rapid.[21] Within a generation of settling in England, the pagan Danish family of Oda and Oswald had produced some of the leading churchmen of the tenth century.

Equally interesting, however, is the fact that Byrhtferth chooses to record their ancestry, and to link them to the army of Ivar and Ubbe. Byrhtferth's tone here is slightly distancing, both in his dry understatement (Oda's pagan father 'did not wholly seek to serve Christ') and in his opening phrase 'certain people say' – a suggestion that he may have considered this legend rather than fact, attributing the information to popular discussion rather than any more authoritative source. He seems to indicate that the link between Oda and Oswald and the ninth-century Danish invasions was a subject of discussion around the turn of the millennium, in the same monastery where Abbo's account of St Edmund had been produced. For Byrhtferth, of course, the story of Oda's pagan origins and his adoption of Christianity provides a clear demonstration of the saint's youthful inclination to holiness, but the naming of Ivar and Ubbe also seems to be a deliberate link to the story of St Edmund: the pairing of these two names suggests that Byrhtferth took his information from Ramsey tradition, either orally or as recorded in Abbo's *Passio*, since other sources (including Byrhtferth himself in his *Historia Regum*) do not name Ubbe among the leaders of the army, but refer instead to Ivar and another brother, Halfdan.[22]

If Dunstan was recalling his memories of St Edmund in Abbo's hearing because the Danes were again becoming a threat, we might wonder whether Oda and Oswald's ancestry was under discussion for the same reason. It has been suggested that it may have been Oda and Oswald who encouraged the renewal of interest in St Edmund at Ramsey, because of their own family history: Antonia Gransden has argued that 'Oda might have fostered St Edmund's cult in expiation for his father's complicity', suggesting that Oswald may have commissioned Abbo's *Passio*.[23] Even if this was their motivation, however, there may have been more at work than the expiation of ancestral sins. Oda might have repudiated his pagan father, but he clearly had not blotted out all memory of his Danish ancestry, nor were those at Ramsey Abbey who discussed the history of Oda and Oswald's family attempting to suppress a link between their saintly patrons and the killers of St Edmund – quite the opposite. Ramsey Abbey seems to have been instrumental in both the renewal of Edmund's cult and in preserving information about Ivar and Ubbe: there is some reason to think that the first reference to these men as the sons of Ragnar Lothbrok occurs in a text whose origins lie at Ramsey Abbey at the end of the tenth century, which will be discussed in further detail in Chapter 2.[24] For Byrhtferth, the narrative of Oda's conversion provides a model for the integration of the descendants of Danish settlers into English society, through the adoption of Christianity and

8. A silver penny of King Cnut (York Museums Trust)

the generosity of their English neighbours. This is not the only moment in the text which shows an awareness of varying kinds of Scandinavian presence within England: later on, Byrhtferth gives a brief description of the city of York, where Oswald was archbishop, saying 'it is inexpressibly filled and enriched by the treasures of merchants, who come there from everywhere, and most of all from the people of Denmark' (*ex Danorum gente*).[25] This view of York as a distinctively Anglo-Scandinavian city is doubtless accurate, and this may have been why Oswald and his kinsman Oscytel, with their Danish connections, were appointed to the archbishopric;[26] but it also offers a nuanced and varied picture of the Danish presence in England, alongside more Jeremiah-quoting rhetoric about the peoples of the north and 'the accursed Danes'.[27] Oda and his family have often been interpreted by modern historians as a paradigmatic model of integrated Danish settlers, and perhaps their story was intended to be read in that way: for readers at Ramsey in the late tenth century, history may have seemed to provide reassurance that the Danes had been absorbed into England before, and might be so again.

ANGLO-DANISH HISTORY AND THE LITERATURE OF CNUT'S COURT

Byrhtferth wrote his *Vita S. Oswaldi* between 997 and 1002. Less than 20 years later, the Danes were ruling England. In the autumn of 1016, after years of bruising warfare, the English finally submitted to the young Danish king Cnut, who ruled until his death in 1035. Cnut's reign was a unique period of cultural and literary interaction between England and Scandinavia, when England formed part of a great North Sea empire hardly equalled before or since. At the height of his power Cnut was king of England, Denmark, Norway and parts of Sweden, and may also have had some authority over Scotland and Ireland. His court was based in England, though the king himself was often absent in Scandinavia, and it must have been frequented by people from across his empire and beyond, including Danes, Norwegians and Icelanders, as well as his Norman wife Emma and her followers.[28]

Cnut went to some lengths to present himself as a successor to previous English kings. In 1018, in a meeting at Oxford, an agreement was reached which declared that Cnut had 'established peace and friendship between the Danes and the English, and put an end to all their former enmity', and both English and Danes agreed to follow the law code of Edgar, Æthelred's father. The king's laws, like those of his Anglo-Saxon predecessors, continued to be issued in English, and during his journeys abroad letters to his people were promulgated in English in the king's name.[29] Cnut also won the support of the English church, and began to present himself as a model Christian king: he made overtures of reconciliation towards the church, becoming a generous patron of monasteries and devotee of English saints.[30]

At the same time, however, and juxtaposed with this display of continuity with the English past, Cnut and his court seem to have been acutely aware of the long history of Danish invasion and rule in England. This is evident from texts composed for Cnut and his wife in Old Norse and Latin, which in their different ways celebrate and commemorate the victories of Cnut's conquest and link them to a larger story about the Danish dynasty now ruling England. Like many Scandinavian kings, Cnut was a generous patron of poetry, and poems were composed for the king in Old Norse by skalds visiting his court in England.[31] These texts, which (since they require knowledge of the Old Norse language) must have been primarily aimed at the king's Scandinavian supporters, reveal some fascinating things about the culture of Cnut's court, casting light on how his followers remembered the conquest in which many of them would have participated. As Matthew Townend has shown, Cnut's patronage of Old Norse poetry continued throughout his reign, reaching its height in the late 1020s. 'There was no jettisoning of Norse traditions – whether suddenly or gradually – as his reign in England progressed', Townend argues, and the poems show Cnut as he wanted to be perceived: 'the gold-giving warrior-king, proud of his Danish origins and by no means metamorphosing into an honorary Englishman'.[32] These poems reveal that Scandinavian culture and literary traditions continued to be prized by Cnut's followers resident in England, but this was a hybrid Anglo-Scandinavian culture, which interacted with and adopted English practices. It has been demonstrated that the poems show some influence from Anglo-Saxon poetic style,[33] and they present Cnut as a Christian emperor, exploiting imagery drawn from both pagan mythology and Christian piety to praise the king;[34] his poets mention his close relationship with the church and his journey to Rome in 1027 as deeds which illustrate his imperial greatness. These poems were probably performed at the English court, but in a language and idiom most speakers of Old English would have found difficult to understand; they show Cnut as ruler of a great Scandinavian empire, simultaneously Christian monarch and triumphant Viking warlord.

9. Cnut (British Library, Royal MS. 14 B VI)

The skaldic corpus reveals that narratives of conquest played an important role in the literary culture of the Anglo-Danish court: stories of Scandinavian invasions of England, both of the immediate and the distant past, were offered to the king by his poets and presumably welcomed by Cnut and his followers. Even as the king made overtures of reconciliation to his conquered English subjects, the skaldic poems commemorate and celebrate that same conquest. Óttarr svarti's *Knútsdrápa*, for instance, celebrates Cnut's battles against the English in detail, hymning Cnut's first voyage to England and cataloguing all the places where the Danes triumphed: Lindsey, Sherston, Brentford, London, Norwich.[35] He extols Cnut's victory over the English, calling them the 'kindred of Edgar' (*ætt Játgeirs*) – though Edgar was the king whose laws Cnut and the Danes had agreed to uphold.[36] Cnut and his followers presumably enjoyed hearing about these triumphs, but the commemoration of the conquest, of course, also serves a political function; it underlines Cnut's power and rewrites the narrative of the conquest in his favour, attributing the glory of the victory to the king and downplaying the role of supporters who might become his rivals.[37]

The evidence of the skaldic verse also reveals that Cnut and his court were aware of the place of the eleventh-century Danish conquest within a longer history of Scandinavian activity in England, and made use of this history for political purposes.[38] The most famous example is Sigvatr Þórðarson's *Knútsdrápa*, which makes reference to Ivar's defeat of Ælla, king of Northumbria, at York in 866–7:

> Ok Ellu bak,
> at, lét, hinns sat,
> Ívarr ara,
> Jórvík, skorit.

(And Ívarr, who resided at York, had Ælla's back cut with an eagle.)[39]

Alluding to Ivar in a poem designed to praise Cnut seems intended to draw an implicit parallel between Cnut's conquest and Ivar's victory over Ælla, suggesting a link between these two Danish invaders and rulers of England.[40] As Roberta Frank argues, this reference not only glorifies Cnut by comparing him to another successful invader, it also implies a historical precedent for Danish rule in England which confers legitimacy on Cnut's own reign, reminding those listening 'that Cnut is heir to Ívarr's conquests, that in possessing England the king has only reclaimed what was his by right.'[41]

Frank has argued that the poets' use of the term *skjöldungr* is intended to have a similar political resonance, associating Cnut with ninth-century Danish conquerors of England and implying his descent from the legendary hero Scyld, who was a common ancestor in the genealogies of both English and Danish royal houses.[42] This too was a term associated with the ninth-century Danish invasions, including in northern English sources: in the

10. Edmund Ironside (British Library, Royal MS. 14 B VI)

Historia de Sancto Cuthberto, the Danish army who invaded Northumbria and defeated Ælla in battle are referred to as *Scaldingi*, apparently a form of 'Scylding'.[43] Kennings which describe Cnut's opponents as the descendants of Edgar, Ælla or Edmund cast the Danish conquest as a struggle between dynasties, the latest and most successful in a long series of battles between the Danes and the English; this must have been reinforced by the fact that Cnut's opponent, Æthelred's son Edmund Ironside, shared his first name with a figure already almost emblematic of Viking defeat of the English, Edmund of East Anglia.[44] This is a radically different interpretation of Anglo-Danish history from any we find in contemporary English sources – the Vikings' own perspective of their right to rule England.

11. Cnut and Emma in the New Minster *Liber Vitae* (British Library, Stowe MS. 944, f. 6)

References to Cnut as *skjöldungr* and to Danish kings who had previously ruled in England are valuable evidence for the knowledge of Anglo-Danish history and legend in Cnut's reign, and its political uses in Danish-ruled England. Some suggestive, though less explicit, evidence is also provided by the *Encomium Emmae Reginae*, a Latin prose narrative commissioned by Cnut's wife Emma during the brief reign of their son Harthacnut, in 1040–2.[45] Emma, the sister of the duke of Normandy, had been the wife of Æthelred before she married Cnut in 1017; some years older than Cnut, with experience of English politics gained during her time as Æthelred's queen, she was a forceful and influential figure at the Anglo-Danish court.[46] The *Encomium* was written for her by an anonymous monk of St Bertin in Flanders, and it tells the story of the Danish conquest, Cnut's reign, and the succession crisis that followed his death in 1035. The author probably had little direct experience of England, and the account he gives must have been largely based on details communicated to him by Emma and other informants at the Anglo-Danish court.[47] The *Encomium* is a highly valuable source, and perhaps the closest thing we can get to an official narrative of the conquest from the Danish perspective, but it is a complex text, extremely selective and partial in the information it provides, particularly when it comes to the details of Emma's own life. It omits to mention, for instance, that Emma had been married to Æthelred before marrying Cnut – a fact of which any contemporary reader of the text would certainly have been aware.[48] Although the *Encomium* tells the story of a successful conquest and a triumphant Danish dynasty, it was written in response to a tense political situation: after Cnut's death in 1035, the throne was disputed between Harthacnut and Harold, Cnut's son by his first wife, and for some years Emma herself was in a difficult position. Her son by Æthelred, Edward, returned to England after more than two decades of exile in Normandy to live at Harthacnut's court, and there seems to have been an uneasy truce between Edward, his mother, and his half-brother. The *Encomium* is evidently an attempt to defend Emma from her detractors and to bolster Harthacnut's claim to the English throne, and in order to do this it looks back to the Danish conquest of 30 years before as a foundational narrative for the Anglo-Danish dynasty now represented by Harthacnut. Its presentation of the past is shaped throughout by the needs of the present, as for instance when the text gives a lengthy account of Cnut making terms with his brother Harold, after their father's death, about sharing the rule of Denmark; this account offers potentially significant information about Cnut's

otherwise obscure brother, but it also seems designed to provide
a parallel to the situation between Harthacnut and Edward at
the time the text was written.

Nonetheless, the *Encomium* gives us a unique and important
perspective on the events of the Danish conquest. The text takes
its shape from the course of Danish rule over England, beginning

12. Cnut's two sons, Harold Harefoot and Harthacnut
(British Library, Royal MS. 14 B VI)

in 1013. The first book describes how Cnut and his father Svein set out to conquer England, the second is a brief account of Cnut's 20-year reign, and the third tells of the political crisis which followed Cnut's death in 1035, which is said to have been brought to an end by the accession of Harthacnut. The three books thus correspond to three generations of Danish rulers of England, the dynasty with which Emma had identified her interests. In its narrative of this period it is in some ways closer to the skaldic poems than to contemporary English sources; it praises Cnut's father Svein, for instance, who is presented as a wise king and an effective military leader, much loved by his men.[49] He is a Christian king, who on his deathbed, in his last words to his son, 'exhorted him much concerning the government of the kingdom and the zealous practice of Christianity, and, thanks be to God, committed the royal sceptre to him, the most worthy of men.'[50] We will see that this is a very different picture of Svein from the one that appears in post-Conquest English sources, where he is presented as a pagan and a tyrant with no redeeming features.[51] Later medieval English historians liked to depict Cnut making atonement to the English for the sins of his pagan father, but there is no hint of this in the *Encomium*; there is no indication here that the Danish conquest is something for which atonement is necessary.

We will have cause to return to the *Encomium* several times over the course of this book, as it provides the first evidence for legendary stories about the Danish conquest which were to become widely known, such as the idea that Cnut and Edmund Ironside fought a duel against each other as the war reached a climax in 1016. Here we can focus on one episode, the account of the final battle of Cnut's conquest in October 1016. The *Encomium* devotes considerable attention to this battle, which was fought in Essex at a place the sources call Assandun (the location has not been identified). In the *Encomium* this battle occurs halfway through Book II, at the mid-point of the text as a whole, and the battle and its aftermath take up five chapters of action and dialogue – almost as much space as is allocated to the two decades of Cnut's reign. Cnut himself plays a fairly limited role in this section of the narrative: more prominence is accorded to Thorkell the Tall, who is given a crucial part to play in the battle, and on the English side to Edmund Ironside and the treacherous earl Eadric Streona. After describing the preparations for the battle, the encomiast says:

> Erat namque eis uexillum miri portenti, quod licet credam posse esse incredibile lectori, tamen, quia uerum est, uerae inseram lectioni. Enimuero dum esset simplissimo candidissimoque intextum serico, nulliusque figurae in eo inserta esset [i]mago, tempore belli semper in eo uidebatur coruus ac si intextus, in uictoria suorum quasi hians ore excutiensque alas instabilisque pedibus, et suis deuictis quietissimus totoque corpore demissus. Quod requirens Turchil, auctor primi prelii, 'Pugnemus', inquit, 'uiriliter, sotii, nihil enim nobis erit periculi: hoc denique testatur instabilis coruus presagientis uexilli.' Quo audito Dani audentiores effecti.

> (Now [the Danes] had a banner of wonderfully strange nature, which though I believe that it may be incredible to the reader, yet since it is true, I will introduce the matter into my true history. For while it was woven of the plainest and whitest silk, and the representation of no figure was inserted into it, in time of war a raven was always seen as if embroidered on it, in the hour of its owners' victory opening its beak, flapping its wings, and restive on its feet, but very subdued and drooping with its whole body when they were defeated. Looking out for this, Thorkell, who had fought the first battle, said: 'Let us fight manfully, comrades, for no danger threatens us: for to this the restive raven of the prophetic banner bears witness.' When the Danes heard this, they were rendered bolder.)[52]

This draws on a motif which appears in various forms in Scandinavian literary tradition: the raven banner which predicts success or failure in battle. In English sources, this banner is linked with the army of Ivar and Ubbe and their brothers, men who were later identified as the sons of Ragnar Lothbrok. The first reference to a raven banner in an English text is in the *Anglo-Saxon Chronicle* entry for 878, which refers to a battle in Devon in which an unnamed brother of Ivar was killed and the Danes' banner was captured, 'which they called "Raven".[53] Although there is no indication of a legend attached to the banner at this point, parallels to the description given in the *Encomium* can be found in later texts from Iceland, Scandinavia and England. In the twelfth-century *Annals of St Neots*, the *Chronicle*'s reference to the events of 878 is expanded with a comment that the banner was woven by the sisters of Ivar and Ubbe, and that the raven moved like a living bird if the army were to be victorious, but hung down motionless if they were to be defeated.[54] Cnut's raven banner therefore seems to derive from the same body of semi-historical legend as the reference to Ivar in Sigvatr's *Knútsdrápa*, and like that reference it may be intended to place Cnut's conquest within the context of a long history of Danish triumphs over English kings.

The *Encomium*'s sense of the importance of Assandun is shared by the *Anglo-Saxon Chronicle* and by Óttarr's *Knútsdrápa*, which both memorialise this climactic battle from their different perspectives.[55] For the chronicler, writing probably early in Cnut's reign, this was the battle by which Cnut won control of the whole English nation: the *Chronicle* lists by name the most important of the English dead, condemning Eadric Streona for betraying king and country with his cowardly flight, and lamenting that all the chief men of the English nation were killed that day.[56] For Cnut's poets, of course, this battle was a great triumph to celebrate. Óttarr extols Cnut's victory:

> Skjǫldungr, vannt und skildi
> skœru verk, inn sterki;
> fekk blóðtrani bráðir
> brúnar Assatúnum.

(Strong Skjǫldungr, you performed a feat of battle under the
shield; the blood-crane [raven/eagle] received dark morsels
at Ashingdon.)[57]

In light of the *Encomium*'s reference to the raven banner, it is
notable that Óttarr also associates Cnut's victory at Assandun
with a battle-hungry bird. This could of course be a straight-
forward instance of the traditional 'beasts of battle' motif, but
the choice of a bird – called a *blóðtrani* 'blood-crane' (probably
a raven, although the kenning could also refer to an eagle) –
is nonetheless strikingly reminiscent of the story told in the
Encomium. It fits well with Óttarr's address to Cnut as *skjöldungr*
in the same verse, conceivably another reference to ninth-
century Danish conquerors of England which would associate
this crucial battle with past Danish victories. It suggests that
there is a historical precedent for Danish rule in England,
and that with his conquest Cnut is following in the footsteps of
great Danish kings of the past; it associates the eleventh-century
king with his larger-than-life predecessors of centuries before,
mythologising his conquest and perhaps (since the raven,
of course, is Odin's bird) conferring some kind of mysterious
supernatural favour upon it.

We need not imagine a direct connection between Óttarr's
verse and the *Encomium*'s story, but there must have been
considerable overlap between the audiences of these two texts,
people to whom the political resonances of these allusions to
England's Viking history were both meaningful and important.
These texts are evidence of a dynamic, high-status Anglo-
Scandinavian culture in England during Cnut's reign, and this
culture can be traced in other kinds of evidence too – not only
in the areas previously associated with Danish settlement, but
in pockets across the country. Cnut gave lands in England to
a handful of high-ranking Danes, who married into English
families and forged a mixed Anglo-Scandinavian elite, and
although their numbers were probably small, in certain areas
they were influential. Perhaps the most interesting example is

the family of Godwine, the young Englishman who rose rapidly under Cnut to become earl of Wessex.[58] Godwine married a Danish noblewoman named Gytha, a close family connection of the king (her brother was married to Cnut's sister). Godwine and Gytha signalled their closeness to Cnut by naming their first children after Cnut's father and grandfather, Svein and Harold, the names Cnut had given to his own two eldest sons. After Cnut's death, the family of Godwine and Gytha would remain at the forefront of English politics, and Harold Godwineson, of course, briefly became king of England in 1066 – a last flare of glory for the Anglo-Danish elite in England. It is one of the ironies of English history that Harold Godwineson, often idolised in modern romantic interpretations of this period as the heroic defender of England against the Norman Conquest, owed his position to his father's support of the Danish conqueror Cnut. Still more ironic, this icon of Englishness bore a name which would have seemed to his contemporaries to be markedly Scandinavian. In later chapters we will explore some of the Scandinavian legends associated with this prominent Anglo-Danish dynasty, whose family origin-myth had a long post-Conquest afterlife.

One telling marker of identity for the Anglo-Scandinavian elite promoted by Cnut seems to have been the foundation of churches in England dedicated to saints popular in the north, particularly St Olaf Haraldson, king of Norway, who was regarded as a martyr after his death in 1030. Cnut, who had been an enemy of Olaf in life, shrewdly promoted the martyr's cult in death, and several churches dedicated to St Olaf in England in the decades after his death can be plausibly connected with powerful Scandinavians.[59] Exeter, Chichester and Southwark, all areas linked with Gytha and Godwine, have eleventh-century churches dedicated to St Olaf; Siward, earl of Northumbria, another of the Danes who rose to prominence under Cnut and married into an English family, founded and dedicated a church to St Olaf in York. We will return to Siward, and his own legendary adventures, later on.

13. A carving from Winchester, perhaps originally part of
a frieze at the Old Minster, where Cnut was buried. It may
represent a scene from the Völsung legend

Siward and the family of Gytha and Godwine – culturally
Scandinavian, but firmly established by interests and by family
ties in England – may well have been the kind of people who
understood and appreciated the view of Anglo-Danish history
put forward by the skaldic poems and the *Encomium*: a dominant

Danish dynasty ruling in England, with its roots in the triumphs of the Viking kings of ninth-century Northumbria. Their understanding of the legendary history of this great dynasty may have stretched back even further than this. In Winchester – the ancient centre of the kings of Wessex, the burial-place of Alfred the Great – there is intriguing evidence for the presence of Cnut and his Scandinavian followers, including a fragmentary carving, probably once part of a larger frieze, which appears to depict a scene from the Norse legend of Sigmund.[60] Sigmund and his son Sigurðr, the dragon-slayer, were part of the greatest heroic cycle of Germanic legend, which is preserved in its fullest form in the later Norse *Völsunga saga*. The carving from Winchester has been interpreted as showing the moment at which Sigmund, bound and about to be devoured by a wolf, smears his mouth with honey to distract her from killing him. Sigmund, who is mentioned in *Beowulf*, was known to the Anglo-Saxons too, but at this time he may have been understood as an ancestor of the Danish kings, and therefore one of Cnut's own forebears.[61]

14. The possible current location of Cnut's remains, in a chest in Winchester Cathedral (Ealdgyth, via Wikimedia Commons)

To find this Scandinavian hero celebrated in Winchester, the spiritual heart of the kingdom of Wessex, is a remarkable testament to the extent of Cnut's cultural and political influence. It is even possible that the carving of Sigmund was made to form part of Cnut's own tomb – it is certainly striking enough for a king.

AFTER 1066: CONQUERORS AND MARTYRS

Exactly 50 years after Cnut's victory at the Battle of Assandun – almost to the very day – England was conquered for the second time in a century. The Norman Conquest which began with the Battle of Hastings in 1066 had a deep and lasting impact on the society, governance, language and culture of England, and has assumed an emblematic status which Cnut's conquest will never achieve: the single date '1066' is still frequently used as a dividing-line, marking the end and beginning of distinct historical epochs, in a way '1016' rarely is. In the decades following 1066, the distinction between the Norman and Danish conquerors was not so clear-cut, and their relative impact could not yet, of course, be perceived. From the end of the eleventh century come a number of thoughtful and influential narratives of Cnut's conquest which link it to earlier Danish invasions, but which evidently interpret these events in the shadow of the more recent conquest. These texts, separated by more than half a century from the events they describe, are influenced in their view of the Danes by pressing contemporary concerns about foreign invasion, oppressive rule and cultural change.

In this period, a legend is first recorded which links the ninth-century Danish invasions of England with the eleventh-century conquest in a particularly dramatic way: the story that Svein Forkbeard was killed by the spirit of St Edmund of East Anglia, who appeared to the Danish king from beyond the grave and pierced him with a lance. Svein's sudden death on 3 February 1014, less than three months after becoming king

15. Svein Forkbeard invades England (British Library,
Harley MS. 2278, f. 98v)

of England, was a remarkable reversal of fortune. The cause
of his death is unknown, and contemporary sources do not
speculate.[62] As we have seen, the *Encomium* gives Svein a
peaceful death, with an exemplary Christian final speech to his
son, but by the end of the century, some writers were offering
a supernatural explanation for this startling – to the English,
almost miraculous – turn of events. The story that Svein was
killed by St Edmund first appears in an account of Edmund's
miracles written at Bury St Edmunds by the monk and
archdeacon Herman, completed in the 1090s.[63] Herman's work
continues St Edmund's story where Abbo's *Passio* had left off,
tracing the saint's posthumous interventions in English politics
from the tenth century up to 1096.

One of the miracles recounted by Herman tells how
St Edmund appeared to Svein to defend his people from the

Danish king's unjust demands for taxation, and suddenly struck Svein dead. This story was to be a highly influential one, shaping the view of Svein and Cnut taken by John of Worcester and other twelfth-century historians.[64] Herman compares it to the death of Julian the Apostate at the hands of St Mercurius, and he seems to have based some elements of his account on that story as told in Ælfric's *Life of St Basil*.[65] This story allows Herman to present Edmund as a powerful enemy of unjust rule in the present day as well as the past, and as the pre-eminent saintly defender of England, and particularly East Anglia, his kingdom in life and death. This unjust rule is imagined not as Viking raiding, but as oppressive taxation: for Herman, Svein's real crime is 'his imposition of the universal tribute: a misfortune still generating much suffering in England, which would be happy, prosperous, and sweet beyond measure were it not for the tributes imposed by its kings.'[66] It is tax-collectors, not

16. St Edmund kills Svein Forkbeard (British Library, Harley MS. 2278, f. 103v)

violent Vikings, who besiege Edmund's city and prompt the saint to take action. This clearly has less to do with the Danes than with contemporary objections to oppressive rule; rather than being stereotypical pagan opponents of Christianity, the Danes are here cast as generic unjust rulers. This seems to have made them almost interchangeable with comparable Norman oppressors: a slightly later story from nearby Ely, probably influenced by the episode of Svein and St Edmund, makes use of a very similar idea – the ghost of a saint appears, threatens an enemy attacking their abbey, and pierces him through with a lance – but replaces Svein Forkbeard with a Norman tax-collector.[67] The impetus behind this legend is clear: Edmund has not only defended his people but avenged his own death from beyond the grave. This suggests a desire to link the earlier history of Danish invasion with later waves of conquest, and positions Edmund as a saint well placed to be the champion of East Anglia's interests against all kinds of foreign oppression.

This is reinforced by the fact that Svein is not the only Dane who is challenged and punished by St Edmund: Herman's *Miracula* contains several other episodes in which the Danes are presented as foreign antagonists to Edmund and his cult. The Danes in these miracle-stories are cast in the role of sceptics, arrogant deniers of Edmund's sanctity, who are miraculously confounded by the power of the saint. In one, a Danish nobleman who dares to peek beneath the cloth covering the saint's litter is instantly blinded, but repents, and presents his golden armlets to Edmund;[68] in another, set in the time of Edward the Confessor, the Danish Osgod Clapa is punished with madness for his presumption in entering Edmund's church drunk and armed.[69] Herman paints a memorable portrait of Osgod swaggering through the church, dressed in 'the skins of wild animals' and gold armlets, with his axe slung *Danico more* ('in Danish fashion') from his shoulder. The recurrence of the gold armlets from the earlier episode suggests they are to be understood as a marker of cultural difference, and the axe and the animal skins

17. Osgod the Dane is punished at St Edmund's tomb
(British Library, Harley MS. 2278, f. 110v)

seem intended to suggest a wild, barbarian violence; Herman's
description of Osgod emphasises the man's Danish identity
and casts it in a distinctly negative light. Herman consistently
characterises the Danes as arrogant and haughty, and repeatedly
shows St Edmund humbling their pride.[70]

Within this context, however, he sets one example of
Edmund's power of conversion: the Danish conqueror Cnut,
who is swiftly converted to the worship of the saint. There is
evidence to suggest that Cnut took a particular interest in
patronising the cult of St Edmund, and perhaps linked it to his
own conquest – he supported the building of a new church at
Bury St Edmunds, which was consecrated on the anniversary
of the Battle of Assandun on 18 October.[71] Herman extensively
praises Cnut's generosity to Edmund's shrine, emphasising his
difference from Svein. To underline this point, he twice uses the
striking image of the wolf: he says that Cnut did not imitate his
father's wickedness, proving the truth of a proverb 'The wolf is

not nearly so big as he is made out to be',[72] and he also includes
a short verse:

> Que Saulum mutauit in Paulum
> in eodem lupum magnum,
> nunc habet ferum hominem
> in Christianissimum regem.[73]

(He who changed Saul into Paul, the great wolf, now has
made a wild man into a most Christian king.)

The image of a wolf acting against its nature is one found
prominently in the hagiography of St Edmund: Abbo's *Passio*
famously tells how a wolf protected Edmund's severed head
when it was hidden by the Danes, allowing it to be found by
his followers and rejoined to his body. With this language,
Cnut is absorbed into the central imagery of Edmund's cult,
though not in a very flattering way: the wild barbarian king,
like the wolf, is converted to the worship of the saint, and
only on such terms can a Dane be accepted.

18. The ruins of the abbey church at Bury St Edmunds, where
St Edmund's shrine stood behind the high altar

It is useful to compare Herman's narrative with a hagiographical text of the same period from Christ Church,
Canterbury, which also engages with the Danish conquest
from the perspective of the late eleventh century, but with a
different and more sympathetic attitude to the Danes. It allows
greater agency to the Danish conquerors, particularly to Cnut,
and although it also shows the Danes converting to the veneration of English saints it does this by redeeming, rather than
scorning, distinctive markers of Scandinavian identity. For
Christ Church, this period of English history was of great
significance, because the community's two chief saints were
archbishops of Canterbury who were both directly linked to the
events of the Danish conquest: St Ælfheah, who was killed by
a Danish army in 1012, after being captured during the Viking
siege of Canterbury the previous year, and St Dunstan, who
was credited with having prophesied the decades of Viking
attacks which followed his death in 988. In the period between
1080 and 1093, accounts of both these saints were composed
by Osbern, precentor of Christ Church. Osbern had been a
member of the community of Christ Church since childhood,
and it has been suggested on the basis of his name that he
may have been of Danish descent.[74] He had a long-standing
personal attachment to the pre-Conquest saints of Christ
Church, and his work attempts to interpret their lives for
the benefit of a new, potentially sceptical audience in Anglo-
Norman Canterbury.[75] His work on Dunstan remained the most
popular hagiographical text on that saint for centuries, and was
responsible for popularising one of the most enduring explanations for the two conquests England suffered in the course
of the eleventh century: Osbern says Dunstan, when conse-
crating Æthelred as king in 978, had prophesied that because
he had come to power through the murder of his half-brother
he would be punished by war and invasion, 'until your kingdom
is given to a foreign power whose customs and language the
people you rule do not know'.[76] As we have seen, Dunstan
was already associated with prophetic knowledge of the

Viking invasions early in the eleventh century; Osbern's more dramatic formulation of Dunstan's prophesy came to be so popular as an interpretation of Æthelred that in the later medieval period it was inscribed on the king's tomb in Old St Paul's, his epitaph and the final word on his reign.[77]

The idea of the Danes as the instruments of divine punishment was, as we have already seen, a widespread one, but elsewhere Osbern explores different potential interpretations of Danish invasion, telling instead how the Danes were converted and integrated into England through their veneration of English saints. In his *Vita* and *Translatio* of Ælfheah, both composed between 1080 and 1089, he describes Ælfheah's death at the hands of the Danes and the return of his body to Canterbury a decade later, with the active involvement of Cnut.[78] In explaining the events leading up to Ælfheah's martyrdom, Osbern presents the Danish leaders Svein and Thorkell as wicked and aggressive pagan pirates, and the English as too weak to resist: 'the land lay at the mercy of the raiders' fury [...] For Æthelred, king of the English, was as weak as he was unwarlike, in his conduct more like a monk than a soldier.'[79] This follows the narrative of Æthelred's reign which by the end of the eleventh century had become conventional, but there are two additional factors at play. As Osbern presents it, the Danes attack Canterbury because they are specifically targeting the archbishop, angry that Ælfheah has been working to convert many ordinary Danish soldiers to Christianity. It is suggested that they are deliberately seeking out Ælfheah, not raiding indiscriminately, and the rank and file of the Danish army are already being distinguished from their leaders, seen as potential subjects for conversion and redemption.

Another significant motivating force is the treachery of Eadric Streona, who incites the Danes to attack Canterbury. In a detail not found in any other source, Osbern claims that Eadric collaborated with the Danes because he sought revenge for his brother (not named by Osbern), a deceitful and proud man killed in a dispute with some noblemen of Canterbury.

After Æthelred refuses to punish the culprits, Eadric goes to the Danes to seek vengeance for his brother. As we will see, the narrative traditions which developed around the Danish invasions in the eleventh century and later frequently provide a personal motive for the decision to invade, and one of the most common is vengeance for the death of a sibling. Comparable explanations for Danish invasion are found in numerous other texts, including the *Encomium Emmae Reginae*, where Thorkell's raiding in England is said to have been motivated by a desire to avenge a brother who had been killed in England.[80] A revised version of Herman's *Miracula*, written at Bury St Edmunds around 1100, adds a detail not found in Herman's text, claiming that Thorkell came to East Anglia to avenge the death of his two sisters, who had been killed at Thetford amid the slaughter on St Brice's Day, and in the following chapters we will see more examples from the twelfth century and afterwards.[81] Osbern's story about Eadric's brother is an early example of this desire to explain the Danish invasions in terms of personal feuds, providing specific motives to provide a narrative justification (and sometimes a moral one) for what might otherwise appear to be random attacks.

Osbern presents Eadric's attempt to recruit the Danes to his cause as a formal pact and a planned invasion. Eadric tells the Danes of the weakness and cowardice of the English, and they agree how to divide up the country once they have conquered it. The result of this pact is the siege and destruction of Canterbury, and the capture of the archbishop. For Osbern these events were a disaster not only for the city but for the whole of England; after describing the burning of the city and the capture of Ælfheah, he observes 'Each singly would have been calamity enough to the kingdom – either the harm done to the priest or the deadly destruction of the city – so that deprived of either glory England would never from that time on regain her former status.'[82] The siege and the death of Ælfheah together form a pivotal moment in the history of Canterbury and of England as a nation – and

19. A twelfth-century window from Canterbury Cathedral, showing
the Viking siege of Canterbury and St Ælfheah being captured
and killed by the Danes

he surely has the Norman Conquest as well as the Danish
invasion in mind here.

After this Ælfheah is taken prisoner by the Danish fleet, and
throughout the months of his captivity he is shown gaining
converts among the Danes, preaching and baptising, until only
the leaders of the army resist his influence. Osbern consistently
distinguishes between the Danish army and its leaders – who
go unnamed after the first reference to Svein and Thorkell –
and indicates that some of the Danes followed and protected
Ælfheah. It is Ælfheah's insistence on making converts, as well as
his refusal (or inability) to pay ransom, which causes the leaders
of the army to decide to kill him, because they fear he is turning
their own men against them. His success in converting the army
brings about his death, but it also sows the seeds for his final
triumph: as sentence of death is pronounced upon him, Ælfheah
speaks a prophecy, telling the Danes that if they do not convert

to Christianity they will not 'take root' in England.[83] Unlike
St Dunstan's prophetic speech to Æthelred, this prophecy is less
a threat than a promise – it suggests that if they *do* convert, they
can take root, and so it proves.

As soon as Ælfheah is dead, his prophecy begins to come true.
It is Ælfheah's Danish converts who are the first to proclaim him
a saint and martyr, and his dying prophetic metaphor is brought
to life with his first posthumous miracle. The few Danes who
remain sceptical propose a trial of his sanctity: if a wooden oar
sprouts new life after it is dipped in Ælfheah's blood, they will
agree that Ælfheah was a holy man and allow his followers to
bury his body. The oar miraculously blooms; the Danish oar has
literally taken root in English land, and the very force which
kept Ælfheah captive, Viking sea-power, becomes the means of
demonstrating his sanctity. It is a living metaphor for the converted Danes who will now, as the narrative goes on to show,
conquer and rule England under Cnut by the guidance of
St Ælfheah. Ælfheah's body is taken for burial in London,
accompanied by crowds of Danes and English.

Osbern shows the archbishop as a figure around whom conquerors and conquered can unite, and this theme is even more
prominent in the fuller account of Ælfheah's translation written
after the *Vita*, in which Osbern develops the central figure of
Cnut as the supreme example of Ælfheah's power at conversion.
The translation of Ælfheah from his first place of burial at
St Paul's back to Canterbury seems to have been one of the
acts Cnut undertook in atonement for the injuries of his conquest, and it involved an elaborate public ceremony, witnessed
by Cnut, Emma and their young son Harthacnut.[84] This was a
politically charged action for a number of reasons: it was not
only a form of reparation for the most high-profile killing of
the Danish conquest, but also an opportunity to remove a
potential focus of anti-Danish feeling in London and to win the
support of Canterbury.[85] The translation took place in 1023 on
8 June – the same date as the first Viking raids on Lindisfarne in
793, which is probably a coincidence, although it is a strikingly

fitting date for an act of atonement for Danish sins against the English.[86] While the *Vita* is anguished and tense, the *Translatio* is cheerful and raucous in tone, emphasising at length the king's personal involvement in the removal of the relics. Osbern presents the translation as an act of propitiation, which is undertaken by Cnut after he witnesses the punishments visited on Thorkell and the other Danish killers of Ælfheah: by the power of God and St Ælfheah the Danes' ships are wrecked at sea and many are drowned, and Thorkell is murdered by his own countrymen when he returns to Denmark. Cnut's decision to translate and honour Ælfheah is motivated by a desire to avoid divine punishment himself, but is also said to be activated by knowledge of Ælfheah's final prophecy. It is his veneration for Ælfheah which wins him control of England: after he has been told about Ælfheah's warning that the Danes will never take root in England unless they convert, he agrees to return the saint's body to Canterbury, 'and a sign of divine propitiation followed the council. For a few days later Cnut made peace and gained, after the peace, half the realm, and later the whole.'[87]

Osbern knew, of course, that the Danes under Cnut did 'take root' in England, so this prophecy helps to explain how it was permitted, and how these events could be interpreted not as punishment for the English (as in Dunstan's prophecy to Æthelred) but more positively, as an example of St Ælfheah's powers of reconciliation and conversion. The translation is presented as Cnut's own decision and arrangement, undertaken with the cooperation of Archbishop Æthelnoth and two Canterbury monks, whom Osbern names as his informants for these events. When Cnut, Æthelnoth and the monks break open Ælfheah's tomb in St Paul's, Cnut addresses the saint's body, asking forgiveness for the injuries inflicted on Ælfheah, and imploring the saint not to blame him for the sins of his 'kinsmen' (*parentes*).[88] Whether this is intended to be a reference to Svein only, or to align Cnut with his more distant Viking forefathers, it is a reminder of Cnut's Danish ancestry as well as his new condition as a penitent Christian king.

The king and archbishop remove the body from its resting-place to Cnut's ship, which is described as 'a royal longship with golden dragon prows'.[89] The king takes the helm himself and steers the ship across the Thames to Southwark, from where he sends Æthelnoth to Canterbury with the body. The *Anglo-Saxon Chronicle* records that Ælfheah's body was taken

20. A modern image of St Ælfheah on a tomb in
Canterbury Cathedral

away from London by boat, but the dragon-ship is Osbern's addition, and this too seems to draw inspiration from Cnut's Danish identity: as in the miracle of the oar, Viking naval power has been converted to serve the glory of the English martyr. The removal is aided by Cnut's own soldiers, 'who are called "housecarls" in the language of the Danes', Osbern notes.[90] The use of this Old Norse word highlights the housecarls' Scandinavian identity, their linguistic and cultural difference – but here they are allies in the service of Ælfheah, joining with the monks of Canterbury against the people of London.

Osbern paints a picture of Cnut as an eager convert, a Danish king who develops a strong personal devotion to Ælfheah. In exchange for his service, Ælfheah grants him rule of a newly united kingdom of England, where Danes and English cooperate in honouring the martyred archbishop. Osbern's two works on Ælfheah offer a narrative in which the violence of the conquest is quickly replaced by unity between conquerors and conquered, achieved through the mutual veneration of English saints. Even more so than in Herman's *Miracula*, Cnut emerges here as an exemplary figure, ready to be guided by English churchmen and to atone for the actions of his Danish ancestors. This is a narrative which imagines a process of conciliation following a disruptive conquest, proposing that even a violent invasion can result in a reign of justice, and that rulers newly rooted in a foreign land may grow and flourish if they align themselves with the people they have conquered. Writing about the Danish conquest provided an opportunity to explore questions of cultural interaction and assimilation in a way that must have been particularly useful in Canterbury after the Norman Conquest, and it is in this context that we should interpret Osbern's narrative of Danish rule as a period in which English identity and continuity with the past had been seriously challenged, almost overcome, but had proved resilient, and able to successfully absorb and work with a new ruling class.

These narratives about saints and Vikings are part of a much larger body of narrative material about the Danish invasions developing and circulating at the end of the eleventh century. Herman's story about Svein's death may already have been in circulation, since Osbern also knew that Svein had been 'killed in a terrible manner by almighty God', although he does not mention Edmund's role;[91] similarly, the revised version of Herman's *Miracula*, which was produced at Bury St Edmunds *c.*1100, adds a number of details which read like the growing elaborations of legend, including the detail of Thorkell's revenge for his sisters and a speech from St Edmund to Svein which sounds remarkably like Byrhtnoth's threat to the Vikings at Maldon, defiantly proffering him weapons in place of the money the Danes have demanded.[92] Osbern has St Ælfheah respond to the Danes' demands for tribute with a similar kind of riddling substitution: instead of money, he says, he will set before them 'the gold of divine wisdom.'[93]

The Danish conquest of 1013–16 had provided new saints and martyrs of Viking invasion, but other kinds of stories were still being told. Not long after Osbern completed his works on Ælfheah, his younger contemporary at Canterbury, Eadmer, wrote the first stand-alone account of St Oda, the Viking's son who became Archbishop of Canterbury. Probably written shortly before 1100, this was one of Eadmer's earliest historical works, and it draws on Byrhtferth's *Vita S. Oswaldi* as well as Osbern's writings on Dunstan.[94] In an attempt to reclaim Oda's cult for Canterbury (where he was buried), Eadmer returned to the saint whose Danish ancestry had, a century before, provided a story of integration and conversion in the aftermath of foreign invasion. Like Byrhtferth, he draws attention to Oda's Danish ancestry as evidence of the pagan origins from which he sprang:

> Venerabilis Christi confessor Odo, nobilibus sed paganis parentibus oriundus, sicut rosa e spinis floruit, uel quasi pretiosum de uilibus uasculis aroma processit. Nam ex impia illa senatorum multitudine fertur genus habuisse quae olim sceleratissimum praedonem Inguarem comitata nauali manu in regnum Anglorum est aducta.

(The venerable confessor of Christ, Oda, who was descended from noble though pagan parents, flourished like a rose among thorns, or, to put it another way, issued forth like a priceless perfume from a worthless vessel. For he is said to have taken his lineage from that horde of godless nobility who were transported long ago in the company of Ivar, a most wicked plunderer, to the kingdom of the English by a naval force.)[95]

The Vikings here are certainly wicked, but Oda's story goes on to show how they were absorbed into England. Later on, Eadmer adds to his source the account of a particularly appropriate and dramatic miracle, performed by Oda for King Æthelstan. He tells how Oda accompanies Æthelstan to the battle of Brunanburh, a fight against 'a vast army of heathens'. Æthelstan's sword breaks at a crucial moment in the battle, and the king is at a loss, left weaponless in the face of his enemies. But Oda is at his side and saves him, miraculously mending his broken sword.[96] This is not the last time we will see a medieval writer reimagining the circumstances of the battle of Brunanburh, or attaching a story to this famous victory. It is not clear what Eadmer's source for this story may have been, but it must have seemed fitting that Oda, the converted son of a pagan Dane, should intervene to help Æthelstan win this great battle over the Vikings.[97] In Chapter 2 we will look at the English legends which developed around what Eadmer calls the 'horde of godless nobility', Ivar and his army, but there is one final point to make about what Oda's story may have suggested to English readers at the close of the eleventh century. At an early stage in the manuscript tradition, including in two (now lost) manuscripts probably written in the 1090s, Eadmer's *Vita Sancti Odonis* is found in a unit of three with Osbern's two works on Ælfheah.[98] These works all deal with saintly archbishops of Canterbury, so they have many overlapping interests and concerns, but these three texts would also incidentally have provided a reader with a narrative of English history bounded by two Danish invasions: the Viking army with which Oda's father came to England, and the conquest of Cnut, who was converted into Ælfheah's most influential supporter. For a reader at the end of the eleventh century, this must have been a powerful story of cultural and religious conversion, giving two saints of Canterbury – Viking's son and Vikings' victim – a central role to play in shaping an England which had survived and absorbed the Viking threat.

CHAPTER 2

THE SONS OF RAGNAR LOTHBROK

The leaders of the Viking armies who invaded England in the second half of the ninth century became the subject of a wide array of later legends, especially the men we have already encountered as the supposed killers of St Edmund of East Anglia: Ivar, Ubbe and their brothers. In time, these men came to be identified as the sons of the semi-legendary warrior Ragnar Lothbrok, one of the most famous Vikings in Scandinavian history. Ragnar and his sons feature in sagas, chronicles and poems from Denmark, Norway, Iceland and elsewhere, with the most extended and colourful stories about them dating from the twelfth century and later. The modern popular image of the Vikings – fearless, ruthless, death-defying – evolved in large part from these Old Norse sagas and poems about Ragnar and his sons, after they were rediscovered by antiquarian scholars in the seventeenth century.[1] It is difficult to separate the sparse facts about Ragnar and his sons from the many legends which grew up around them, but the historical origins of these figures have been the subject of a considerable amount of investigation from scholars, who have worked to untangle history from legend and to trace the development of these stories as they spread around the Scandinavian world and beyond.[2]

The fullest versions of these legends are the vivid and detailed Scandinavian texts, but a few sources – preserved

mostly in short summary form, in Latin chronicles and saints'
lives – suggest there were also various stories about Ragnar
Lothbrok and his offspring circulating in medieval England. It
has been argued that these narratives may have had their ultimate origin in the Anglo-Scandinavian society of the Danelaw,
as settlers and their descendants attempted to explain or justify
the Viking invasions of northern and eastern England in the
ninth century.[3] Whether we think of this as taking place in the
early days after the settlement, as was the traditional view, or
in the twelfth century, as has more recently been suggested,[4]
these short English narratives are often discussed primarily in
relationship to the Scandinavian tradition, rather than in their
own right. In this chapter we will attempt to do something
different: we will trace the development of these stories within
their English context, to explore what they could have meant
for English audiences at a time when the Viking Age was an
increasingly distant memory.

THE LOTHBROK LEGEND

The Ragnar Lothbrok of the Norse legends is a Viking warrior
and king, a serpent-slayer and the father of many warlike sons.
One of his adventures explains how he got his nickname: to
defend himself in a fight against two poisonous serpents, he
coated his legs in woolly breeches covered with tar, and so
earned himself the name *loðbrók*, 'shaggy breeches'. Various
sources give him at least three wives, one of whom he wins by
this serpent-slaying exploit; another wife is a dauntless female
warrior who fights alongside him in battle, and the third is the
daughter of the great hero Sigurðr the Völsung. By these wives
Ragnar has at least eight sons, who all embark on adventures of
their own, raiding and ruling across northern Europe. In the
end, the legend goes, Ragnar meets his death in England after
raiding in Northumbria. He is captured by the Northumbrian
king Ælla and put to a cruel death in a snake-pit. With his last

words as he lies dying he laughs in the face of death, declaring
that his sons will come to avenge him. They do, and Ælla is made
to pay dearly for Ragnar's death.[5]

This is the story as told by a range of Scandinavian sources,
including the thirteenth-century Old Norse *Ragnars saga
loðbrókar*, the Danish historian Saxo Grammaticus, writing
between *c*.1188 and *c*.1208, and numerous others.[6] These narratives are a synthesis of what may originally have been a variety of
disparate legends, attached to the names of a number of Viking
leaders who were probably the ultimate historical antecedents of
Ragnar and his sons: Reginheri, who sacked Paris in 845, a man
named Björn who was raiding around the Seine in 857–9, and
the Ivar, Ubbe and Halfdan who were active in France, Ireland
and England in the second half of the ninth century.[7] However,
it is evident even from this brief summary that the legends about
these men developed very far from any likely historical origins.
Although the English traditions about Ragnar and his sons are
related to these legends, they in fact share very few of the details
of the story summarised above, and have their own interpretation of the details they do share. The name Ragnar does not
even appear in the English sources (with one possible exception, which will be discussed below). The equivalent figure in
England is named only Lothbrok, with no explanation for how
he got that name. In place of the large number of sons attributed
to Ragnar in the Scandinavian traditions, the Lothbrok of the
English sources is usually credited with just two or three: Ivar
(whose name usually appears in medieval English texts as Inguar
or Hinguar), Ubbe and Beorn. Another brother, Halfdan, who
features among the sons of Ragnar in the Scandinavian legends,
is identified in Anglo-Saxon sources as a brother of Ivar, but is
never made the son of Lothbrok in an English source.

In their earliest appearances in the historical record, the Viking
leaders who may have been the origins of these legendary
figures are not linked to any named father, nor are they always
identified as brothers. In the second half of the eleventh
century, however, they began to be named as the sons of a man

called 'Lothbrok'. The first to make this identification was the Norman historian William of Jumièges, writing around 1070. In his *Gesta Normannorum Ducum*, writing about Viking raids on northern France in the middle of the ninth century, William mentions a warrior named Bier (Björn), son of King Lothbrok. This Bier, he says, was known as 'Ironside', because his mother had protected him with magic spells of invulnerability which meant he could fight unarmed on a battlefield and yet not be injured by any weapons.[8] William says it was the law among the Danes that a father would exile all his sons from his land except one, who would be his heir, and so Lothbrok exiled Bier, who left home to conquer lands for himself. Accompanied by his tutor Hasting, he gathered an army of other young men and raided across France and Italy. Bier was subsequently shipwrecked on the coast of England as he was sailing back to Denmark, and finally met his death in Frisia. Nothing else is said of his father Lothbrok. It has been argued that William's identification of Bier as the son of Lothbrok came from English or Anglo-Scandinavian tradition, rather than from Normandy, especially in light of the fact that the nickname 'Ironside' may have been borrowed from the name of Cnut's opponent, Æthelred's son Edmund Ironside.[9]

A few years later, around 1076, Adam of Bremen identifies Ivar, whom he calls the cruellest of Norse warriors, as the son of 'Lodparchus', evidently a form of Lothbrok.[10] Adam attributes this information to a history of the Franks, although his specific source is unknown. Adam used a variety of written sources for his *History* but he had impressively well-connected oral sources, too: he was in close contact with the Danish king Svein Estrithson, Cnut's nephew, who provided Adam with information about his ancestors among the kings of Denmark. At this stage, then, a man named Lothbrok was being identified as the father of some Viking leaders, although it is the sons, rather than the father, who are the focus of these references. The names Ragnar and Lothbrok are not recorded in combination until a few decades later, when the link was made by the Icelandic scholar

Ari Þorgilsson in his *Íslendingabók* (written between 1120 and 1133), a history of the settlement and conversion of Iceland. In his first chapter, Ari says that 'Ivar, son of Ragnar Lothbrok', had St Edmund killed, 'according to what is written in his saga'. This reference to Edmund's 'saga' probably suggests Ari had access to one of the works on St Edmund written in England, although his exact source has not been identified; he may have used Abbo or Herman, or a composite version of the two containing some additional information (neither of those sources, in their surviving form, identifies Ivar's father).[11]

From the twelfth century onwards, these brief references to Ragnar Lothbrok and his sons grew into a forest of legends. It is in the twelfth century, too, that the first signs appear of a legend about Lothbrok in England, but this branch of the tradition was to develop in different ways and in very different contexts from the Scandinavian legends.

LOTHBROK IN ENGLAND: THE BEGINNINGS OF THE LEGEND

The first mention of Lothbrok in England appears in a Latin text known as the *Annals of St Neots*, a compilation of annals based largely on the *Anglo-Saxon Chronicle* but also incorporating details from other sources and from oral tradition. Its reference to Lothbrok is brief, but very suggestive. In an entry for the year 878, based on the *Chronicle*, it describes how one of the leaders of the Danes was killed in battle against the English and the Danes' banner 'Raven' was captured. It goes on to explain:

> In quo etiam acceperunt illud uexillum quod Reafan nominant. Dicunt enim quod tres sorores Hynguari et Hubbe, filie uidelicet Lodebrochi, illud uexillum tex`u´erunt et totum parauerunt illud uno meridiano tempore. Dicunt etiam quod, in omni bello ubi praecederet idem signum, si uictoriam adepturi essent, appareret in

medio signi quasi coruus uiuus uolitans; si uero uincendi
in futuro fuissent, penderet directe nichil mouens – et hoc
sepe probatum est.[12]

(In that battle they took the banner which is called 'Raven.'
For it is said that the three sisters of Ivar and Ubbe, that is,
the daughters of Lodebroch, wove that banner and prepared
the whole thing in the space of one noon-tide. And it is
also said that in every battle where this banner is carried,
if the victory is to be theirs there appears in the middle of
the banner what seems to be a living raven flying; but if they
are to be defeated, then it hangs down motionless – and this
has often been proved.)

The precise date and composition of this text are difficult
to establish, but the sole manuscript was written at Bury St
Edmunds between *c.*1120 and *c.*1140 (it is known as the *Annals
of St Neots* because by the sixteenth century the manuscript
belonged to the priory of St Neots in Cambridgeshire).[13] It has
been argued that the annals were originally compiled at Ramsey
Abbey at the end of the tenth century, although this information may be a later addition – the composite nature of the text
makes it difficult to ascertain when it was added to the annals.[14]
We have already seen that there was a particular interest in
St Edmund and his Danish enemies both at Ramsey and at
Bury St Edmunds, and it is not surprising that this first English
reference to Lothbrok should occur in this context.

In other ways, however, this appearance of Lothbrok *is* surprising. He is mentioned in passing, as if the English audience
could be expected to recognise the name, and associated with
three daughters who do not appear in any other source from
England or Scandinavia. The two sentences describing the
banner both begin *dicunt*, 'it is said', perhaps intending to attribute
this information to popular oral tradition, and it may be that
this is a local legend from East Anglia.[15] However, the association of Ivar and Ubbe as a pair here suggests influence from
the hagiography of St Edmund (the *Chronicle* entry which is the

basis for this passage instead mentions an unnamed 'brother of Ivar and Halfdan'), and a written source is also a possibility.[16] We have already seen a comparable magical, prophetic raven banner attributed to Cnut in the *Encomium*, so this may be linked to a story already known in England rather than an independent version of the legend. There are parallels to the description here in later Norse sagas – including the detail that the raven banner was woven by a female relative of the warrior who bears it – but since the English examples of the motif pre-date any of the Scandinavian ones, it has been suggested that the story travelled from Anglo-Danish England to the north rather than the other way around.[17]

As the East Anglian context for this first reference to Lothbrok suggests, it was the cult which grew up around St Edmund which provided the richest source for English legends about Lothbrok and his sons. Abbo's tenth-century account of Edmund's death was hugely influential, and we have already seen that Abbo has little interest in exploring the part played by the Danes. His interpretation of their behaviour – pagan ferocity and northern savagery – remained a common and widespread interpretation of the Danes' motivation, when writers troubled to give them any motivation at all. Many later texts about St Edmund followed Abbo's lead; the account of St Edmund's death in the *South English Legendary* gives a perfunctory but fairly typical explanation of how and why Ivar and Ubbe came to England:

Tuei princes of anoþer lond þat were of liþer þo3t
Faste here red togadere nome to bringe Engelond to no3t.
Hubba was þoþer ihote & þoþer het Hyngar.
Wiþ grete furde hi come to Engelond er eni man were iwar.
In Norþhumberland hi bigonne & þer hi slo3e to grounde,
Robbede also & brende to no3t & destruyde al þat hi founde.[18]

(Two princes of another country, who were of hostile thought, made the decision together to bring England to nothing. One was called Ubbe and the other called Ivar. They came to England with a great army before anyone was aware. They began in Northumberland and slew widely there, and stole and burned and destroyed to nothing all that they found.)

Although this text is concerned to promote Edmund as an English saint – not only a saint of East Anglia – there is no interest here in the origins of his killers. Ubbe and Ivar are named, but they are only 'princes of another country', and are not even identified as Danes. This is fairly typical of the presentation of Ivar and Ubbe in vernacular saints' lives of this period; by this date they often feature not as Danish invaders but as a much more general kind of threat, savage pagans of indeterminate racial origin, who attain, in John Frankis' description, 'almost mythic status as archetypal opponents of Christianity.'[19] In the *South English Legendary*, one brief reference to Northumberland is all we hear of their existence before or after Edmund's death: they come out of nowhere, manifest themselves only to wantonly kill, steal and destroy, and afterwards disappear again.

In the former Danelaw, however, the role played by the Danes in Edmund's death and veneration was a much more complex matter. This had been true from the very earliest days of Edmund's cult: although a Viking army was responsible for Edmund's death, it was the Danish invaders who were the first to recognise and acknowledge the power of the martyr. Some 25 years after the king's death, coins bearing St Edmund's name were being minted and circulated by the new Danish rulers of East Anglia. This may have been a shrewd political move to win the support of the local population, an act of expiation for the king's death or, as Susan Ridyard suggests, 'a product of diplomacy, a negotiated, perhaps enforced, concession which might help to stabilise their political power' and legitimise the new Danish regime.[20] By the eleventh century, Edmund's cult was still benefitting from the patronage of Danish kings. As we have seen, Cnut seems to have taken an interest in St Edmund, which post-Conquest writers like Herman interpreted in the context of the king's Danish heritage: it was as his pagan father's son, and the descendant of Danes, that Cnut was converted to the worship of Edmund. This focus on Cnut as a figure of the penitent Danish king does not, however, allow room for much discussion of the previous invaders for whose sins he is atoning, or what brought them to England in the first place.

This began to change in the middle of the twelfth century. From that date onwards, we start to see versions of Edmund's story which offer a variety of different interpretations to answer exactly that question: why did Ivar and Ubbe come to England, and why did they kill St Edmund? It is in these sources that we first find narratives in which not only Ivar and Ubbe, but also their father, Lothbrok, play a crucial role in the king's death.

Lothbrok is not mentioned by Abbo, Herman, or other early writers on Edmund, although the *Annals of St Neots* show that Lothbrok was a name associated with Ivar and Ubbe in England by the twelfth century. A decade or so after the manuscript of the *Annals of St Neots* was written, an account of the early life of Edmund was composed for the monks of Bury St Edmunds by Geoffrey of Wells.[21] The main purpose of this text was to fill in some of the gaps in St Edmund's legend: the earliest sources provide no information about Edmund's parentage or youth, or anything before the events immediately leading up to his death, and in the twelfth century this was a space his hagiographers did their best to fill.

Geoffrey explains that he wrote his *De Infantia S. Eadmundi* at the urging of Sihtric, the prior of Bury St Edmunds, and Goscelin, the sub-prior; his work is dedicated to Ording, who was abbot between 1148 and 1156, and so can be dated to those years. Geoffrey himself was probably a canon of Thetford Priory, and his name suggests he came from Wells-next-the-Sea in Norfolk.[22] He claims that he had discussed Edmund's parentage and youth with the monks of Bury St Edmunds, and that on these occasions everyone would share the information they had learned about the saint, while Geoffrey would contribute what he had heard from oral tradition or from reading.[23] This is all the information he gives us about his sources for the *De Infantia S. Eadmundi*.

Geoffrey's contribution to the legend of St Edmund is, as the title of his text suggests, to tell the story of Edmund's youth, and to explain how he came to be king of East Anglia. He says that Edmund was born on the continent, the son of the king of Saxony, and a relative of Offa, king of East Anglia.[24] Offa has no heir, and decides to go on pilgrimage in the hope that God will provide him with a successor. On his journey, he visits Saxony and stays with his kinsman, Edmund's father. He is impressed by Edmund's conversation and manner, and decides to adopt the young man as his son and heir. Offa dies on his journey soon afterwards, bequeathing his kingdom to Edmund.

Edmund sets out for East Anglia, and lands on the north Norfolk coast. From the moment of his landing, miracles begin to occur: twelve healing streams spring up from the earth, and the area around Hunstanton, the place of his arrival, becomes the most fertile land for crops in the whole of East Anglia. With his taste for etymologising, and a touch of Norfolk pride, Geoffrey explains that Hunstanton means 'town of the honeyed-stone' – a fitting name, he says, for a town whose inhabitants are sweet-tongued and sturdy as stone.[25] Geoffrey comments that these rivers and this fruitful land can still be seen in the region, bearing enduring witness to Edmund's holy presence there.

Edmund is accepted by the people as a legitimate heir to Offa, and the kingdom flourishes under its new saintly king. His fame spreads and reaches Denmark, where it comes to the ears of a man named Lothbrok, 'a very rich and famous, but wicked and deceitful man'. Geoffrey asserts that the name Lothbrok means *odiosus rivus*, 'loathsome brook', interpreting the name as if it were an English compound, from *lōth* 'hateful' and *brōk* 'brook'.[26] For an English-speaker this would have been a logical assumption, and, while probably inaccurate, it is not the most fanciful of all the etymologies which have been proposed for 'Lothbrok' over the years.[27] It does, however, suggest that nothing like the story attached to the nickname in Scandinavian tradition was known to Geoffrey.

From this loathsome brook, Geoffrey says, flows a stream of hateful progeny: three sons, Ivar, Ubbe and Beorn. This family originate in the north of Denmark, and are members of a people known for their physical strength, height and fortitude in battle, as well as their cruel acts of piracy and plunder. Geoffrey comments that they are descended from the Goths, their neighbours, and that they interpret their own name (*dacos*, 'Danes') as related to *dagos* (i.e. *de gothorum*, 'from the Goths'); the idea that the Danes were descended from the Goths was a common one.[28] Geoffrey goes on to say that Ubbe was particularly known for his skill in magic and the 'devilish arts' of witchcraft. He had the power to cast spells over an opposing army, and when he approached his enemy he would say to his men 'Lift me up on high, that I may overlook the army' (*superuideam*).[29] If he was able to 'overlook' them in this way, their luck would fail them and Ubbe's army would triumph. This is a supernatural power which has several parallels in Norse literature, as well as in the *Gesta Herwardi*.[30]

Unfortunately we learn no more from Geoffrey of these powers of Ubbe's. He does tell, however, how Lothbrok heard of King Edmund's rise to power in East Anglia. One day when Lothbrok and his sons are talking and the brothers are boasting of their brave deeds, Lothbrok taunts his sons by comparing them unfavourably to the English king:

> [P]ro nichilo inflati estis et in uentum uerba profertis. Quid enim dignum adepti estis memoria inter preliorum discrimina? Certe quidam inuuenis Ædmundus ante non multos hos annos a saxonia descendit, anglicos ad sinus cum paucis apulit et regnum Estangle pro uelle disponit. Quid uos unquam simile peregistis? O qualis genitura mea in uobis!

> (Much reason you have to be so boastful, and to make the air ring with your proud words! What, I should like to know, have you ever achieved worth remembrance as the result

of all your hard-fought battles? Why, there is a young man named Eadmund, who, not many years ago, embarked from Saxony, and landed in an English haven with a few followers, and now he has the realm of East Anglia under his absolute control! What have you ever accomplished like that? Oh! how inferior are you whom I have begotten!)[31]

Enraged by their father's taunts, Ubbe and his brothers decide to prove their worth by invading England.

At this point Geoffrey abruptly concludes his text, referring the reader to Abbo for further information; his own narrative is intended to be a prequel to that authoritative account of Edmund's death. He leaves Lothbrok's sons in the act of plotting against Edmund and collecting an army, but the story breaks off before they actually set sail for England.

The *De Infantia* is clearly not a positive portrayal of Lothbrok and his sons and their history with Edmund, but it is a much fuller one than any previous source had provided. In this text Geoffrey does spend some time describing and characterising the Danes, and provides them with a motive for attacking England – and Edmund specifically – beyond greed for plunder and love of battle. The way in which Geoffrey has Lothbrok encourage his sons to compare themselves with Edmund leads the reader, too, to compare the saint with his Danish opponents, to weigh up their contrasting characters and rival claims to the throne of East Anglia. The Danes appear as a negative, inverse reflection of Edmund and his family: as a demanding and taunting father, Lothbrok stands in opposition to the two kings who feature as loving and supportive father-figures to Edmund (his birth father, the king of Saxony, and his adoptive father Offa). Both aspire to rule the kingdom because of the urging of a father-figure, and although Geoffrey has been careful to point out that Edmund has a legitimate claim to the throne through Offa, Lothbrok's speech explicitly presents them as rival conquerors.

In this text, neither Edmund nor the sons of Lothbrok are natives of East Anglia; both belong to Germanic tribes, related to the Anglo-Saxons, but originating from the continent and coming to claim the throne from across the sea.[32] The native line of kings seems about to die with Offa (perhaps this is Geoffrey's way of explaining why it did in fact die out with Edmund).[33] This means that Edmund, like the Danes, is a newcomer to England – a foreign ruler, even if his kinship with Offa is emphasised. It is Edmund whose landing in England is dwelt upon by the text – his immediately fruitful interaction with the land functions as both a revelation of his saintly power and an omen for the prosperity of his future reign. It is a moment of peaceful conquest. The healing rivers which spring from the Norfolk soil as soon as Edmund sets foot upon it present an implied contrast with the 'loathsome brook' and his stream of hateful progeny, the meaning Geoffrey draws from his interpretation of Lothbrok's name. Geoffrey's etymologising makes sense in this context, encouraging the reader to see a contrast between the streams originating from Edmund and from Lothbrok.[34] Whatever the origins of Geoffrey's information about Lothbrok and his sons, he puts it to imaginative work in constructing his narrative about St Edmund's youth.

LOTHBROK AND THE HUNTSMAN: DEATH AND DANISH VENGEANCE

Just as Geoffrey of Wells provides St Edmund with a lineage, a family and a narrative of his youth, so he gives the fullest picture to date of Ubbe, Ivar and Beorn. Later sources build further on this desire to provide origins and motivations for both Edmund and his enemies, and the figure of Lothbrok comes to the fore. In Scandinavian tradition, Ragnar famously meets his death in England, captured by the Northumbrian king Ælla and put to death in a snake-pit. The death of Ragnar in England is a crucial part of the Norse legends, because it explains why his sons decide to come and invade Northumbria: they come to get vengeance on King Ælla. In *Ragnars saga*,

21a. Lothbrok and his dog set sail from Denmark to England

Ragnar, with his dying words, predicts his sons will be angry at his death: 'The piglets would grunt if they knew the boar's plight', he says.[35] The Norse legends tell how each of the sons reacts on hearing the news, their responses revealing their different characters: one son, Sigvard, cuts himself with a knife without noticing the pain; another, Hvitserk, is playing a game when he hears the news and squeezes a game-piece so tightly that his hand bleeds; Ivar turns red, then white, but is able to control himself enough to ask for every detail of his father's death. Saxo Grammaticus says that Ivar's reaction reveals he is the most dangerous of Ragnar's sons – the one with the most self-control and courage.[36]

Medieval English sources also have a story about Lothbrok's death and his sons' revenge, but the English version of the narrative has some significant differences from the Norse tradition. The most important is that in England the story is linked to St Edmund, rather than to Ælla, and so it came to be combined with Geoffrey of Wells' explanation of the Danes' motives and promulgated as part of Edmund's popular cult. The link between Lothbrok's murder and the Danish invasion is first made by the chronicler Roger of Wendover, a monk of St Albans, writing in the early thirteenth century.[37] Roger tells of a Danish man named Lothbrok, who goes out in a little boat, hunting for birds with a hawk. His boat is carried out to sea by a sudden storm, which drives him to the coast of East Anglia. He lands at Reedham in Norfolk and is taken to the court of King Edmund; Edmund receives him kindly, and 'as the Danish tongue is very like the English', Roger says, Lothbrok and Edmund are able to talk to each other. Lothbrok is greatly impressed by the elegant lifestyle he observes at Edmund's court, and asks to stay so that he can learn to imitate courtly manners. He takes lessons in hunting and hawking from Edmund's huntsman Bern, but Bern soon becomes jealous of Lothbrok's favour with the king and one day while they are out hunting Bern murders Lothbrok and hides his body in a thicket. Lothbrok's faithful greyhound leads Edmund and the rest of the court to discover the body, and Bern is found to be guilty of the crime. He is punished by being set adrift at sea in Lothbrok's boat and comes ashore on the coast of Denmark, where he meets Lothbrok's sons, Ivar and Ubbe, and maliciously lies that their father has been murdered by Edmund. They swear to take revenge on the English king, and so decide to invade his kingdom. From this point on, the story follows the familiar lines of Abbo's *Passio*.

This story is clearly related in some ways to the Norse versions of Ragnar's death, but the characterisation of Lothbrok and the shape of the narrative are very different. This

21b. Lothbrok is received at Edmund's court

Lothbrok is an innocent victim of Bern's jealousy, and in his admiration for St Edmund and his desire to imitate the courtly life of the East Anglian kingdom he is evidently intended to be a sympathetic character, a protégé of the saintly English king. Perhaps the most striking feature of this story is how it reduplicates aspects of Edmund's martyrdom in Lothbrok's murder, particularly in the role given to the protective greyhound who leads to the discovery of the murdered man's body – this seems to replay the motif of the wolf who guards Edmund's head in the usual accounts of Edmund's death. The repetition of one of the most famous elements of Edmund's story seems to position Lothbrok and Edmund in parallel roles, both innocent victims of undeserved murder, rather than in opposition or contrast to each other as in Geoffrey of Wells. A similar kind of structural repetition also occurs in the two journeys, in which characters travel between Denmark and England, in each case driven by the winds of chance (or fate, or divine providence). First Lothbrok is carried out to sea and driven to the coast of East Anglia, then Bern is set adrift in the same boat as a form of ordeal, 'that it might be proved whether God would deliver him from the danger'.[38] This narrative's use of such accidental journeys recalls William of Jumièges' reference to Björn Ironside being shipwrecked in England on his way home to Denmark, but in Roger's story the name Beorn belongs not to one of Lothbrok's sons but to the man whose intervention brings the Danes to England – a detail we shall encounter again.

Lothbrok's character and role are therefore conceived quite differently in this story from those of the 'loathsome brook' of Geoffrey of Wells, but the function of the Danes in both narratives is comparable. In each case, Denmark is imagined as a kind of mirror to East Anglia – whether directly or inversely – rather than as a distant or alien country. Edmund's characteristics as a saint, and some of the key images of his cult, are refigured in the presentation of his Danish enemies, allowing for the saintly king to be defined and exalted by contrast or by analogy. As well as explaining why the Danes came to England,

21c. The murder of Lothbrok by Bern the huntsman

these stories make use of the Danes to serve their purpose of praising Edmund, and they envisage Denmark as a near neighbour, a rival or a relative to East Anglia. Although the narratives still end in Edmund's death, Roger of Wendover's story, in particular, imagines a positive interaction between Lothbrok and the English king. Presenting Lothbrok's sons as avenging their father's murder (and blaming Edmund for it only because they have been misled by Bern), explains their behaviour, even if it does not quite justify it, while the innocent Lothbrok himself is an entirely sympathetic character.

In the ravenous search for material about St Edmund, these two distinct stories were in time combined into one narrative. A fourteenth-century compilation of hagiographical material, produced at Bury St Edmunds around 1377, contains a life of St Edmund which joins these two versions of the Lothbrok story into one.[39] Here, as in Geoffrey's narrative, the fame of the glorious King Edmund spreads to Denmark and causes Lothbrok to incite his sons to jealous anger against Edmund. After this, Lothbrok, out hunting at sea, is blown off course to England, taken to Edmund's court, and murdered by Bern the huntsman as in Roger of Wendover's tale. This composite version of the story was then used by John Lydgate, monk of Bury St Edmunds, in his *Life of St Edmund*, which was

commissioned to celebrate the occasion of Henry VI's stay at the
abbey in 1433–4.[40] A lavishly decorated manuscript of Lydgate's
poem, with more than a hundred miniatures illustrating the
story, was presented to the young king shortly afterwards.
This manuscript, which has been called 'one of the most
accomplished works of English illustration of the fifteenth
century',[41] shows Lothbrok and his sons in richly ornamented
costumes, and here they are clearly figured as foreign pagans.
Now the story of Lothbrok is fully incorporated into the narrative
of Edmund's death, but any sympathy for Lothbrok found in
Roger of Wendover's story is done away with; Lydgate presents
him as a cruel and envious pagan king, and his sons as bloodthirsty pirates.[42] In a poem which is intended to affirm the link
between Bury St Edmunds and royal power, the elements of
Lothbrok's story which are emphasised are his wicked kingship
and the dangers of envy at court – not only exemplified by
Lothbrok himself, but also by the murderer Bern. The pagan
Danes serve to exalt the saintly Edmund by contrast, and
Lothbrok is not the only Danish king cast in that role; Lydgate
also includes Herman's stories of Svein Forkbeard's death as a
result of Edmund's supernatural intervention and of Osgod's
hostility to Edmund, so the narrative includes a number of
Danes acting as Edmund's enemies.

21d. Bern tells Lothbrok's sons that Edmund has killed their father

Lydgate's poem became popular and widely read, and it survives in a large number of fifteenth-century manuscripts.[43] It circulated the story of Lothbrok's murder to a much wider audience than any previous version of the legend, and made it part of the standard late-medieval narrative of Edmund's death. The English branch of the Lothbrok story is often treated as a minor offshoot of the Norse saga tradition, but it is worth remembering that by the fifteenth century it had become an established part of one of the most high-status saintly cults in England; the idea of the teenage Henry VI reading about Lothbrok and his sons provides an important indication of how very different the context of the English strand of Lothbrok-lore is from its Scandinavian analogues, whatever their shared origins may have been.

Finally, there remains to be considered one further version of the revenge legend centring on St Edmund and the Danes. This was recorded by the monastic historian Thomas Elmham, writing in the second decade of the fifteenth century. He wrote at the monastery of St Augustine's in Canterbury, but his name suggests he came originally from North Elmham in Norfolk, so there may be a link to the East Anglian traditions.[44] Lord Francis Hervey, nineteenth-century editor of hagiographical texts on

21e. The Danes invade England

Edmund, called this version of the story 'the stupid and revolt-
ing figment which Thomas of Elmham has perpetuated', and
was so horrified by it that he consigned it to an appendix and
refused to translate it;[45] it is, however, a particularly interesting –
if lurid – variant of the usual story explaining the connection
between Edmund and the Danes.

This story tells how Edmund married the daughter of the
king of Denmark (no other source gives Edmund a wife; he was
considered a virgin saint).[46] His new wife already has two sons,
Ivar and Ubbe, whom she has conceived 'against nature', with a
bear. After their marriage Edmund catches his wife in bed with
the bear, and he kills it, rejects his wife, and returns to England.
When Ivar and Ubbe grow up, their mother tells them Edmund
is their father's murderer, and they cross the sea to England in
search of vengeance.

The motif of descent from a bear reflects a legend found in
Norse sagas, where the bear is usually either half-human or a
man magically transfigured into a bear. The element of the bear's
adult sons taking revenge for the killing of their father frequently
appears in those versions of the story, too, and in Chapter 3 we
will consider some more examples of this bear-descent motif –
in England it is always attached to Scandinavian characters,
suggesting that to English audiences the story had a particularly Norse flavour. It is not a motif linked to Ivar and Ubbe in
the Scandinavian legends (since their father there is Ragnar),
although one reference to Ivar says that he could shape-shift
into a bear, and the name of their brother Beorn – who does
not appear in this story – means 'bear'.[47] It seems that this is
a unique English combination of a story about Edmund with
an idea elsewhere associated with the Danes in England, which
is independent both of the Scandinavian legends and the
East Anglian stories about Edmund. It has parallels to
that tradition, but it involves a very different view of King
Edmund from the official version of his cult promoted at Bury
St Edmunds – he is not a virgin saint, and is actually the killer of
Ivar and Ubbe's father.

All these stories suggest that the character of Lothbrok was conceived of in England entirely in relation to the story of St Edmund's death. Although his sons feature in other contexts, Lothbrok never appears in a story unrelated to Edmund. This in itself sets the English Lothbrok legends apart from their Scandinavian analogues, and it means they reflect a specifically East Anglian perspective on the relationship between England and Denmark: Denmark is a close neighbour, just across the sea, and although the intervention of the Danes in East Anglian affairs is generally hostile there is also space for sympathy towards Lothbrok when he submits to the influence of St Edmund. Although Lothbrok shares the name of the great hero of Scandinavian legend, he is essentially a different character; whether imagined as the envious king of Geoffrey of Wells, or the humble victim of Roger of Wendover's story, he is no hero in his own right, but simply an adjunct to East Anglia's greater hero, St Edmund.

St Ragner

This brings us to one of the stranger offshoots of this legend in England, which seems to be the only appearance of the name Ragnar in English sources. A man named 'Ragner' appears to have been venerated – in one town at least – as a martyr and a saint. A short Latin text, the *Inventio cum translatione S. Ragnerii*, describes how the relics of a saint Ragner, 'soldier and martyr', were supposedly discovered at St Peter's church in Northampton.[48] In the text we learn very little about this Ragner or who he was thought to have been, although the circumstances of the finding of his relics are described in detail – and they are of interest in themselves.

The text survives in a manuscript of Bede's *Historia Ecclesiastica* which was made at Kirkham Priory in Yorkshire,[49] and another copy appears in a fourteenth-century manuscript, probably originating from the Northampton area, containing saints'

lives and other hagiographical material.[50] The *Inventio* claims
that the relics of St Ragner came to light in the middle of the
eleventh century, during the reign of Edward the Confessor.
At that time, it says, the priest of St Peter's was a man named
Bruning, and among Bruning's servants was a man of Norwegian
birth, so simple and patient that many people laughed at him as
a fool.[51] This Norwegian man, who is not named, conceives a
great desire to go on a pilgrimage to Rome to seek the tomb of
St Peter – he wants to seek out the man he is accustomed to call,
in his own language, 'drotin', which the text translates as *dominus*,
'lord'. He sets out, but during his journey he has a sequence of
three dreams telling him he must turn back: his real 'drotin' is to
be found not in Rome, but in his own church in Northampton.
The man obeys his visions and returns home, much to the
mockery of his companions, and after more than a year his
humble devotion is rewarded by a vision showing him a spot
in the church where the relics of an unknown martyr lie buried.
When the tomb is excavated crowds gather to see the discovery
and miracles take place: a woman named Alfgiva is healed from
illness after praying at the tomb, bells ring by some divine
power, and dazzling light shines from the church in the middle
of the night. It is only after these miracles that Bruning finally
opens the tomb, and there he finds the body and an inscription
identifying the saint as 'Ragener, holy martyr of Christ', a
nephew of St Edmund who died in the same persecution as
the king. More miracles occur, and the fame of Ragner spreads.
Pilgrims come from far and wide, and King Edward sends
generous gifts to the newly built shrine. The text then closes
with an attempt to put these events in some historical context:
Edmund and Ragner both died in 870, it says, and seven years
later his persecutor Ivar was killed along with another unnamed
pagan king. The date of Edward the Confessor's death, 1066, is
also noted as an indication of when these relics were thought to
have been discovered.

Apart from this one short account, there are very few other
references to this mysterious saint Ragner. Ragner is mentioned

in a list of saints' resting-places which was compiled c.1155 by Hugh Candidus, monk and chronicler of Peterborough. This list includes a saint named 'St Ragaher, king' whose relics are in 'Hamtune' (i.e. Northampton).[52] No other details are given. Although there is no evidence that this saint was venerated anywhere other than Northampton, his cult seems to have endured there for some time: from the fifteenth and sixteenth centuries there are references in the church records to a 'fraternytye of Seynt Reginary in the church of Seynt Peter' and a chapel of 'St Eregiar', apparently the same saint.[53] In the fifteenth century the feast of St Ragner was being celebrated at St Peter's on 21 November, the day after St Edmund's.[54]

Who was St Ragner? The *Inventio* gives no details about the saint's life or death, except to say that he was Edmund's nephew and died with him. Where, why, or how he was killed is not stated. The focus of the text is entirely on the discovery of his relics, and not on the activities of the saint himself; the link to Edmund and the supernatural elements of the narrative are sufficient to demonstrate his sanctity. There is not much to go on, then, except his name – which is, of course, a suggestive one. It seems possible that there may be a connection between this Ragner and Ragnar Lothbrok, especially as there are no other obvious candidates for this supposed relative of St Edmund. Since the figure named in Scandinavian sources as Ragnar Lothbrok is usually called only Lothbrok in England, it would be unusual to find him appearing under the name Ragnar; as noted above, however, the first time the two names occur together is in a twelfth-century text from Iceland, apparently attributing the information to English sources on St Edmund's death, so it may be that this link had already been made in England and is simply not recorded in any of the surviving sources. As Edmund's legend grew, he was provided with numerous saintly relations for whom there is no historical basis – over the centuries he acquired a hermit brother named Eadwold and a nephew named Fremund, in addition to St Ragner.[55] We have seen how Lothbrok, originally Edmund's antagonist, became reinterpreted in legend as his friend and even his protégé, cruelly and innocently murdered; it would not be a great stretch to make that into a family relationship, or to interpret Lothbrok's murder as a kind of martyrdom.

If these were indeed the origins of St Ragner, however, the text which recounts the discovery of his relics does not seem aware of it. Although Ivar is mentioned at the very end, the *Inventio* does not suggest any link between these pagan kings and the 'holy martyr of Christ'. However, there is one intriguing connection with Scandinavia in the *Inventio*: the Norwegian servant. The simple, devout man to whom Ragner's relics are revealed is not just of Norwegian birth, but is explicitly said to be a Norse-speaker – he refers to St Peter in his native language as *drotin*, 'lord', and by the miraculous discovery of the martyr's relics he learns that Ragner, not St Peter, is the real *drotin* he has been seeking. This must represent the Old Norse word *dróttinn*, a common word for 'lord', which was also frequently used in medieval Christian contexts to refer to God and to saints. The appearance of this word in the *Inventio* is an interesting moment of linguistic self-consciousness: the text treats it as a foreign and unfamiliar word, worth noting and translating as a marker of this Norwegian man's distinctive language.[56] The meaning of the word then becomes crucial to the story of the man's revelation and spiritual enlightenment, as he is shown the identity of his true 'lord' and leads others to venerate him.

In some elusive way, then, the Norwegian identity of this man seems to be important, but the *Inventio* tells us far less about him than we would like to know – unlike the priest Bruning and the healed Alfgiva, the Norwegian servant does not even have a name. Could it have been a man from Scandinavia, living in Northampton, who decided to promote the story of St Ragner the martyr? If so, when did this happen? The text places these events in the reign of Edward the Confessor (about a hundred years before the earliest records of St Ragner), giving it an air of antiquity and an association with not one but two saintly

Anglo-Saxon kings. A more likely time for this story to emerge might, however, be the middle of the twelfth century, around the time in the 1140s when the church of St Peter's was rebuilt in splendid Romanesque style, probably under the patronage of Simon de Senlis, earl of Huntingdon and Northampton. The church boasts a rich array of Norman carvings, including an elaborately decorated grave-cover which may be connected to St Ragner's shrine.[57] In Chapter 3 we will see how the earldom of Huntingdon and Northampton became linked to a legendary origin-story drawn from Anglo-Scandinavian narrative material, attached to Simon's maternal grandfather Waltheof. This narrative, which is also set in the reign of Edward the Confessor, was recorded at Crowland and at Delapré Abbey, on the outskirts of Northampton, in the early thirteenth century. It is impossible to be sure if there is any relationship between this narrative and the cult of St Ragner, but the Northampton and Senlis connection is suggestive. If nothing else, it is a reminder that the elaborate Bury St Edmunds version of the Lothbrok legend was probably only the tip of the iceberg – there may have been other traditions about Ragnar and his sons circulating in England, for which we now have only incomplete and tantalising evidence.

THE DEATHS OF LOTHBROK'S SONS

The *Inventio* closes with a note that Ivar and 'another pagan king' died in 877.[58] No information is given here except the date, but other English sources show an interest not only in Lothbrok's death – the motivator of the Danish invasion – but also in the death and burial of his sons at various places in England. Some time in the first half of the thirteenth century, on the blank leaf of a manuscript of Bede's *Historia Ecclesiastica*, a number of brief notes in Latin and English were added on an assortment of historical subjects.[59] They include two lines of verse in English on the sons of Lothbrok:

Yngvar and vbbe beorn wæs þe þridde
loþebrokes sunnes loþe weren criste

(Ivar and Ubbe, Beorn was the third, Lothbrok's sons, hateful
to Christ.)

These two lines draw the same connection between *Lothbrok*
and the Middle English word *lōth*, 'hateful, wicked', which
was noted by Geoffrey of Wells; they may be the remains of a
longer poem, or simply a brief verse tag. The lines are followed
by a short passage in Latin describing the deaths of Ubbe and
Beorn. It says that Ubbe, after killing many Christians, was
killed at 'Ubbelawe' in Yorkshire by the will of God, while his
brother Beorn destroyed the church at 'Scapeia' (apparently
Sheppey in Kent) and violated the nuns there. In a sudden act
of divine punishment Beorn was swallowed up by the earth –
horse and armour and all – at Frindsbury near Rochester. To
this day, the note goes on, there is a deep fissure in the road
there, 20 feet wide, where Beorn was engulfed by the earth,
and the water at the bottom of it is always tinged red as if
with blood.

This manuscript, originally made around the end of the
twelfth century, may have belonged to Tynemouth Priory in
Northumbria. The other notes on the leaf include some details
on King Osred of Northumbria (who was buried at Tynemouth)
and the Anglo-Saxon boy-martyr St Kenelm, about whom there
is also a line of English verse. In addition, there is a short passage
in Latin about Siward, earl of Northumbria, which is taken from
Henry of Huntingdon's *Historia Anglorum*. This briefly notes
Siward's conquest of Scotland in 1054 and reproduces Henry's
account of his death, in which Henry tells how Siward, after
a long military career, insisted on dying in his armour rather
than 'in bed like a cow'. This story and others about Siward, and
their connection to English legends about the sons of Ragnar
Lothbrok, will be discussed in more detail in Chapter 3; what
is particularly interesting in the context of this manuscript

is that the Siward story and the note on Ubbe and Beorn are found together, and that they both concern the unusual deaths of these Danish warriors. There is some comparison in the style of their deaths: Beorn, like Siward, dies in full armour, with his lance held upright. A final comment, added to Henry's story about Siward's death, makes the link to Tynemouth by noting that Siward's successor as earl of Northumbria was Tostig Godwineson, who 'laid the foundations of the church at Tynemouth'.[60]

Tynemouth was a cell of St Albans, the monastic community to which Roger of Wendover belonged, so there may be a connection between this knowledge of Lothbrok in Tynemouth and Roger's story; there are differences, however, since in Roger's version of the Lothbrok legend Beorn is not Lothbrok's son, but his murderer. Like the information about Siward, the extract about Ubbe and Beorn seems to have been copied from another source, since there are close verbal parallels with a passage found in one thirteenth-century manuscript of the *Chronica* of Roger of Howden (London, British Library, Arundel MS. 69). This manuscript contains a number of additions to Roger of Howden's chronicle, some of which are connected with the history of Bury St Edmunds, although all that is known of the provenance of the manuscript is that it belonged to Netley Abbey, near Southampton, by the fifteenth century.[61]

The Tynemouth manuscript also contains a marginal note (probably a later addition, and not present in the Arundel manuscript) connecting the story of Beorn's death to Hoo St Werburgh, on the Hoo peninsula near Frindsbury in Kent. This link to Kent is particularly interesting, because most of the evidence we have looked at so far for English traditions about the sons of Lothbrok has come from East Anglia and the East Midlands; the references to Kent are therefore surprising, and not easily explained. There are, however, other comparable references to the violent deaths of Lothbrok's sons from elsewhere in England. A late-medieval text found only in

a manuscript from Hyde Abbey, Winchester, says that it was
Ubbe who was swallowed up by the earth with his horse while
he was riding, and Ivar (here called, as is common in English
medieval sources, Hinguar) was drowned while crossing a
ford in Berkshire. The place where he died came to be named
after him, *Hyngarford* – modern Hungerford.[62] This suggests
that a variety of legends had grown up around the deaths
of Lothbrok's sons, focusing particularly on how they were
punished for their wickedness by divine intervention. These
seem to belong to an alternative tradition from the Lothbrok
legend of East Anglia, and it may be significant that they come
from areas of the country which had a very different history
of Viking activity (although this may also simply be an acci-
dent of survival). The link made in these stories with English
place-names like Hungerford, or with distinctive features of
the landscape – the pit with its water tinged with blood –
suggest they may be precursors to legends about the Danes
which are recorded more fully from the early modern period,
and which we will return to in the epilogue.

THE KING BY THE SEA: BURIAL-MOUNDS
AND THE DANES IN ENGLAND

As well as these references to the deaths of the sons of Lothbrok,
there may also have been legends about their places of burial,
although the evidence for this is more scanty. The Tynemouth
text mentions 'Ubbelawe' as the place of Ubbe's death in
Yorkshire, and this is a name which also occurs in passing in
Geffrei Gaimar's *Estoire des Engleis*, an Anglo-Norman chronicle
written c.1136–7. Gaimar records that after Ubbe was killed
in battle in Devon he was buried in a mound which took his
name, *Ubbelawe*.[63] The name-element *lawe* derives from Old
English *hlæw*, and refers to artificial elevations in the landscape,
especially barrows and burial-mounds.[64] Gaimar calls it a *hoge*,
a word meaning 'burial-mound'; this word was borrowed into

northern dialects of English (and in this case Anglo-Norman) from Old Norse *haugr*, and it is found in place-names in the north of England in the form *howe*. This battle in Devon is the one in which the *Anglo-Saxon Chronicle* says that the raven banner was captured (and also the point at which the *Annals of St Neots* adds its note about Lothbrok's daughters weaving the banner in one noon-tide). However, the detail of Ubbe's death and burial and the name of his barrow-mound are Gaimar's additions to his source, and are not recorded elsewhere. The *Anglo-Saxon Chronicle* only says that a brother of Ivar and Halfdan was killed; Gaimar adds Ubbe's name and the location of the battle at 'Pene' (perhaps Penwood or Penselwood). There have been attempts to identify *Ubbelawe* with a landmark near Appledore, on the Devon coast, which has now been lost to the sea, but which as late as the eighteenth century was known as Ubbaston or Whibblestan.[65]

Wherever this mound may have been (if it really existed), Gaimar may have learned its name in Lincolnshire, where he was probably writing. It may be that there was never any particular legend attached to this burial-mound, but it is worth noting that the Norse legends about the sons of Ragnar make a point of saying that Ivar was buried by the sea in England. Ivar's burial-mound features prominently in Old Norse narratives of Anglo-Scandinavian history, because it is given a crucial and dramatic role to play in the two conquests which England faced in 1066. Its construction, on Ivar's own orders, is described in *Ragnars saga*:

> Ok þa er hann la i banasott, mellti hann, at hann skylldi þangat fera, er herskat veri, ok þess kvazt hann venta, at þeir mundi eigi sigr fa, er þar kemi at landinu. Ok er hann andaz, var sva giort, sem hann mellti fyrir, ok var þa i haug lagidr. Ok þat segia margir menn, þa er Haralldr konungr Sigurdarson kom til Englandz, at hann kemi þar at, er Ivar var fyrir, ok fellr hann i þeirre faur. Ok er Vilhialmr bastardr kom i land, for hann til ok braut haug Ivars ok sa Ivar ofuinn.

Þa let hann giora bal mikit ok lętr Ivar brenna á balinu. Ok
eptir þat berzt hann til landsins ok fęrr gagn.[66]

(And when [Ivar] lay in his last illness, he said that he
should be carried to the place where armies came to harry,
and he said he thought they should not have the victory
when they came to the land. And when he died, it was
done as he had said, and he was laid in a barrow (*haugr*).
And many people say that when King Harald Sigurðarson
[i.e. Harald Hardrada] came to England, he landed at the
place where Ivar was, and he died on that expedition. And
when William the Bastard came to the land, he went to
the place and opened Ivar's howe and saw Ivar, undecayed.
Then he had a great fire made and had Ivar burned in the
flames. After that he fought battles across the country and
won the victory.)

This burial-mound also appears in *Hemings þáttr*, a narrative written in Iceland in the thirteenth century, which deals
at greater length with the attempted Norwegian invasion of
England, the Norman Conquest, and its aftermath. It draws on a
range of sources, some of which may have included information
ultimately of English provenance; it includes, for instance, a version of the legend that Harold Godwineson survived the Battle
of Hastings and lived on as a hermit in England.[67] It also seems
to have used a version of *Ragnars saga*, from which the story of
Ivar's burial-mound may have been borrowed. In *Hemings þáttr*,
Harald Hardrada and Tostig Godwineson see a mound as they
arrive on the coast of Cleveland in 1066, and Harald asks for the
name of it:

Þeir taka land ok ganga þar vpp sem Kliflond heita konvngr
spyr T(osta) hvat heitir hæð sv er þar er norðr a landit.
T(osti) s(egir) eigi er her hverri hæð nafn gefit. konvngr
s(egir) nafn man þo þersi eiga ok skalltv segia mer. T(osti)
s(egir) þat er havgr Ivars beinlavsa. konvngr svarar fair hafa

þeir sigrað England er at hans havgi hafa fyrst komit. T(osti)
s(egir) forneskia er nv at trva slikv.[68]

(They reached land and came ashore at a place called
Cleveland. The king asked Tostig, 'What is the name of the
hill which is along the land to the north?' Tostig said, 'Not
every hill has a name given to it.' The king said, 'But this one
has a name, and you shall tell it to me.' Tostig said, 'That is
the howe of Ivar the boneless.' The king replied, 'Few who
have landed in England near this howe have been victorious.'
Tostig said, 'It's superstition to believe such things now.')

In these texts, the difference between the two invaders of 1066
is shown by how they react to Ivar's burial-mound: William is
prepared to risk the wrath of the great Viking by burning his
bones, but Harald, who is convinced he is doomed to die on his
expedition, accepts the bad omen as his fate. The connection
between the mound, the act of naming, and success or failure
in conquest is significant here, drawing a powerful link between
the invader's burial and the land he has conquered. Ivar's ability
to defend his kingdom endures after his death, and the burial-
mound, standing on the cliffs above the sea, is a visible symbol
of his supernatural control over it.

Norse literature is rich in legends linked to barrows and
burial-mounds, which are the location of encounters with the
otherworld, with supernatural beings, and with the dead.[69]
There is a variety of evidence from Anglo-Saxon England, too,
for the cultural importance of burial-mounds: as meeting-
places and as landmarks, as the home of dragons and demons,
and as the site of hidden treasure, such mounds seem to have
been interpreted as profoundly meaningful sites of encounter,
a liminal space for coming face to face with the past.[70] The
most famous burial-mound in Anglo-Saxon literature appears
at the end of *Beowulf*, when the hero is buried in a barrow on
a headland, according to the instructions he has given before
his death.[71] As described in the poem, this barrow serves as
a memorial to Beowulf and a landmark to sailors, but its

function appears to be mnemonic, not defensive – there is no explicit warning to future invaders.[72] The idea of the defensive burial-mound seems to represent a particular offshoot of this wider literary tradition which connects the burial-mound with invasion and conquest. This may be linked to the role of mounds in king-making, the claiming of inheritance, and the enacting of royal power: there are numerous examples in Old Norse literature of kings being formally elected or accepted as king on a mound, as well as of mounds being used as the sites of assemblies and the proclamation of laws.[73] It has been suggested that the story about Ivar's burial-mound recorded in *Ragnars saga* may have originated in an area of England with strong Anglo-Scandinavian heritage, since this was, as Rory McTurk puts it, 'surely the most likely environment for the development of a story in which a Viking leader seems to be presented as a guardian spirit of the English people.'[74] There is no trace of this from any surviving English source; if some kind of legend was ever attached to the burial-mound that is recorded in English sources, Ubbelawe, it was not preserved.

However, there are two examples of burial-mound stories worth discussing here which occur in sources written in late Anglo-Saxon England, both in the context of interaction between the English and an army of invading Danes. One is a miracle-story in the *Historia de Sancto Cuthberto*, written in Northumbria in the late tenth or eleventh century.[75] This story takes place after the Viking conquest of York, after Ælla and Osberht have been defeated by the Danes. The Viking leader, Halfdan – in Norse tradition, though not here, one of the sons of Ragnar Lothbrok – has been forced to flee. He has been driven mad by the wrath of God in punishment for his sins, perhaps an early example of the kinds of stories about the violent deaths of Ubbe, Ivar and Beorn considered above. As a result, there is a power vacuum, and by the supernatural intervention of St Cuthbert a young slave-boy named Guthred is chosen to become king of the Danes. Cuthbert appears in a vision to Eadred, the abbot of Carlisle, to announce to him how Guthred should be elected and made king: 'lead him with the whole army upon the hill which is called *Oswigesdune* and there place upon his right arm a golden armlet, and thus they shall all constitute him king'.[76] The body of St Cuthbert is brought to the hill for the king-making ceremony, and Guthred and the army swear on the relics that they will keep peace and fidelity with the community of St Cuthbert. As the saint has instructed, Guthred grants all the land between the Tyne and the Wear to St Cuthbert's community.

This is a remarkable episode, which seems to show the Christian leaders of Northumbria making a political and religious accommodation with the pagan Danes.[77] Guthred is presumably the Guthfrith who ruled in York between c.883 and 895, and here he is cast in the role of Cuthbert's anointed king – a second King David, plucked from humble origins to become a Christian ruler. Guthfrith was buried in York Minster, so by the end of his reign he must have accepted Christianity. However, although the new king and his army swear an oath on the relics of St Cuthbert, the details of this king-making ceremony – the location on *Oswigesdune*, the use of a symbolic armlet – reflect pagan Scandinavian custom.[78] The mound of *Oswigesdune* was presumably a meeting-place associated with a king named Oswiu, perhaps the brother of King Oswald who reigned in Northumbria between 642 and 670. It is necessary to be cautious in using a miracle-story like this as evidence for the situation in ninth-century Northumbria, but whatever lies behind this episode, it offers an example of a Norse king-making ceremony involving a burial-mound, associated with the Danish invasions, which became part of English historio-graphical accounts of this period.[79]

A similar connection between the supernatural power of a *hlæw* and a Danish invasion seems to lie behind an intriguing passage in the *Anglo-Saxon Chronicle* entry for 1006. A Danish army raided in Wessex that year with devastating effect, and the chronicler is scathing about the lack of resistance they met with from the English:

Þa ofer þone midne sumor com þa se micla flota to Sandwic,
7 dydon eal swa hi ær gewuna wæron, heregodon 7 bærndon
7 slogon swa swa hi ferdon. Þa het se cyng abannan ut ealne
þeodscipe of Wesseaxum 7 of Myrcnum, 7 hi lagon ute þa
ealne ðone hærfest on fyrdinge ongean þone here, ac hit naht
ne beheold þe ma ðe hit oftor ær dide, ac for eallum þissum
se here ferde swa he sylf wolde [...] Þa to ðam middan
wintran eodan him to heora gearwan feorme ut þuruh
Hamtunscire into Bearrucscire to Readingon, 7 hi a dydon
heora ealdan gewunan, atendon hiora herebeacen swa hi
ferdon. Wendon þa to Wealingaforda 7 þæt eall forswældon,
7 wæron him ða ane niht æt Ceolesige, 7 wendon him þa (i)
andlang Æscesdune to Cwicelmeshlæwe, 7 þær onbidedon
beotra gylpa, forðon oft man cwæð gif hi Cwicelmeshlæw
gesohton þæt hi næfre to sæ gan ne scoldon; wendon him
þa oðres weges hamwerd. Þa wæs ðær fyrd gesomnod æt
Cynetan, 7 hi þær togædere fengon, 7 sona þæt wered on
fleame gebrohton 7 syþþan hiora herehyþe to sæ feredan. Ac
þær mihton geseon Wincesterleode rancne here 7 unearhne
ða hi be hiora gate to sæ eodon.[80]

(Then after midsummer the great fleet came to Sandwich,
and acted just as was their custom: they harried and burned
and slew as they went. Then the king summoned out all
the nation from Wessex and Mercia, and they stayed out in
military service against the army all through the autumn,
but it did no more good that it had often done before,
because for all this the army went about exactly as they chose
[...] Then towards midwinter they went to the provision
prepared for them, out through Hampshire into Berkshire
to Reading, and they followed their old custom, lighting
war-beacons as they went. Then they turned to Wallingford
and burned it all, and spent one night at Cholsey, and then
went along Ashdown to *Cwichelmeshlæw*, and there they
waited for what they had been proudly threatened with,
because it had often been said that if they reached
Cwichelmeshlæw they would never get to the sea. Then they

went home another way. The English army was then gathered
at the Kennet, and [the Danes] came together there and at
once put that troop to flight, and afterwards carried their
booty to the sea. There the people of Winchester could see
the proud and undaunted army as they went past their gates
to the sea.)

Cwichelmeshlæw (now called Cuckhamsley Barrow or
Scutchamer Knob) is a significant site. It is a mound standing
in a prominent position on the ancient track of the Ridgeway,
high on the Berkshire Downs, commanding a view over the
surrounding country for miles around.[81] Although a prehistoric
barrow probably dating to the Bronze Age, it takes its name
from Cwichelm, seventh-century king of Wessex;[82] early Anglo-
Saxon sources record Cwichelm's battles against the Welsh and
Mercians alongside his brother Cynegils, and *Cwichelmeshlæw*
may have been believed to be his burial-mound, or perhaps the
site of one of his battles.[83]

The mound was a meeting-place for the shire assembly of
Berkshire, and an important local landmark set in a particularly
meaningful landscape. In the early Anglo-Saxon period, this
region was the heart of the kingdom of Wessex, the site of royal
settlements and its first episcopal see at Dorchester-on-Thames,
where Cwichelm was baptised in 636.[84] Although by the early
eleventh century the political centre of the kingdom had shifted
south, the name *Cwichelmeshlæw* preserved these resonant
associations with the early history of the West Saxon kings. To
a reader of the *Anglo-Saxon Chronicle*, there would have been
echoes here too of earlier conflicts against the Vikings: the army
travelled 'along Ashdown', where Alfred the Great had won a
memorable victory against the Danes in 871, and this is an area
with which Alfred himself was strongly associated – Cuckhamsley
Barrow is less than five miles from Alfred's birthplace at Wantage.
For the chronicler, the bitter point is that the Danes were so
dominant in Wessex at this period that they were confident
enough to flout English threats of resistance – not only did the

vaunted opposition not materialise, but they were able to raid across Wessex at will and deliberately defy the proud English boast that 'if they reached *Cwichelmeshlæw* they would never get to the sea.' They proceeded to carry their booty past the very gates of Winchester, by this time the political and spiritual centre of Wessex. In the perspective of the chronicler, the Danes were consciously using the landscape of West Saxon power to humiliate the English and demonstrate their control.[85] The threat about *Cwichelmeshlæw* is framed as a boast but it might equally be interpreted as a superstition, even a curse, reflecting the power Cwichelm was supposed to hold over the mound which bore his name. The Danes defy not only a living king but a dead one: so fallen is the kingdom of Wessex from its former greatness (the chronicler implies) that King Æthelred is helpless to resist these invaders, and even the supernatural power of the once mighty Cwichelm has no ability to restrain them.

22. The remains of *Cwichelmshlæw* (now called Cuckhamsley Barrow or Scutchamer Knob), once a prominent mound on the Berkshire Downs, where the Vikings defied Anglo-Saxon threats in 1006

What is interesting in both these stories is that the burial-mounds in question belong to Anglo-Saxon kings – Oswiu and Cwichelm – but retain their meaning in the context of a Danish invasion. In each case the Danes are perceived as making use of the power of the landscape and showing an awareness of the cultural and political resonance such monuments might have for their Anglo-Saxon enemies. Perhaps this provides one possible environment in which the story of Ivar's howe may have arisen, for an English audience more sympathetic to the Danes than the writer of the *Anglo-Saxon Chronicle*; a tradition significant in an English context becomes the means by which power is transferred to the invading Danes.

An even stronger parallel occurs in the context of another narrative about the invasions of 1066 which, like *Ragnars saga*, links a burial-mound legend to the Norman Conquest. The *Carmen de Hastingae Proelio* says that after his death at Hastings Harold Godwineson was buried, on William's orders, under a heap of stones on a cliff by the seashore. His tomb bore the epitaph 'You rest here, King Harold, by order of the duke, so that you may still be guardian of the shore and sea.'[86] William of Poitiers adds that this was done in mockery of Harold, and in spite of his mother's petition that his body be returned to her for burial.[87]

Harold's fate after the Battle of Hastings is a contested issue in the medieval sources, and became the subject of legend. In addition to this tradition of burial by the shore, different sources claim he was buried at Waltham Abbey, or that he survived the battle to live as a hermit in Chester.[88] The legend of his survival reached Scandinavia and Iceland, and *Hemings þáttr*, which takes the story of Ivar's burial-mound from *Ragnars saga*, is also one of several Norse texts to tell of Harold being rescued from the battlefield at Hastings and recovering from his wounds to live as a hermit.[89] Elisabeth van Houts has persuasively argued that the *Carmen*'s description of seashore burial is likely to originate from Scandinavian England, rather than from Normandy, and she even suggests that the *Carmen* describes a form of

23. Harold Godwineson on the
Bayeux Tapestry (Wikimedia
Commons)

king-making ceremony, in which William declares himself king on the burial-mound of his defeated enemy.[90] If this is the case, the idea finds its strongest resonance within the particular context of Anglo-Scandinavian England and the complex and contested identity of Harold and his family. Through their Danish mother Gytha, Harold and his siblings had strong family ties to Scandinavia: at the time of Harold's death in 1066 his cousin, Svein Estrithson, was king of Denmark, and he and his siblings represented the most powerful Anglo-Scandinavian dynasty in England. Gytha, whose request to William prompted this 'mockery' of a burial, returned to Denmark after the Conquest, with the remaining members of her family and some of Harold's children, to seek refuge with her nephew Svein.[91] In the years that followed, Svein and his brothers took an active part in aiding English rebellion against Norman rule, and there was a serious threat of Danish invasion in the decades after 1066, the period in which the *Carmen* and William of Poitiers' *Gesta Guillelmi* were written.[92]

In Chapter 3 we will see how an origin-myth associated with Gytha's family and the Danish royal dynasty appears in post-Conquest England in a disparaging, anti-Danish (though also anti-Norman) context. It might be possible to read the references to Harold's burial by the sea as a mocking assault on the Danish side of the king's identity, casting the defeated

Harold – whose legitimacy and claim to the throne were so roundly attacked by Norman writers in the immediate aftermath of the Conquest – in the role of a pagan Viking invader. Despite the claims of *Ragnars saga*, William doubtless did *not* trouble to seek and out destroy Ivar's burial-mound, but this story of Harold's burial seems to imagine the Norman conqueror flouting the protective power of the barrow in a not dissimilar way.

Saints and sagas: conclusions

In this chapter we have looked at the English traditions relating to Ragnar Lothbrok and his sons within a medieval English context, rather than attempting to assess their relationship to the historical facts or to the much more extensive legends recorded in the Scandinavian sources. In part this is because both those avenues of inquiry have already been fully and profitably explored, but it is also because there are advantages in re-situating these traditions within their English context, and in relation to the particular communities and texts where they are recorded. Because the English narratives about Lothbrok and his sons are scattered and brief by comparison with the Norse tradition, they have often been interpreted within the context of that larger body of material, in order either to hypothesise about the origins of the later Norse traditions or to explain what might otherwise be cryptic references in the English sources. In this approach, the people for whom these traditions are assumed to be most meaningful, for whose cultural identity they are perceived to be most relevant, are the early Scandinavian settlers in northern England, in the first decades after the settlement when a sense of Norse identity might be strongest. Alfred Smyth's judgement is typical, commenting that the English traditions about Lothbrok and his sons 'are independent survivals in a greatly altered form of the saga of Ragnar which began life among the Northumbrian Danes before these had lost their identity in medieval England.'[93]

These may, indeed, be the origins of the stories about Lothbrok and his sons – we will never really know for sure. However, the context in which they are preserved in English sources is very distant from these hypothetical beginnings. They appear in a range of hagiographical and historical sources, predominantly linked to the history of East Anglia, although with a few other isolated references. In the hagiography of St Edmund, expanding the role of Lothbrok in Edmund's death allowed space for an exploration of kingship and royal power, with Edmund's Danish antagonists cast variously as contrasts or as complements to the central figure of St Edmund. They were given a role in the increasing promotion of Edmund as not only a regional but also a national saint, a patron of England, whose cult was particularly linked to the royal family – a trend culminating in Lothbrok's appearance among the brightly-dressed pagan Danes of Lydgate's fifteenth-century poem.[94] At the same time, the two main versions of the Lothbrok story, eventually combined into one narrative, both have strong links with eastern England, particularly with East Anglia, and explore some possible reasons why the Danes might have come to that region in the Anglo-Saxon period.

Other references to the various fates of Ivar, Ubbe and Beorn are less interested in motive than in punishment – colourful stories which prove that the invaders got what they deserved. In contrast to the East Anglian traditions (though perhaps descending from them), they are more widely scattered throughout the country: the notes on the fates of Lothbrok's sons survive in manuscripts which could hardly have belonged to places further apart, from Tynemouth in the north to Netley Abbey on the coast of Hampshire. They are added to other, more authoritative sources for English history, perhaps because they were perceived to be relevant to local concerns, perhaps simply out of interest. The wickedness of Ivar and Ubbe and their brothers formed a standard part of later medieval narratives about the Viking Age, mostly following the Anglo-Saxon sources; what we see in these brief references, however, seems to be evidence of a tradition which continued to develop, rather than a simple reproduction of previous narratives. They are an indication that narratives about the Danes in England should not be viewed simply as imperfect or derivative survivals of older legends, but as a living tradition in their own right, with continuing meaning and relevance to English audiences throughout the medieval period.

CHAPTER 3

THE STORY OF SIWARD

The tales of the ancients tell that a certain noble man, Ursus (whom the Lord, contrary to the usual manner of human procreation, allowed to be begotten with a white bear as his father and a woman of noble birth as his mother), begot Spratlingus; Spratlingus begot Ulsius; and Ulsius begot Beorn, nicknamed Beresune, that is, 'Bear's Son'. This Beorn was Danish by race, a distinguished earl and illustrious soldier. As a sign, however, of the difference of species on the part of his ancestors, nature had given him the ears of his father, that is, those of a bear. In all other ways he resembled his mother's species. And after many acts of valour and military adventures, he begot a brave son, a noble imitator of his father's strength and military skill. His name was Siward.[1]

This is the beginning of a text which survives in a thirteenth-century manuscript, probably written at Crowland Abbey in the Fenlands of Lincolnshire.[2] What follows is an eventful story about the life of Siward, the grandson of a bear, telling how he travelled from Denmark to Britain in search of adventures, fought a dragon, and tricked Edward the Confessor into giving him an earldom. Many of the episodes in this narrative have marked parallels in Old Norse literature, and it has sometimes been described as the closest thing to saga to have survived from medieval England.[3] But the context in which it survives is, perhaps, surprising: this text, known as the *Gesta antecessorum comitis Waldevi*, is presented as an account of the ancestors of Waltheof, earl of Huntingdon and Northampton, who was venerated as a saint at Crowland Abbey. This suggests that the story of Siward, with his bear ancestry and his exotic adventures, was apparently intended to reflect glory on one of the abbey's saintly patrons. What did this tale about the exploits of a Danish warrior have to offer to an audience in thirteenth-century Lincolnshire? In this chapter we will explore this story within the context of related narratives from the East Midlands and the Fens, including the legends of the sons of Ragnar Lothbrok and tales of Hereward the Wake, and see how the story of Siward may have come into being.

THE HISTORICAL SIWARD

Unlike some of the Viking warriors we have considered so far, Siward is a well-attested historical figure. His origins are obscure, although he was probably born in Denmark (the name Siward is a common anglicisation of the Norse name Sigurðr). He seems to have risen to prominence in the reign of Cnut: he first appears in English sources in 1033, two years before Cnut's death, holding the title of earl of southern Northumbria.[4] His predecessor in that role was Erik Hakonarson, Cnut's brother-in-law, earl of Hlaðir and ruler of western Norway. Erik had played an important role in the Danish conquest of England in 1015–16, and was rewarded by Cnut with the huge and powerful earldom of Northumbria. Erik appears to have died around five years later (the precise year is unknown), but it is not clear exactly when Siward succeeded him as earl.[5]

Given the care with which Cnut made his appointments, it is surprising that such an important earldom should have been entrusted to a man whose family origins are so unclear; the speed of Siward's rise might suggest his ancestry was more distinguished than we can now reconstruct. It has been speculated that he may have been related either to Erik or to

24. St Olave's, York, the church founded by Siward, earl of
Northumbria, where he was buried in 1055

Cnut himself,[6] but no such relationship is mentioned in any
contemporary source. The only evidence we have for his family
history is the 'bear's son' genealogy quoted above – and that
presents numerous problems, as we shall see.

In any case, Siward outlasted the Danish king who had
appointed him, and remained an important figure in English
politics well into the reign of Edward the Confessor. At first he
was ruler only of southern Northumbria, the region centred on
York, but in 1041 the rest of Northumbria north of the Tees was
added to his earldom. This was the old pre-Viking kingdom
of Bernicia, with its centre at Bamburgh, and Siward allied
himself with the house of Bamburgh by marrying a woman
named Ælfflæd, whose great-grandfather, Waltheof, had been
ealdorman of Bamburgh at the end of the tenth century. The
twelfth-century writer Symeon of Durham claims that Siward
obtained control of northern Northumbria by murdering his
predecessor Eadulf, a member of the house of Bamburgh.[7]

By the early 1050s, in addition to his earldom in the north, Siward also held lands in the East Midlands, ruling an earldom centred on Northampton and Huntingdon.[8]

We do not have a great deal of information about Siward's time as earl, although we know that he offended the community of St Cuthbert at Durham by appropriating some of their lands and challenging their ancient privilege to elect their own bishop,[9] and that he supported Malcolm III in his struggle for the Scottish throne. Perhaps Siward's most significant act as earl was to lead an expedition to Scotland in 1054 on behalf of Edward the Confessor, in support of Malcolm and against Macbeth. During this campaign, as the *Anglo-Saxon Chronicle* records, Siward's son Osbeorn and his nephew were killed in battle.[10]

Siward himself died the following year, more peacefully than most of his predecessors (it has been said that Siward is the only one of the 14 men who ruled in Northumbria between 993 and 1076 to have died from natural causes).[11] The *Anglo-Saxon Chronicle* says that he was buried in a church in York, which he had founded and dedicated to the Norwegian king St Olaf Haraldsson.[12] This is a particularly interesting dedication, since at the time of Siward's death in 1055 Olaf was a very recent saint. Olaf fought against Cnut for rule over Norway and was killed by his own people in 1030. Soon after his death he was venerated as a martyr and his cult was swiftly encouraged by his former rival, in a shrewd tactical move which was doubtless an attempt to prevent Olaf being used as a figurehead for Norwegian rebellion against Danish rule.[13] Of the pre-Conquest churches in England dedicated to St Olaf, a number are linked to Anglo-Scandinavian aristocratic families, including Earl Godwine and his Danish wife Gytha, and Siward's dedication of a church to St Olaf may, therefore, be a marker of his Danish identity, or at least his continuing interest in contemporary Scandinavian politics. The church still stands in York, adjoining the probable former location of the earls' palace in the Bootham area of the city. A site on Heslington Hill, outside York, was later known as 'Siward's Howe', suggesting that it was believed in popular tradition to be the earl's burial-mound; it may perhaps have been a location for meetings presided over by Siward in his time as earl.[14]

Siward seems to have employed men of Scandinavian descent among his followers: the account of his 1054 expedition to Scotland records that many English and Danish soldiers were killed there, and these Danes were probably among Siward's men.[15] He was known to his contemporaries under the byname *digri*, an Old Norse word meaning 'big, stout'.[16] The author of the *Vita Ædwardi Regis*, writing around ten years after Siward's death, not only records this nickname but also identifies it as a Danish term: he refers to 'Siward, earl of the Northumbrians, called in the Danish tongue "digri", that is "strong".[17] This Norse byname, taken together with Siward's patronage of the cult of St Olaf, suggests that Siward retained – at least in the eyes of his contemporaries – a noticeable Scandinavian identity, even after settling in England. This does not explain, however, how his colourful genealogy and daring adventures came to be recorded by the monks of thirteenth-century Crowland. That was the result of a strange sequence of events which led to the son of this Danish warrior being venerated as a saint – a martyr of the Norman Conquest.

WALTHEOF, TRAITOR AND MARTYR

After the death of his elder son Osbeorn in 1054, Siward appears to have had only one surviving child, his son Waltheof. Waltheof was born late in his father's life, the product of Siward's marriage to Ælfflæd, the descendant of the earls of Bamburgh, and he was named for one of his mother's distinguished ancestors.[18] He was apparently too young to succeed to the rule of Northumbria on his father's death, and Edward the Confessor instead gave the earldom to Tostig Godwineson, a decision with far-reaching consequences: Tostig's harsh rule of Northumbria sparked uprisings and revolts, caused conflict with his brother Harold after the latter became king in 1066, and ultimately resulted in Tostig joining the Norwegian invasion attempt against Harold.[19] At the time of the Norman Conquest, young Waltheof was earl of Northampton and Huntingdon, the southern part of his father's earldom. It is not recorded whether he fought at the Battle of Hastings, but in the immediate aftermath of the Conquest he swore allegiance to William.[20]

Over the turbulent decade which followed, however, Waltheof twice took part in rebellions against the Norman king. In 1069 he participated in the northern uprising against William and, joining forces with a fleet sent by the Danish king Svein Estrithson, was in the army which captured York from the Normans. When the rebellion failed, Waltheof made peace with the king, married William's niece Judith, and was given his father's earldom of Northumbria.[21] But in 1075 he rebelled again: he became involved in the Revolt of the Earls and this time, although he once more submitted to William and apparently repented of his crime, he was sentenced to death. Waltheof was

25. The ruined west front of Crowland Abbey, Lincolnshire

beheaded as a traitor on St Giles' Hill in Winchester on 31 May 1076, in the only recorded political execution of William's reign. His body was at first thrown into a ditch, but was later retrieved by the monks of Crowland Abbey and taken there for burial – Crowland lay within Waltheof's southern earldom, and the earl had been a generous patron of the abbey. There, in 1092, 16 years after his death, his body was translated and found to be incorrupt, miracles were reported at his tomb, and he began to be regarded by the monks of Crowland as a martyr.[22]

In Old Norse literature, Waltheof was commemorated as a warrior. Like his father, Waltheof had Scandinavian men among his retainers, including a skald named Thorkell Skallason who, after Waltheof's execution, composed memorial poetry for the earl in Old Norse. This indicates that Siward and his family not only retained some kind of Scandinavian identity but that they also continued to value and practise Norse cultural and literary traditions: as Judith Jesch comments, Thorkell's poem reveals the existence of 'an audience conversant with that language, attuned to the cultural values of skaldic poetry, imbued with Norse concepts of loyalty and treachery, and politically in opposition to the new regime, somewhere in England in the late 1070s.'[23] Two verses survive of Thorkell's poem in memory of Waltheof. One celebrates his victory at York in 1069, proclaiming in bloodthirsty triumph that Waltheof caused 100 of William's soldiers to be burned to death in the city, leaving the Normans to become carrion for the wolf. The second verse mourns Waltheof's death: 'William, who reddened weapons, the one who cut the rime-flecked sea from the south, has indeed betrayed the bold Waltheof,' Thorkell laments. 'Killings will be slow to cease in England, but my lord was brave; a more splendid munificent prince will not die.'[24] From these verses, later Scandinavian historians spun a compelling story about Waltheof's relationship with William the Conqueror: in these accounts Waltheof is represented as a son of Godwine, an honourable brother of the doomed English king and the traitor Tostig, unjustly murdered by the Normans. This made for a more dramatic story, but it means that Norse sources have nothing to say about Waltheof's real father, Siward.[25]

In England, however, Waltheof was remembered as a traitor or as a martyr, and the manner of his death made him a controversial saint. The monks of Crowland engaged in the production of texts in support of his claim to sanctity, but his cult remained a predominantly local one and never became popular outside Crowland's sphere of influence. In the first half of the twelfth century the abbot of Crowland commissioned the historian Orderic Vitalis (who stayed at the abbey some time between 1109 and 1124) to write an account of Waltheof's life and death, as well as of the abbey's early history and its other saint, Guthlac.[26] Orderic incorporated these works into his *Ecclesiastical History*, but copies also remained at Crowland and formed the basis of later accounts of the earl's life. Orderic, presumably following what the monks had told him during his visit to the abbey, lays heavy stress on the idea that Waltheof was an innocent victim of Norman malice: they had executed him because they were envious of him, and feared him for his integrity.[27] He also records the story of a Norman monk named Ouen who denied Waltheof's sanctity on the grounds that the earl was a traitor who had deserved to be executed for his crime. The monk died a few days later, a punishment from God for doubting Waltheof's holiness.[28]

Around the same time, William of Malmesbury comments in his *Gesta Regum* that there were two versions of Waltheof's story: while the Normans considered Waltheof a traitor, the English said he had been forced to join the plot against the Conqueror and repented of it before his death.[29] In his *Gesta Pontificum*, William further records that when he visited Crowland the prior tried to persuade him of Waltheof's sanctity, and he remarks 'God, it seems, signifies his assent to the English version, for He manifests many extraordinary miracles at the tomb.'[30]

This emphasis on Norman hatred of Waltheof's cult is almost certainly an exaggeration. Unlike some of the Fenland abbeys – such as Ely, which actively supported rebellions against the Normans – Crowland does not seem to have been hostile to Norman influence. Geoffrey, the abbot who commissioned Orderic and challenged the Norman monk's scepticism, was himself of Norman origin.[31] However, the accusation of Norman prejudice must have served a useful purpose for the promoters of the cult, helping to exonerate Waltheof from the charge of treachery attached to his ignominious death, and the presentation of the debate in these terms, in this early period when the first literary records of the cult were being produced, must reflect the narrative which was accepted at Crowland in the first half of the twelfth century. In this narrative, Norman-English rivalries were central to the proof of Waltheof's innocence and therefore of his sanctity; these texts display a readiness to frame Waltheof as an English saint, a victim of Norman prejudice.

But Waltheof's identity was a more complicated matter than this, as the monks of Crowland seem to have been well aware. Although born in England, he was the son of a Danish warrior, and in building up the materials of Waltheof's cult the monks also found space to explore their saint's Scandinavian lineage. At the beginning of the thirteenth century, a manuscript was compiled which preserves a cycle of texts related to Waltheof, his cult, and his family, together with works on two other Crowland saints, Guthlac and Neot. It is in a variety of twelfth- and thirteenth-century

26. A medieval statue of Earl Waltheof, with hunting-dog, on the west front of Crowland Abbey

hands, and may have been compiled to mark the second translation of Waltheof's relics in 1219.[32] The texts about Waltheof
include the *Gesta antecessorum comitis Waldevi*, which opens
with the genealogy quoted at the beginning of this chapter. In
this text, Waltheof's Danish heritage is foregrounded: Waltheof's
grandfather Beorn is 'Danish by race' and his ancestors bear
the distinctly Norse names Ulf and Spratling (we will return to
these names in a moment). Not only this, but the importance of
ancestry is highlighted by the detail of the bear's ears, a genetic
marker of paternal identity which ensures that Beorn is recognisable as his father's son. This suggests an interest in ancestry and
inheritance for their own sake, and particularly in the
Scandinavian side of Waltheof's ancestry, a story the monks of
Crowland seem to have been eager to tell.

THE 'SAGA OF SIWARD'

The monks of Crowland were not the only people with an
interest in Waltheof's ancestry; his descendants, too, may have
taken some part in creating or preserving stories about Siward
and his Danish forebears. The *Gesta antecessorum* is followed in
the manuscript by a text entitled *De Comitissa*, which continues the story of Waltheof's widow Judith and their daughters,
tracing the descent of their lands, especially the honour of
Huntingdon, through three generations.[33] By the marriages of
Waltheof's eldest daughter Maud – first to the Norman earl
Simon de Senlis and then to David, king of Scotland from
1124 to 1153 – the honour of Huntingdon passed to the Senlis
earls and then to the Scottish royal house. The narrative about
Siward is, therefore, part of the history of this important Anglo-
Norman family. The Crowland text is not the only witness to the
narrative about Siward: a version of the text in Anglo-Norman
survives from Delapré Abbey, near Northampton, and seems to
have been written by a nun of Delapré around 1237.[34] The first
part of this narrative deals with Siward and Waltheof and is very

closely related to the Latin version in the Crowland manuscript, but there is an additional section dealing with the Senlis and Scottish earls of Huntingdon, Waltheof's descendants, which is unique. This text also makes reference to stories about Siward in 'books of the English' belonging to 'Richard le Chauntour de Notyngham', and it has been suggested this may have been an English version of the Siward narrative in the *Gesta antecessorum*; if so, it no longer survives.[35] Like the Crowland *Gesta antecessorum*, the text from Delapré was produced for a particular purpose: to demonstrate that the earldom of Huntingdon was held by right of the king of Scotland, not the king of England, an issue which affected the abbey's own land rights.[36] In both versions of the text, therefore, the history of Siward's acquisition of the earldom of Huntingdon occurs in a context where ancestral rights and inheritance are not simply matters of antiquarian curiosity, but are directly relevant to contemporary interests. As we shall see, this affects how we should read this narrative's approach to Siward's adventures and Waltheof's heredity.

The structure of the *Gesta antecessorum* falls into two parts: the first is a tightly structured and internally consistent account of Siward's youthful adventures, and the second is a summary of his years as earl of Northumbria which contains two distinct, unconnected narrative episodes. It will be helpful to provide a brief overview of these two parts of the narrative, before discussing them separately.[37] After the opening genealogy which introduces Siward, the narrative tells how the young warrior sets out from his father's house with 50 companions and a well-stocked ship. He sails from Denmark to the Orkneys, where he lands on an island and is told that its inhabitants are being terrorised by a dragon. Siward fights the dragon and puts it to flight from the island. Triumphant, he sets sail again, this time to Northumbria, where he has heard tell of another dragon to fight.

But when he lands in Northumbria, instead of finding a dragon, he finds his destiny. He meets an old man sitting on a steep hill, who greets him by name. The old man tells Siward that he knows he has come to test his strength against the dragon, but his fate lies elsewhere: he must go instead to London, where the king will welcome him and grant him land. Siward is understandably sceptical, and says that his companions will not believe him if he tells them what the old man has said. To prove that the encounter has taken place, the mysterious old man gives him a banner named Ravenlandeye (the narrator notes that the name means *corvus terre terror*, 'raven, terror of the land').

Siward accordingly sails to London. He meets King Edward (that is, Edward the Confessor), who has heard of his coming, and the king accepts Siward into his service. Siward distinguishes himself so much that the king promises that the first high honour which becomes available in the land will be given to him, and soon his opportunity arrives. One day it happens that Siward is travelling from Westminster to London when he encounters an enemy of the king, a Danish man named Tostig, earl of Huntingdon. It is said that the king hates Tostig because he is married to the queen's sister, a daughter of Earl Godwine. Siward and Tostig meet at a bridge over the river, which is so narrow that as haughty Tostig passes he splashes Siward's cloak with mud. (In those days, the Crowland narrator adds, the fashion was for men to wear long fur cloaks.) Siward takes Tostig's behaviour as an insult, and decides to get revenge. He lies in wait for Tostig, and as the earl returns across the bridge Siward draws his sword and cuts off his head. Concealing the head beneath his cloak, he goes to the court and asks the king to make him earl of Huntingdon, because that earldom is vacant. The king assumes this must be a joke – the earldom cannot be vacant, as the earl has only just left his presence. Siward produces Tostig's head from beneath his cloak and throws it at the king's feet, and the king, remembering his promise, has no choice but to grant the vacant earldom to Siward. Siward leaves the court and seeks out his companions, and finds them fighting against Tostig's men. They kill them all and bury them near London, at a place which becomes known as the 'Danes' Church' – 'as it is still called to this day', the Crowland narrator adds, presumably referring to St Clement Danes in London. Siward, who is now earl of

Huntingdon, is shortly afterwards made earl of Northumbria, Cumberland and Westmoreland too.

It is clear even from this summary that the first part of the narrative has little basis in the historical facts of Siward's life – apart from the statement that Siward was of Danish origin, which there seems no reason to doubt. It is just possible, as has been suggested in the past, that his murder of Tostig recalls the murder by which he may have obtained the rule of northern Northumbria in 1041;[38] however, the story surrounding the murder, with the insult on the bridge and the folkloric 'rash promise' which the king is forced to fulfil, is pure fiction.[39] The name Tostig suggests some knowledge of Siward's historical career, but the role attributed to him is extremely confused: Tostig was Siward's successor, not his predecessor, as earl (and of Northumbria, not Huntingdon); he was the brother of the king's wife, not the husband of the queen's sister; and in a reversal of the order given in the *Gesta*, Siward had probably been earl of Northumbria for more than 20 years before he gained the earldom of Huntingdon in the early 1050s.

So far, then, the *Gesta antecessorum* is almost entirely fiction, but from the point when Siward is granted his earldom the narrative agrees more closely with what can be verified about his career. The break in the story is marked in the Delapré text with the statement that more of Siward's deeds are recorded in the English book belonging to 'Richard le Chauntour de Notyngham', and the *Gesta* acknowledges the change with a general observation that Siward maintained peace in Northumbria for many years, in accordance with a prophecy recorded by some unnamed 'ancient histories of the English' that a man born of a union between a rational and an irrational being – that is, the woman and the bear – should defend England from its enemies. It then recounts how Siward leads an army to Scotland in support of its deposed king, named as 'Duneval'. During his absence his son Osbeorn 'Bulax' is killed, and on hearing of his death, Siward reacts so violently that he smashes a stone sphere with his axe. Many years later (in fact he died the year after his expedition to Scotland), Siward feels his own death approaching and chooses to die in his armour rather than in bed 'like a cow' (*more vaccino*). He is buried at York, having given his banner Ravenlandeye to the church he founded there.

All the Siward material is, as we will see, a composite of numerous motifs drawn principally from Anglo-Scandinavian tradition; however, there is a clear distinction between the two parts of the narrative, and the two stories told in the second part have some grounding in other sources. Both the death of Siward's son and Siward's own death are recorded in the *Anglo-Saxon Chronicle*, and versions of the two stories in the *Gesta* are also told by Henry of Huntingdon, with some additional details and dialogue which do not appear in the *Gesta*. Henry records Siward's reaction to Osbeorn's death in 1054 as follows:

Circa hoc tempus Siwardus consul fortissimus Nordhymbre, pene gigas statura, manu uero et mente predura, misit filium suum in Scotiam conquirendam. Quem cum bello cesum patri renuntiassant, ait, 'Recepitne uulnus letale in anteriori uel posteriori corporis parte?' Dixerunt nuntii, 'In anteriori.' At ille, 'Gaudeo plane, non enim alio me uel filius meum digner funere.' Siwardus igitur in Scotiam proficiscens, regem bello uicit, regnum totum destruxit, destructum sibi subiugauit.

(Around this time Siward, the mighty earl of Northumbria, almost a giant in stature, very strong mentally and physically, sent his son to conquer Scotland. When they came back and reported to his father that he had been killed in battle, he asked, 'Did he receive his fatal wound in the front or the back of his body?' The messengers said, 'In the front.' Then he said, 'I am completely happy, for I consider no other death worthy for me or my son.' So Siward set out for Scotland, and defeated the king in battle, destroyed the whole realm, and having destroyed it, subjected it to himself.)[40]

Henry was writing 70 years after Osbeorn's death, and it is clear that by this time the story had already taken on a distinctly literary shape. The idea here is that wounds in the front of the body are a mark of honour, because they show that Osbeorn died fighting – not running away – and thus met a worthy death. It is an idea with analogues in various cultures, but it has often been noted that there is a close Norse parallel to this conversation, which also draws an explicit connection between the manner of the wounds and vengeance for the killing (Siward's questions about Osbeorn's death are followed by what is apparently a revenge attack on Scotland). This appears in *Egils saga*, when Kveld-Ulf asks for details of the death of his son Thorolf, who has been killed in battle against the Norwegian king:

> Kveld-Úlfr spurði Ǫlvi vandliga frá atburðum þeim er gjǫrzk hǫfðu á Sandnesi þá er Þórólfr fell, svá at því hvat Þórólfr vann til frama áðr hann felli, svá ok hverir vápn báru á hann, eða hvar hann hafði mest sár, eða hverneg fall hans yrði. Ǫlvir sagði allt þat er hann spurði, svá þat at Haraldr konungr veitti honum sár þat er œrit mundi eitt til bana, ok Þórólfr fell nær á foetr konungi á grúfu. Þá svaraði Kveld-Úlfr: 'Vel hefir þú sagt, því at þat hafa gamlir menn mælt, at þess manns mundi hefnt verða ef hann felli á grúfu, ok þeim nær koma hefndin er fyrir yrði er hinn felli. En ólíkligt er at oss verði þeirar hamingju auðit.'[41]

> (Kveld-Ulf questioned Ölvir closely about everything that had happened at Sandnes when Thorolf fell: what brave deeds Thorolf did before he fell, whose weapon injured him, where he received his worst wounds, and how his death occurred. Ölvir told him everything he asked, that King Harald gave him the wound which alone was enough to kill him, and that Thorolf fell forwards at the foot of the king. Then Kveld-Ulf replied, 'You have said well, because old men say that he who falls forwards will be avenged, and that vengeance will come near to the one before whom he falls. But it is not likely that such will be our luck.')

The idea that the details of wounds received in battle have meaning, and can be interpreted, is presented in the saga as a traditional belief or superstition (what 'old men say'). However, it is also a literary motif, appropriate for the story of a father's reaction to his son's untimely but honourable death. The *Anglo-Saxon Chronicle* agrees that Osbeorn died in battle, but the stories of Siward's reaction told by Henry and the *Gesta* differ in some details from the earlier account: the *Chronicle* says that Osbeorn died on campaign with his father in Scotland, but both the stories told by Henry and the *Gesta* have it that Siward is apart from his son and hears of his death from messengers. This allows for the introduction of a conventional reaction motif: in Henry's story it is the dialogue about the placement of the wounds, while in the *Gesta* it is the separate but related motif of violent reaction to news of a death.

The *Gesta*'s story of Siward's emotional response to his son's death – smashing the stone sphere – has been compared to perhaps the most famous example of this motif in Norse literature, the reactions of the sons of Ragnar Lothbrok to the news of their father's death.[42] As we shall see, this is not the only potential connection between the Siward material and legends about the sons of Ragnar. Meanwhile, Henry's story, repeated by later chroniclers, had a long afterlife: Siward's questioning and his judgement on his son's death appear in *Macbeth*, which is distantly based on Siward's Scottish campaign of 1054. Towards the end of the play Siward's son (here called Young Siward) valiantly but vainly tries to kill Macbeth, and is killed himself. When the news comes to his father, Siward questions the messenger, asking where he got his wounds. He is told they were in the front of his body and so, Siward declares, he will not mourn him: 'Had I as many sons as I have hairs, I would not wish them to a fairer death', he says.[43] Siward's stoic reaction and his ability to rejoice in the face of death are in a clear line of inheritance from Henry of Huntingdon's story.

In fact, both of Henry's two stories about Siward involve the earl's reaction to death. The second deals with Siward's approach to his own death, and bears a close resemblance to the version in the *Gesta antecessorum*, although once again, Henry preserves it in the form of speech:

> Siwardus, consul rigidissimus, pro fluuio uentris ductus mortem sensit inminere. Dixitque, 'Quantus pudor me tot in bellis mori non potuisse, ut uaccarum morti cum dedecore reseruarer! Induite me saltem lorica mea inpenetrabili, precingite gladio. Sullimate galea. Scutum in leua. Securim auratam michi ponite in dextra, ut militum fortissimus modo militis moriar.' Dixerat, et ut dixerat armatus honorifice spiritum exalauit.

(Siward, the stalwart earl, being seized by dysentery, felt that death was near. And he said, 'How shameful it is that I, who could not die in so many battles, should have been saved for the ignominious death of a cow! At least clothe me in my impenetrable breastplate, gird me with my sword, place my helmet on my head, my shield in my left hand, my gilded battle-axe in my right, that I, the bravest of soldiers, may die like a soldier.' He spoke, and armed as he had requested, he gave up his spirit with honour.)[44]

27. The death of Earl Siward, by James Smetham, 1861 (©Wellcome Library, London, CC BY-SA 4.0)

Again, there are numerous parallels between this story and Norse examples of warriors choosing the manner of their death,[45] and we have already seen that one medieval reader may have found a comparison between Siward's death and the death of Beorn the son of Ragnar, swallowed up by the earth while in full armour.

Where did Henry of Huntingdon come across these two stories? It seems significant that they have several features in common. Both of them, each telling of a memorable reaction to death, appear in Henry's *Historia* and in the *Gesta antecessorum* (with enough differences to suggest that the *Gesta* has not borrowed directly from Henry); in the *Gesta* these two episodes essentially comprise the second part of the narrative, and are more closely tied to the known events of Siward's life than any other part of the text. Both episodes make substantial use of direct speech, and in each case the words attributed to Siward are effectively the point of the story. The core of each narrative may therefore originally have been a legend about a memorable utterance, and these two stories about Siward may already have been in circulation at the time Henry was writing, in the second quarter of the twelfth century. The first part of the *Gesta*'s narrative, telling how Siward came to England, has quite a different character – there is, for example, only one instance of direct speech in this section, and that is attributed not to Siward but to the old man on the mound, who tells Siward to go to London and seek his fortune. This is a particularly powerful speech, reflecting the old man's mysterious knowledge of Siward's name, his prophetic telling of his future, and the naming of the banner, and it is not really comparable to the memorable sayings of the other two episodes. It seems that the two stories told by Henry of Huntingdon – memorialising the old warrior's indomitable courage in the face of death – were already circulating together by the twelfth century, but the first section of the narrative seems to have had different origins. It is to the first section that we will now turn.

Prophets and dragons

With the exception of the two stories about reaction to death, the *Gesta antecessorum* is very vague about the latter part of Siward's life. By contrast, the early part of the text forms a cohesive narrative, covering a brief period of time and possessing its own internal causal logic: Siward's youthful dragon-fighting, his encounter with the old man on the mound, and his killing of Tostig are not a series of unrelated episodic adventures but a structured account which purports to explain how the Danish warrior Siward came to obtain an earldom in England. Such a narrative must have been compiled, at least in outline, at the same time and as a single unit. It draws motifs from traditions about the Danes in England and knits them together to compile a narrative of Siward's early life; it gives the impression of being composed to explain how Waltheof's Danish father came to possess his earldom, and to convey the idea that in coming to England Siward – and his son and descendants – in some way fulfilled their appointed destiny.

This is most clearly illustrated by Siward's encounter with the old man on the mound, which takes place at the moment of his first landing in England. This episode contains some elements we have already encountered in legends about the Vikings in England, although used here in a slightly different way, and it places Siward in an established tradition of Norse heroes who receive supernatural help from a figure like this enigmatic old man. In Old Norse literature Odin frequently manifests himself in this form, appearing in disguise to guide young warriors to their destiny and bestow gifts upon them – precisely what this old man does for Siward.[46] Siward meets this Odinic figure sitting on a mound, and the act of sitting on a burial-mound frequently occurs in Norse tradition as a means of accessing wisdom or supernatural aid. To take one famous example, the whole great line of the family of the Völsungs begins when King Rerir, unable to have a child with his wife, sits on a mound and prays to Odin and Frigg, who send him an apple which enables his wife to conceive a son.[47] This son, Völsung, becomes the progenitor of a family of heroes and warriors, including Sigurðr the dragon-slayer, who himself has mysterious and life-changing encounters with an old man who turns out to be Odin.

In the English narrative the old man has prophetic knowledge of Siward's name and destiny, and guides him towards
achieving it with the gift of the banner. This banner, which is
named 'Ravenlandeye', suggests a link to the raven banner which
appears in legends about Cnut, the sons of Ragnar Lothbrok,
and other Scandinavian warriors. As we have seen, the story of
the prophetic raven banner was known at Cnut's court, since
it appears in the *Encomium Emmae Reginae*, and it is linked
with the sons of Lothbrok in the twelfth-century *Annals of
St Neots*. All three raven banners in English sources are therefore
associated with Danes, and two of them have similar prophetic
properties which suggest a likely common origin. Siward's is not
said to have any distinctively supernatural qualities, but the old
man's comment that the banner will convince Siward's companions of the truth of his words, that is, of their prospects for
success in London, might be a remnant of the banner's prophetic
qualities in the other sources, its ability to predict victory or
defeat. In those texts the prophecy concerns success in battle,
and in an invasion of England; Siward is not an invader, but
he is a Danish warrior who has come to prove himself and win
lands in England. The placing of this encounter at the moment
of landing in Northumbria suggests he is here in a parallel position to Cnut and the sons of Lothbrok, although his destiny
is an earldom and not a kingdom. Interestingly, this narrative
does not present Siward coming to England as part of a Danish
invasion, or as a result of Cnut's reign in England (as must have
been the case in reality); his is an independent enterprise, and
the king who grants him promotion is Edward the Confessor.
This might suggest a desire in this narrative to present Siward
not as a Viking invader, but as an adventurous young Danish
warrior who finds success in England and becomes a
trustworthy supporter of the English king.

It is worth noting that one of the Norse parallels to the raven
banner story, in *Orkneyinga saga*, says that the Orkney earl
Sigurðr Hlöðvisson owned a raven banner, which was carried
before him at the Battle of Clontarf,[48] and there is a specific

connection between this story and the Crowland narrative in the fact that Sigurðr not only bears a name cognate with that of Siward of Northumbria, but also shares Siward's byname *digri*. This may simply be a coincidence: the nickname, although rare in England, was fairly common in Scandinavia.[49] However, Judith Jesch suggests that if the story of a raven banner was known in royal circles during the reign of Cnut and his sons, as its appearance in the *Encomium* indicates, it may have travelled to Orkney from there;[50] the banners of Siward and Sigurðr would then most probably be independent outgrowths of the same English stories about the sons of Ragnar Lothbrok. The court of Cnut was, of course, the specific milieu in which Siward of Northumbria first came to prominence, although the later Crowland narrative does not show any awareness of this.

Siward's story also seems to draw on a detail associated with another would-be Scandinavian invader of England: it has been suggested that the name of Siward's banner, Ravenlandeye, appears to be a blend between the raven banner and the banner *Landøyðan* ('land-waster'), which belonged to the Norwegian king Harald Hardrada.[51] According to later Norse sources, this banner was Harald's most valuable possession, since (like the raven banner) it brought victory to the one for whom it was borne into battle.[52] It was said to have been carried by Harald's army in England in 1066, both at Fulford and at Stamford Bridge.[53] Tales about Harald were apparently circulating in England in the twelfth century – a story of his semi-legendary exploits in the East is told by William of Malmesbury, who describes how Harald strangled a lion with his bare hands,[54] and it may be that the name of his banner was also known in England.

The connection of the raven banner motif with the figure of the old man sitting on the mound is unique to the Siward story, but both elements are reminiscent of other legends about the Danes in England. We have seen that a connection between burial-mounds and arrival in England features in *Ragnars saga* in the form of Ivar's howe, which had the power to defend

England from later invaders; in some Norse accounts of 1066,
Ivar's burial-mound on the coast of Cleveland is said to be the
first place where Harald Hardrada landed when he came to
conquer England – the expedition on which he carried the
banner *Landøyðan*. Siward's version of the story is slightly different, but this mound too seems to be situated near the sea, since
Siward encounters it immediately on landing in Northumbria. The
connection between the appearance of a raven banner/mound
episode in the Siward material, the legend of the sons of Ragnar,
and traditions about the last campaign of Harald Hardrada in
England is extremely suggestive, especially as later Icelandic
tradition connected Waltheof and Harald, naming Waltheof as
one of those who fought against Harald and Tostig in England
in 1066.[55]

There is one further possible point of contact between
the legends of the sons of Ragnar Lothbrok and the Siward
narrative in the *Gesta antecessorum*. According to the *Gesta*,
Siward's Danish father was named 'Beorn Beresune', and both
Siward (Sigurðr) and Beorn feature among the names of the
sons of Ragnar in Scandinavian tradition. These are among the
most common Old Norse names, but we may briefly consider
whether there is any connection between the Siward material
and these two characters in the Ragnarssons legend, especially
Sigurðr. The two are sometimes grouped together: in Saxo's
Gesta Danorum, Bjorn and Sigvard are said to have killed Ælla
of Northumbria, an act more usually attributed to Ivar and
Ubbe.[56] Sigurðr does not appear in any of the English versions
of the Ragnar legend, but Beorn features several times, although
not always as one of Ragnar's sons: Geoffrey of Wells gives the
names of the three sons of Lothbrok as 'Inguar, Hubba, et Bern',
but we have seen that in Roger of Wendover's story, the man who
is responsible for bringing the Danes to England is named Bern.
Beorn, although identified in continental sources as one of the
sons of Lothbrok, was not always grouped with his brothers
in the English traditions, and his role seems to have been
reinterpreted in varying ways.

As for Sigurðr, known as *ormr-í-auga* ('snake in the eye'), his absence from the English sources makes it difficult to tell what part, if any, he took in the Ragnar legend in its earlier stages of development.[57] His role may have been expanded in Scandinavia at a later date after a link was made between the Ragnar tradition and the Völsung legend, which made Áslaug/Kráka, the daughter of Sigurðr the Völsung, Ragnar's second wife; the coincidence of the names encouraged, and may perhaps have inspired, this link.[58] There are no strong narrative parallels between the stories of Siward of Northumbria and the Sigurðr of the Ragnar legend, but Sigurðr is the only one of the sons of Ragnar to have a direct encounter with an Odinic figure comparable to the old man on the mound who offers Siward patronage and protection. Saxo's *Gesta Danorum* tells how Sigvard is wounded in battle and healed by a man who gives his name as Rostar (i.e. Hroptr, a name of Odin[59]) in return for a promise to consecrate to him all the souls of the men Sigvard will afterwards kill. Rostar pours dust on Sigvard's eyes and little snakes appear in them, and this, says Saxo, is how Sigvard got the nickname *ormr-í-auga*.[60]

This means that Sigvard, as well as being the only one of the sons of Ragnar to be assisted by Odin in disguise, is also the only one to be associated with snakes – a feature which appears prominently in the stories about Ragnar himself, and which may have helped to make the link between the Ragnar legend and that of Sigurðr the Völsung, the slayer of the dragon Fafnir. There is no evidence that the serpent-slaying exploits of Ragnar, recorded by Saxo and *Ragnars saga*, were known in England, but those of Sigurðr the Völsung certainly were, at least as early as the tenth century.[61] Sigurðr was the most famous dragon-slayer of Germanic legend, and an association between the name Sigurðr and serpents may have helped contribute to the narrative which grew up around Siward of Northumbria. Although it is treated fairly succinctly in the *Gesta antecessorum*, Siward begins his career by fighting with dragons: when he meets the old man on the mound, he has already encountered one serpent in the Orkneys and is in search of another to fight. Like both his legendary namesakes, Sigurðr the Völsung and Sigurðr the son of Ragnar, the dragon-fighting Siward is given assistance and patronage by an Odinic figure, who promises him a favourable wind to guide his ship to London and tells him what to do to achieve success there.

All this suggests that the narrative about Siward may have been forged out of elements drawn from Anglo-Scandinavian tradition, probably in the East Midlands. Although the historical Siward's strongest connections were with Northumbria, all the evidence for interest in the Siward legend comes from the Midlands: the Crowland *Gesta antecessorum*, the text from Delapré, Henry of Huntingdon, and the reference to 'Richard the Chauntour' of Nottingham. We have seen that while the legend of Lothbrok and his sons belongs to a tradition shared by England and Scandinavia, the distribution of the surviving evidence suggests that in England it was particularly popular in East Anglia and the East Midlands, so it is not difficult to believe a writer at Crowland might have encountered such legends. The story in the *Gesta* is clearly told from a southern perspective, not a Northumbrian one, and the references to Northumbria in the early part of the narrative suggest an attitude to the region more likely to resonate with a southern audience: Northumbria is used as the setting of Siward's landing in England, but in a way which suggests it is seen as a distant and exotic location, where supernatural monsters are more easily to be met with than in the Fenland. It is in Northumbria that Siward seeks the dragon to fight after killing one in the Orkneys, and there that he meets the old man on the mound who directs him south to London. This use of Northumbria as a wild, liminal country suggests the attitude of an audience to whom Northumbria was as alien and unknown as the Orkneys. It is also suggestive that the story about the acquisition of Siward's earldom of Huntingdon takes place in London and Westminster, concentrating on the king's decision to grant the earldom to Siward. The complete absence of any reference to the ancestral earls of Northumbria, into whose family Siward married (and who were actually the more distinguished of Earl Waltheof's ancestors), suggests ignorance on this subject.[62] The earldom of Huntingdon was obviously of more significance to the compiler of the *Gesta antecessorum* than Siward's role in Northumbria, and his account of Siward's life has been influenced by the concerns of an audience nearer to the place where the manuscript was produced at Crowland. This seems to reveal that story-telling traditions of Anglo-Scandinavian origin – dragons, raven banners, Odinic guides and all – were not just being preserved but were continuing to thrive and grow in this part of England in the twelfth and thirteenth centuries.

The bear's son: 'wild blood' and the Danes

In the case of the prophetic old man and the raven banner, it is difficult to be sure about the form in which the Crowland compiler might have encountered these narratives about the Danes in England – if they were legends circulating in the East Midlands, whether orally or in written texts, it is probably impossible to pin down any particular source. It is a different matter with the other most strikingly Scandinavian element of Siward's story: the genealogy of the bear's son, with which this chapter began.[63] The legend of a man descended from a bear is a widespread folk-tale, and it appears in various forms in Scandinavian tradition. Common versions of the story tell, for instance, of a man magically turned into a bear who begets a son while in bear form, or of a woman kidnapped by a bear who has a child by it; often the bear is killed and the son seeks revenge for his father.[64] We have seen that one variant of this story features in a strand of the English legends about the sons of Lothbrok, Thomas Elmham's fifteenth-century tale about St Edmund becoming stepfather to the bear's sons through his marriage to a Danish princess. That version contains some parallels with the usual form of the story, such as the idea that the bear's sons wreak vengeance on their father's killers.

In the Crowland text we hear nothing of the woman involved other than that she was of noble birth, but we are given a genealogy of Siward's father, Beorn 'Bear's Son'. The Crowland version of this genealogy is muddled, since Ursus and Beorn are clearly meant to be the same person: both names mean 'bear', the usual name for the bear's son in this kind of story, and it is Beorn who has the ears of a bear as a sign of his ancestry. (In Old English *beorn* means 'man, warrior', but Old Norse *björn* means 'bear', the equivalent of the Latin *ursus*.) The Crowland *Gesta* has added two extra steps to Siward's ancestry, but the version of the text from Delapré has a simpler and probably correct genealogy: Bear-Beorn-Siward, without the addition of Spratling and Ulf. These additions in the *Gesta* have been copied from a genealogy attached to another aristocratic Scandinavian family, more famous and influential than Siward's otherwise unknown father – the family of the eleventh-century nobleman Ulf Thorgilsson, who was connected by marriage to both Cnut and Earl Godwine. Ulf was married to Cnut's sister, while his own sister Gytha was married to Godwine and was the mother of Harold and Tostig Godwineson and their siblings. The genealogy of Ulf and Gytha is recorded in both English and Danish sources, and Saxo Grammaticus gives the story of their bear ancestry in the *Gesta Danorum*. He tells how the daughter of a Swedish farmer was captured by a bear and bore him a son – 'wild blood was invested with the features of a human body'.[65] This son, named for his father (i.e. Beorn), became the father of Thorgils Sprakalegg, who was the father of Ulf and Gytha. Saxo says that Ulf betrayed in his character his descent from a wild beast – evidently a rationalisation of the motif which gives the descendant of the bear physical features belonging to his ancestry, such as a bear's ears.

This genealogy was also known in England, although the *Gesta antecessorum* is the only source to share Saxo's connection between it and the 'bear's son' motif. John of Worcester records it (without the bear) in giving the ancestry of Ulf's son Beorn, while describing how Beorn was murdered by his cousin Svein

Godwineson in 1049. John identifies Beorn as the son of 'the
Danish Earl Ulf, son of Spracling, son of Urse, and brother of
Svein, king of the Danes'.[66] Ulf's father is referred to here as *filii
Ursi*, which might be a translation either of the name Beorn
or, perhaps, of an epithet, 'bear's son'. The naming traditions of
the family suggest a link with the legend of bear ancestry: Ulf
had a son named Beorn and one named Osbeorn (Old Norse
Ásbjörn), which means 'god-like bear'.

This is obviously the genealogy which lies behind the extra
names added to the *Gesta antecessorum*. The *Gesta's* version of it
cannot be accurate, as Siward and Ulf were contemporaries and
Ulf's son Beorn certainly could not have been Siward's father.
It has been suggested that Siward was related to the family of
Ulf, although no sources record this, but it may be that Siward
simply also had a father named Beorn – especially since Siward
too had a son named Osbeorn, the son killed fighting against
Macbeth in 1054.[67] The scribe of the *Gesta* presumably copied this
genealogy from a text of John of Worcester, thereby introducing
several superfluous generations into Siward's ancestry, as a result
of confusing Siward's father Beorn with Beorn the son of Ulf.

Why borrow this genealogy for Siward, in the process of
constructing a history for Siward's acquisition of the earldom
of Huntingdon? Ulf and his family had close links to England,
and played prominent roles in the political crises of the eleventh
century in England and Scandinavia. Ulf's career in England
was short-lived, although he briefly held an English earldom
under Cnut. He was involved in the conquest of England and
witnessed several charters between 1020 and 1024, but returned
to Denmark soon after 1024 and was murdered on Cnut's orders
in 1027.[68] His brother Eilaf held an earldom in Gloucestershire
under Cnut, but it was their sister Gytha whose presence in
England had the most lasting effect. She probably married Earl
Godwine around 1020, and her husband and sons dominated
politics in England in the middle decades of the eleventh
century. Her nephews, Ulf's sons Beorn and Osbeorn, also made
their careers in England. Osbeorn held an earldom in England

under Harthacnut, but was exiled on the accession of Edward the Confessor.[69] Beorn was given an earldom by Edward in 1045, which he held until he was murdered by his cousin Svein Godwineson in 1049; this earldom covered eastern Mercia, including part of Lincolnshire and Huntingdonshire.[70]

The eldest brother Svein became king of Denmark in 1047, on the strength of his relationship to his maternal uncle, Cnut, and his descendants ruled Denmark until the fifteenth century. For a brief period in 1066, two of the grandsons of Thorgils – Gytha's son Harold and Ulf's son Svein – were ruling England and Denmark. The family's connections with England continued after the Conquest, and they took part in English rebellions against the Normans; the Danish fleet which came to the aid of English rebels (including Waltheof) in 1069–70 was sent by one of Ulf's sons, Svein, and led by another, Osbeorn, and three of Svein's sons also took part.[71] William of Malmesbury and John of Worcester claim that Osbeorn was bribed by William the Conqueror to leave England, angering Svein and leading in time to his exile from Denmark.[72] In 1075 two of Svein's sons returned to England to support the Revolt of the Earls, the rebellion that led to Waltheof's execution. As a result of their family connection with Earl Godwine and their involvement in the rebellions of the 1070s, Ulf's sons must have been fairly well-known in England, especially in East Anglia and the Fenland.

There is also some evidence to suggest that legendary stories about Ulf and Godwine circulated in Anglo-Scandinavian tradition, in which similar narratives were attached to both earls or transferred from one to the other. For instance, a story told by Walter Map about how Godwine came to marry Cnut's sister through trickery with the king's seal has close parallels with a similar tale attached to Ulf by Saxo Grammaticus.[73] Walter Map tells how Cnut plots to kill Godwine by sending him to Denmark on the pretence of wanting him to share the rule with Cnut's sister, but on the voyage Godwine opens the sealed letters containing Cnut's orders, and finds his death-warrant.

He amends the letters so that they entrust him with the government of Denmark and arrange for his marriage with the king's sister.[74] This story, which appears in a very similar form in the *Vita Haroldi*,[75] makes use of a familiar motif in the secret changing of the letter, which is also found in the context of a journey between Denmark and England in Saxo Grammaticus's story of Amleth, from where it eventually reached *Hamlet*.[76] Godwine was the subject of a number of such legendary narratives by the twelfth century, some of which appear in Norse sources too.[77] The thirteenth-century *Knýtlinga saga* tells a story in which Ulf encounters Godwine, the son of a Wiltshire farmer, while taking refuge in his father's house after the battle of Sherston in 1016. Impressed by the boy's attentive hospitality, the Danish earl takes Godwine to join Cnut's fleet, marries him to his sister, and arranges for him to be appointed earl.[78] This might be dismissed as a late fiction were it not for the fact that Walter Map also tells a very similar story about Godwine's origins, although he says that it was King Æthelred who spotted Godwine's potential.[79] It is likely that *Knýtlinga saga* preserves the earlier story, and that at some point in English tradition the name of Æthelred came to replace that of the less familiar Danish earl; the story may have originated as an explanation for how Godwine came to marry Ulf's sister.

The connection between Godwine and Ulf was not very well remembered in English sources, with the exception of John of Worcester. Even the *Vita Ædwardi Regis*, although it was commissioned by Eadgyth, daughter of Godwine and Gytha, and written while Gytha was still alive, does not mention Ulf and calls Gytha the sister of Cnut.[80] But some information about Godwine and his family seems to have been available at Worcester, and John of Worcester has additional information about a number of Anglo-Danish families in the period of his chronicle in which Ulf's genealogy appears.[81] John is the only source to note the parentage of Svein ('son of Godwine and Gytha') as well as the genealogy of Beorn in his account of Beorn's murder, clarifying the relationship between the cousins as well as Beorn's link to Svein, king of Denmark. The genealogy appears

in the context of a narrative of treachery and betrayal, in which
Svein Godwineson, returning from exile in Denmark and
dishonestly promising to remain faithful to the king, murders
his cousin, who has offered to intercede with King Edward
on his behalf.[82] Some of these elements recur in the *Gesta*'s
narrative about Siward and Tostig, in which Siward takes
his revenge on Tostig for an insult and gains his earldom by
exploiting an unconscious promise from the king. Since the
Crowland writer clearly had access to John of Worcester's
Chronicle, he may have been influenced by it in this respect too.

It is hardly surprising that the Crowland writer confused
these two Danish families, with their plethora of similar names,
but it is interesting that he chose to elaborate on Siward's
genealogy by borrowing from such a prominent Anglo-Danish
dynasty. It suggests that in composing an origin narrative for
Siward, the compiler of the *Gesta antecessorum* was deliberately
taking names from eleventh-century history, locating his story
in the reign of Edward the Confessor and during a period of
particularly intense Anglo-Danish interaction. This probably
also explains why he used the name Tostig for Siward's Danish
predecessor, whom Siward murders by trickery – this story
lets Siward defeat Tostig, presenting Siward as braver, brighter
and more loyal than the Godwinesons, as well as borrowing
their genealogy.

This offers an important context for the narrative of Siward's
ancestry and adventures. What this narrative provides is not
just the tale of a daring Viking settler, but the origin-myth of
an aristocratic Anglo-Danish dynasty. The lineage of the bear
lives on through Waltheof's descendants, and so does their
connection with the earldom to which Siward was super-
naturally guided. This also explains how the story of Siward fits
together with the other texts in the same manuscript, providing
a narrative of both family history and the history of the honour
of Huntingdon. The emphasis in the *Gesta antecessorum* on
Siward's acquisition of Huntingdon acts as a form of prologue
to the later history of the earldom under the Senlis earls and the

Scottish royal line, and Siward's story provides a foundational myth for the dynasty, hinting at some supernatural agency at work in the link between Waltheof's family and Huntingdon. The story of bear ancestry is assimilated to this purpose, too, through the reference to a prophecy in the 'ancient histories of the English' which says that a man born of a rational and irrational being would defend England from its enemies. This Scandinavian legend provides Waltheof and his descendants (including the royal line of Scotland and later, through them, the royal family of England too) with an incomparable ancestry – a distinguished line of forebears with more than human power and ferocity.

HEREWARD AND THE BEAR

There are two final relevant comparisons for the bear ancestry element in the story of Siward, which suggest how in medieval England this kind of Scandinavian legend could be used in different ways for different audiences. The first is the *Gesta Herwardi*, a twelfth-century account of the adventures of the anti-Norman rebel Hereward, which features a related narrative about a Scandinavian family and descent from a bear.[83] The *Gesta Herwardi* is a Latin prose text preserved at the end of a thirteenth-century collection of legal documents from Peterborough Abbey (Peterborough Cathedral Manuscript 1, folios 320–39),[84] and based on the fact that it was used in the compilation of the *Liber Eliensis*, it is possible to date its composition to between 1107 and 1131.[85]

Like Siward, Hereward was a historical figure who came to be the subject of a colourful narrative of his early adventures. The evidence for Hereward's life is confined to the Domesday record of his possible land-holdings and to the chronicle records of two events, the plundering of Peterborough Abbey by his 'gang' in 1070 and the siege of Ely by the Normans in the following year, which Hereward stoutly resisted.[86] The *Gesta Herwardi*, however, offers an expansive account of Hereward's adventures as a young man, set during the 1060s in Northumbria, Cornwall, Dublin and Flanders, and then goes on to record numerous stratagems and tricks played by Hereward against the Normans, claiming to be based on a variety of first-hand accounts of his life. The *Gesta Herwardi* is a mixture of historical fact and romantic adventures, many of which went on to influence later outlaw legends such as the stories of Robin Hood. Hereward, like Robin Hood, is a young nobleman unjustly dispossessed of his inheritance, who wages a mischievous campaign of guerrilla warfare against his enemies while living a comfortable life in an inaccessible hideout. Hereward takes refuge in the Fens rather than the greenwood, but he has Robin Hood's taste for tricks – putting the shoes on his horse backwards, so as to send his pursuers in the wrong direction – and a similar retinue of assorted outlaws with their own individual stories.[87]

It is Hereward's very first adventure that concerns us here. The *Gesta Herwardi* tells how, as a young man, Hereward is forced to leave his native Lincolnshire because his behaviour is too riotous for his family to handle. He goes to stay with his godfather somewhere in the far north 'beyond Northumbria'. His godfather keeps wild beasts in cages for the entertainment of his knights, and among these beasts is a very large bear. But this is not an ordinary bear – it is, the *Gesta Herwardi* says, the offspring of a famous Norwegian bear, which is said to have had the head and feet of a man and human intelligence. This bear understood human speech and was cunning in battle, and according to 'the stories of the Danes' (*fabula Danorum*), it had fathered Beorn, king of Norway, on a human woman. The point of the story is that the bear breaks loose and young Hereward is the only one strong enough to fight and kill it; he saves the lives of his host's wife and daughters and earns their gratitude, and songs are composed in his honour.[88]

This motif of bear–human hybrid ancestry is clearly related to the stories we have been looking at, although there are some differences in detail. Neither this text nor the Siward narrative tells the whole legend as it appears in the Scandinavian sources:

both lack elements such as the abduction of the woman, the killing of the bear, and the son's revenge on its killers (which Thomas Elmham's later story does include). They only deal with the offspring of the bear and the physical characteristics which reveal its animal parentage. Both, however, indicate that the story is traditional: the *Gesta Herwardi* attributes it to 'the stories of the Danes', and the *Gesta antecessorum* to 'the tales of the ancients' (*relaciones antiquorum*).[89] The presentation of the story in the *Gesta Herwardi* is particularly self-aware, as it not only makes use of the bear story, but explicitly identifies it within the text *as* a story, and one associated with Scandinavia – specifically Norway, where Beorn, the bear's son, is said to have been king. The Scandinavian identity of the story is clearly marked, and in framing the story like this the *Gesta Herwardi* seems to be deliberately directing our attention to the way in which it is weaving a legendary narrative into the life of its historical hero. The part of the *Gesta Herwardi* which deals with Hereward's youthful adventures is closely related to other early romance narratives, and we could interpret the comment here as a self-referential aside, a wink at the fictionality of this part of the text: Hereward, in his first adventure away from the Fenland, goes north and encounters legends brought to life. We are told in the prologue to the *Gesta Herwardi* that the author of the Old English text on which the Latin version claims to be based, Hereward's chaplain Leofric, was something of an expert in fables and legends: it says that he would gather the deeds of giants and warriors *ex fabulis antiquorum*, 'out of the stories of the ancients', for the edification of his audience, and commit them to writing in English.[90] The text seems to be reminding us of this assertion about its own origins – its own complicated ancestry-story – by associating Hereward's first adventure with such *fabulae*, and offering a literary context within which to interpret this narrative of Hereward's early career.

More than this, however, the *Gesta* makes it clear that the monster Hereward encounters is not just a creature *like* something from Danish legend; it is a genetic relation of a bear who is a figure from an existing narrative – a narrative that was the ancestral origin-myth associated with a noble, by this time a royal, dynasty. Although written early in the twelfth century, Hereward's adventure with the bear is set on the eve of the Norman Conquest, at a time when the family with whom this myth of bear ancestry was apparently linked were at the height of their power. This may not be a coincidence. The historical Hereward collaborated closely with the Danish army led by Ulf's son Osbeorn: the interpolation in the *Peterborough Chronicle* describing the plunder of Peterborough in 1070 by Hereward and his gang of outlaws tells how, after stripping the church, Hereward gave its treasures to Osbeorn's army, who were camped at Ely and later sailed away with them back to Denmark.[91] This collaboration between Hereward and the Danish army is not mentioned at all in the *Gesta Herwardi* – a striking omission, which perhaps indicates not only that plundering churches did not fit with the *Gesta*'s view of Hereward as a fair-minded hero, but also that collaboration with the Danes might have sullied this text's presentation of him as an *English* hero. The *Gesta Herwardi,* a text full of stories about post-Conquest conflict between the English and the Normans, is keenly alert to questions of national and cultural identity, and in light of its unwillingness to mention Hereward's Danish allies, the text's one explicit reference to a Scandinavian legend – a legend associated in twelfth-century sources with the family of Hereward's allies – might be interpreted as derisive, or at best dismissive. This cousin of a Scandinavian royal family is a savage half-human bear, kept in a cage for the amusement of a nobleman and then unceremoniously killed by Hereward. By making Hereward confront this creature from Danish legend at the very beginning of the text, the *Gesta Herwardi* seems to be putting Hereward into the Scandinavian world only to demonstrate his distance from it. Its attitude to the bear story is quite different from that of the Crowland narrative about Siward; while the *Gesta Herwardi* keeps a sceptical distance from the Danes and their *fabulae* about half-human bears, the monks of

Crowland seem to have been glad to claim similar ancestry for their own hero, Earl Waltheof.

The final point to mention here concerns a short episode in the *Roman de Waldef*, an Anglo-Norman verse romance composed in East Anglia, probably in the first decade of the thirteenth century.[92] This romance is set in an imagined version of pre-Conquest East Anglia, which is presented as a world of small regional kingdoms and warring kings, and the titular hero, Waldef, is said to be the ruler of a kingdom in Norfolk. The *Roman de Waldef* is the earliest and (although unfinished) the longest of the Anglo-Norman ancestral romances, and the episode in question takes place just over halfway through this very lengthy story, as attention turns from Waldef to the next generation, his twin sons Gudlac and Guiac. The children are kidnapped as infants, and grow up apart and far from their East Anglian homeland. Gudlac is brought up in Morocco, but is exiled from that country after killing the nephew of the king in a fight, and he ends up shipwrecked on the coast of Denmark. This initiates a brief Scandinavian interlude in the romance: Gudlac seeks out the court of the Danish king, Svein, and while riding with the king and other nobles rescues the king's son from a giant white bear. This act of heroism brings Gudlac into favour with the king; he remains in Denmark and aids the Danes in fighting off a Norwegian invasion, and in return Svein provides him with ships and men for his return to England, where he is eventually reunited with his parents and brother.[93]

Gudlac's adventure with the white bear seems to have been borrowed more or less wholesale from the *Gesta Herwardi*, in a manner which is characteristic of the narrative composition of the *Roman de Waldef* – this romance takes stories, motifs and character names from a variety of historiographical and romance sources, reusing them and recombining them at will. The name 'Hereward' is used for an unconnected character in the romance, and there are some other parallels between the two texts.[94] The links between the two bear episodes are clear, both in the narrative details and in the function of the episode within the text: the encounter with the bear takes place when the young hero has been exiled for violent behaviour, he saves innocent victims from an out-of-control bear, proving his valour for the first time, and he is rewarded highly for this deed by the local ruler.

The most important difference between this text and the others we have been looking at is that the bear in the *Roman de Waldef* is not sentient, and does not come equipped with a story of human–bear progeny like that referenced in the *Gesta Herwardi* and the narrative about Siward. However, all three texts bear some relation to each other, even if the exact direction of influence is difficult to reconstruct. In all three, the bear motif appears in roughly comparable narrative contexts: it occurs early in the career of a young hero, who has left home and is setting out into the world to try his prowess, and in all three texts it is associated explicitly with Scandinavia and Scandinavian men.[95] In plundering his stock of character names from other sources, the Anglo-Norman poet seems to have borrowed the name Waldef from Crowland's Waltheof, although there are no similarities between the plot of the romance and any surviving stories about the earl. (Similarly, Gudlac gets his name from the Anglo-Saxon hermit St Guthlac, Crowland's other saint, with whom he has even less in common than Waldef does with Waltheof.) The *Roman de Waldef* has been dated to c.1200–10, and it is probably not a coincidence that interest in Waltheof as a saint appears to have been at its height in the early part of the thirteenth century: the 1219 translation of his relics doubtless encouraged this interest, which seems to have also led to the production of the Crowland manuscript where the Siward story is recorded. All three texts have a Crowland connection, since Crowland also had a particular interest in Hereward, who had been a tenant of the abbey. The *Gesta Herwardi* says that Hereward's first wife took the veil at Crowland, and the later chronicle of Pseudo-Ingulf, written at Crowland, gives its own version of the Hereward story which shows knowledge of the *Gesta Herwardi*.[96] Since the hero of *Waldef* and one of his sons share their names with the two principal saints of Crowland Abbey, it seems possible that the author might have had a connection to that house and knowledge of the texts being produced there.

These three texts, then, suggest different ways in which legends about the Danes might retain meaning and use for English audiences into the twelfth and thirteenth centuries. The narrative element of bear ancestry is reused in three geographically close but very different contexts, yet in each case is still marked out as Scandinavian. In the first place, a particular version of a widespread story seems to have been introduced to England as an origin-myth for an aristocratic dynasty, in the mid-eleventh century when ties between English and Danish noble families were closer than ever before, and when elite Scandinavian literary culture was known and practised in England. In the Crowland narrative about Siward, it retains some of its original power, providing a foundational myth for the abbey's past and current aristocratic patrons. The *Gesta Herwardi*, written in a different and tense political context in the decades immediately after the Norman Conquest, repurposes this Danish story for its own ends, and in doing so makes it available as narrative material for later romance such as the *Roman de Waldef*. There the episode is in part simply a useful way to launch a story about Gudlac's Scandinavian adventures, but the *Roman de Waldef* is also interested in a much longer and more wide-ranging narrative of pre-Conquest history than either of the other two texts. This romance's use of narratives about the English past, as Rosalind Field has argued, 'goes beyond a casual plundering of commonplace motifs' to create something that amounts almost to 'a national corpus of literary material', imagining pre-Conquest England not as a single unified Anglo-Saxon world but as a space occupied by multiple competing interests, kingdoms and nationalities.[97] Within this corpus, narratives about the history of interaction between England and Denmark have their own place, as we will see in Chapter 4.

CHAPTER 4

DANISH SOVEREIGNTY AND THE RIGHT TO RULE

The relationship between the legends of Siward and Hereward and the Anglo-Norman romance *Waldef* suggests how, in the fertile literary culture of post-Conquest England, narrative material could freely pass between Anglo-Scandinavian legend, historical writing, hagiography and romance. What we see in these texts is narratives and legends about England's Viking history becoming part of the material of romance, reshaped and adapted to fit new audiences. In Middle English romance, narratives of Anglo-Danish interaction feature most often as tales of Viking aggression – with the important exception of *Havelok*, which will be discussed in the next chapter.[1] However, even in texts where the Danes appear primarily as adversaries, it is sometimes possible to see a more nuanced interest in the history of their relationship with England. In this chapter we will look at how the Danes feature in the story of one of the most popular heroes of medieval romance, Guy of Warwick. Guy's long and varied career takes him from dragon-slayer and chivalrous knight to a repentant pilgrim and hermit, but his final and most famous victory comes when he defeats a Viking invasion through single combat against the Danes' champion. The Guy story uses the threat of

Danish invasion as a national conflict in which the defender of
the English can win a patriotic triumph, but it also seems to
show knowledge of a belief, found in other sources, that in the
Anglo-Saxon period the Danes had some kind of historical right
to claim sovereignty in England. Rather than framing the idea of
Danish invasion and settlement in solely personal terms – as we
have seen in many of the stories about Lothbrok and his sons,
and in the tale of Siward – this tradition takes an interest in the
political and legal history of Danish rule in England.

GAIMAR AND THE DANISH CLAIM

One of the earliest writers to explore this idea is the twelfth-
century writer Geffrei Gaimar in his *Estoire des Engleis*. Gaimar's
Estoire was written c.1136–7 and narrates the history of the
English, in Anglo-Norman verse, from the coming of the Saxons
to the death of William Rufus in 1100.[2] An earlier section of the
chronicle, dealing with the origins of the British, is referenced
by Gaimar but no longer survives. Gaimar wrote under the
patronage of Constance, the wife of Ralph fitz Gilbert, a member
of a family characterised by Ian Short as 'well-connected
members of the minor aristocracy of Lincolnshire'; unlike many
of the texts we have been considering so far, therefore, Gaimar's
Estoire is intended primarily for a secular, aristocratic audience.[3]
Gaimar presents a narrative of English and British history
freely drawn not only from his two main sources, Geoffrey of
Monmouth's *Historia Regum Britanniae* and the *Anglo-Saxon
Chronicle*, but also from romance and oral tradition which he
probably encountered in Lincolnshire.

In a series of passages not derived from either of his two main
sources, Gaimar mentions a number of semi-legendary Danish
kings who ruled in England.[4] The first is Havelok, whose legend
will be dealt with at greater length in the next chapter, and he
also refers to a king named Wasing, a Danish ruler of Norfolk
not found in any other source, as well as to the better-attested
periods of Danish rule under Svein and Cnut.[5] He claims that

the Danes believed they had a right to rule England dating back
to before the arrival of the Saxons, when England was ruled
by a king named Dan, from whom later Danish kings were
descended. This belief in an ancient Danish right to England
is discussed in the *Estoire* on two separate occasions. The first
comes as an explanation for the beginning of Viking raids
in England, prompted by the reference in the *Anglo-Saxon
Chronicle* to the arrival of a small number of ships on the coast
of Wessex in 789:[6]

> E en cel tens vindrent Daneis
> pur guereier sur les Engleis:
> un senesçal al rei oscistrent,
> la terre saisirent e pristrent,
> mult firent mal par les contrees,
> si nen u[re]nt ke treis navees.
> Puis realerent en lur païs
> si asemblerent lur amis;
> en Bretaigne voldrent venir,
> as Engleis la voldrent tolir
> car entr'els eurent esgardé
> e dit ke ço est lur herité,
> e mulz homes de lur linage,
> urent le regne en heritage
> ainceis kë Engleis i entrast
> ne home de Sessoigne i habitast:
> li reis Danes tint le regnez,
> ki de Denemarch[e] fu nez:
> si fist Ailbrith e Haveloc,
> e plus en nomerent ovoc,
> purquai il distrent pur verité,
> Bretaigne ert lur dreit herité.
> (2065–86)

(It was during this time that the Danes arrived to wage war
on the English. They killed a certain royal steward, seized
and secured the land and, despite their only having three
ships, caused a great deal of damage throughout the region.

They then returned home and enlisted their allies with the
intention of coming to Britain to seize the island from the
English, for they had reached the decision between them,
and claimed that this country was part of their heritage, and
that many of their ancestors had established an inheritance
claim before any English had even arrived or before anyone
from Saxony came to live there. King Danr, who was born in
Denmark, had ruled over the kingdom, as had Adelbricht[7]
and Haveloc, and they named others in addition who had
done so. It was on this basis that they claimed it to be true
that Britain was their rightful inheritance.)[8]

Gaimar provides this as an explanation for all Danish attacks
on England from the ninth century onwards, rationalising
Viking activity as a coordinated attempt at national expansion.
The Danes are imagined not as opportunistic plunderers but as
would-be conquerors who target England specifically because
their ancestors had once ruled there. Gaimar returns to this
subject in his account of the meeting between Cnut and
Edmund Ironside at Deerhurst in Gloucestershire in 1016. In
common with a number of medieval historians, Gaimar says
that on this occasion the two kings made preparations for a
single combat to determine which of them should rule England,
and in the middle of the duel he has them debating their
respective rights to the English throne. As they face each other
before beginning the combat, Cnut interrupts and speaks *mult
sagement*, 'very wisely' (4307), about his grounds for claiming
to rule England. He tells Edmund that they are both the sons
of kings who have ruled the country, but that his ancestors held
England many years before the coming of the Saxons:

> e bien sachez loi[n]gtenement
> l'urent Daneis nostre parent:
> prés de mil anz l'out Dane aince[i]s
> ke unc i entrast Certiz li reis.
> Certiz, ço fu vostre ancïen,
> e li reis Danes fu le mien.

Daneis le tint en chef de Deu,
Modret donat Certiz son feu:
il ne tint unkes chevalment,
de lui vindrent vostre parent.
Pur ço vus di, si nel savez,
si vus od mai [vus] combatez,
l[i] un de nus ad greignur tort,
ne savom liquels en ert mort.
Pur ço vus vol un offre fere
e ne m'en voil de rien retrere:
partum la terre dreit en dous,
l'une partie en aiez vus,
l'altre partie me remaigne!
(4315–33)

(Our Danish ancestors, I'll have you know, have been ruling here for a very long time. Almost a thousand years before king Cerdic came to the throne, Danr was king. Cerdic was your ancestor, and king Danr was mine. A Dane held the land in chief from God. It was Mordred who granted Cerdic his fief; he never held it in chief, and your family is descended from him. In case you don't already know, I'll tell you that if you fight me, one of us is going to be in the wrong more than the other, though we don't know which one of us will die as a result. This is why I'm willing to make you an offer – one that I will not seek to back down from: let us divide the kingdom exactly in two, with one part going to you and the other remaining with me.)[9]

Cnut repeats the argument attributed to the Danes by Gaimar as the first cause of Viking activity in England, and here the circumstances seem to validate it as a fair argument indicating a legitimate claim to rule the country. For Gaimar, the story of Dan explains why Cnut and Edmund chose to divide the country between them instead of proceeding with the planned single combat, because both have a well-founded right to claim sovereignty.

There are significant differences here from other contemporary narratives of this single combat, which do not engage in this way with the question of the justice of the Danish claim. The legend that Cnut and Edmund Ironside fought a duel in the wars of 1015–16 first appears as early as the *Encomium Emmae Reginae*, and became a story repeated in many different iterations by later historians.[10] The *Anglo-Saxon Chronicle* says that the kings *comon togædere*, 'came together', to reach a settlement that would divide England between them, a phrase which probably only means that they met, but which seems later to have been interpreted to mean that they fought a duel.[11] The *Encomium* says that single combat was proposed by Edmund, but never took place, because Cnut was too wise to fight when he could not be sure of victory. Here the challenge and Cnut's refusal are set during the winter of 1015–16, and there is no connection between this episode and the partition of the kingdom; that division takes place several months later, after the battle at Assandun, and the *Encomium* says it was proposed by the traitor Eadric Streona. Apparently unwilling to support the principle of shared rule as a long-term solution to a contested kingdom, the *Encomium* casts both duel and division in a very negative light.[12]

By the twelfth century, however, a number of historians were claiming that this proposed single combat had actually taken place, usually at the very end of the war and after Assandun. Where Gaimar has Cnut arguing eloquently and, the narrative suggests, correctly about the right of both kings to rule England, most other chroniclers agree that Cnut stopped the combat because he was intimidated by his valiant English opponent. Of all the accounts of this supposed single combat, Gaimar's is the most favourable to Cnut (except, of course, for the pro-Danish *Encomium*). William of Malmesbury has Cnut refuse to enter into combat because he is physically smaller than Edmund and fears the English king's strength,[13] while Henry of Huntingdon says that Edmund was winning the combat when Cnut stopped it to propose a settlement.[14] Walter Map provides a dialogue between the two in which Cnut taunts Edmund for being short-winded, to which Edmund replies, 'Not too short, if I can bring so great a king off his feet'; Map calls this a 'memorable phrase'.[15] By the early thirteenth century, Roger of Wendover has Cnut claiming to be so overwhelmingly impressed by Edmund's virtues that he cannot fight him and is eager to be Edmund's joint-king and sworn brother.[16] In Gaimar's account, it is rather the other way around: Edmund admires 'how humbly and how justly the good king spoke to him',[17] and agrees to the division of the country along the lines proposed by the Danish king. His response to Cnut's argument implicitly accepts it as a valid interpretation of the history, and Cnut's offer to divide the kingdom, in this light, is a magnanimous one: he has a prior claim to rule the whole country, but chooses to reach a settlement to prevent either himself or Edmund from being killed in the combat.

In some of these versions of the story Cnut stakes his claim to England on the grounds that his father had ruled the kingdom (if only for two months), and he, like Edmund, can therefore claim to be his father's heir.[18] The argument put forward by Gaimar's Cnut is more complex than this, however, and reiterates what Gaimar has already said about the motivation behind Danish raids on England. This speech, like that earlier passage, is Gaimar's attempt to explain why the Danes believed themselves to have a prior right to the country, dating back to before the foundation of the kingdom of Wessex. The idea that the Saxons were granted land in England by Mordred, nephew of King Arthur, is found in Geoffrey of Monmouth, but it is Gaimar's innovation to claim there was a period of Danish rule in England long pre-dating the coming of the Saxons.[19]

This seems to be an instance where Gaimar is closer to Scandinavian or Anglo-Danish tradition than to the English sources. King Dan does not appear in any other sources from England, but there are several references in Scandinavian historical writing to a king named Dan, progenitor of the Danes.[20] Saxo Grammaticus begins the first book of the *Gesta Danorum* by naming Dan and Angul, sons of Humbli, as the originators

of the Danish and English nations, respectively. According
to Saxo, this Dan was the grandfather of Sciold (Scyld), from
whom the Scyldings were descended.[21] Although various other
etymological interpretations of the name 'Danes' were current
(Saxo himself mentions that Dudo of St Quentin derives the
name from 'Danaans'), Dan is found in a number of other
Scandinavian sources too. A King Dan is also mentioned in
the twelfth-century *Chronicon Lethrense* (*c.*1170), as the son
of a king of Sweden, who ruled Denmark in the time of the
Emperor Augustus and gave his name to the Danes.[22] Snorri
Sturluson, in the prologue to *Heimskringla* and in *Ynglinga
saga*, says that Dan was the first person to be called king by
the Danes.[23] King Dan is probably a purely legendary figure,
a back-formation from the name of the Danes, as Angul is
from the English.[24] Although these brief references do not say
whether Dan was thought to have ever held land in England,
it seems possible that the ultimate source of Gaimar's information may have been connected to these Scandinavian traditions. The idea that the Danes ruled in England before the
invasions of the ninth century does also appear in some late
Norse sagas; *Hrólfs saga kraka*, for instance, has a Danish man
as the second king to rule Northumbria after the foundation
of that kingdom.[25] In England, the idea of a historical Danish
claim to rule is mentioned in some other sources of the later
twelfth century: Richard FitzNigel, writing in the 1170s, says in
his *Dialogue of the Exchequer* that the Danes invaded England
in the Anglo-Saxon period not just for plunder but because, 'as
the history of Britain tells more fully', they claimed an ancient
legal right to rule England.[26] It is possible, however, that this is
a reference to Gaimar's *Estoire* (or the lost portion of it dealing
with the history of the Britons) so it may not be independent
evidence for the idea.

This is not the only occasion where Gaimar seems to have had
access to sources for Viking Age history which were unknown
to other chroniclers, and which give a different slant to his
interpretation of England's Danish past. Particularly notable

is his lengthy narrative about the Viking capture of York in 866–7, which describes how the Danes were invited to invade Northumbria as part of a feud between the Northumbrian nobles and their king.[27] In this story, Gaimar tells how the Northumbrian king Osberht (here called Osbryht) rapes the wife of a man named Buern Butsecarl, a noble and valiant sailor. Buern, seeking to avenge his wife, goes to the Danes and incites them to attack Northumbria to punish Osbryht. Buern's supporters depose Osbryht and replace him with Ælla, and Buern brings the Danes to York, where they capture and kill Osbryht. While this is going on, the new king Ælla is out in the woods hunting. He boasts to his knights about how many deer he has caught and killed, and a mysterious blind man, overhearing them, tells him the Danes have caught more – they have captured York and killed many men. Ælla refuses to believe him, but the blind man says that the truth of his words will be proved by this: Ælla's nephew Orrum will be the first one killed in the next battle at York. In a vain effort to defeat this prophecy, Ælla shuts up his nephew in a tower and returns to York, but his nephew escapes by jumping out of the tower, using two shields as makeshift wings. He rushes off to fight against the Danes and he and Ælla are both killed in battle – and as the blind man foretold, the Danes triumph. Gaimar notes that Ælla was killed at a place called Ellecroft, and adds that 'in the very centre of England' stands a cross which the English call Ellecross (neither place has been identified).

Gaimar probably learned of this story from Lincolnshire sources, but it seems possible that it was in origin a Northumbrian tradition, as York and the two Northumbrian kings feature so prominently. There are some points of contact here with the East Anglian traditions about Ivar and Ubbe which we looked at in Chapter 2, but there are numerous important differences too. This is also a story of revenge, but in this case the Danes are not the ones injured – they are merely the instruments of Buern's vengeance on the king.[28] As in the story of Lothbrok's murder, it is a man named Beorn who is responsible for bringing the Danes to England, but Gaimar's Buern Butsecarl is envisaged very differently from Edmund's murderous huntsman – he is the hero of the story, a noble man standing up against a tyrannous king. The most significant difference is, of course, the culpability attached to the English kings, Osbryht and (to a much lesser degree) Ælla, and in this respect Gaimar again seems to be closer to Norse tradition than to the English stories about Lothbrok and the innocent Edmund. In Scandinavian tradition, it is Ælla who is responsible for bringing about the Danish invasion because he puts Ragnar to death in a snake-pit. Here, however, this take on the story aligns with Gaimar's own broader interest in figures like Buern as rebels against the unjust exercise of royal power – he favours stories which emphasise that kings must be subject to the law and respect the rights of their vassals.[29]

The story of the blind man's prophecy is also an intriguing element, which suggests without stating outright that the fate of the wicked king Osbryht had some kind of divine sanction. Ian Short notes that this is one of the rare moments where super-natural influences appear in Gaimar's narrative, apart from in the Havelok story, his other extended narrative about the Danes.[30] We might compare the blind man to the mysterious prophet Siward meets who tells him of his destiny; in Old Norse literature an encounter with a mysterious, prophetic old man, one-eyed or blind, is often a sign that someone has met Odin, who walks the world in disguise helping his favoured heroes and foretelling the fates of men. Ælla's blind man might be drawn from a version of this trope, but Gaimar again adapts it to suit his interest in the punishment of kings who violate the law – there is perhaps a sense that Ælla, in attempting to defy the prophecy and save his nephew from his appointed fate, has sinned against the proper workings of divine justice.

Some of this narrative may have come from local legend about the Danish invasions, and there is similar legendary material in the story that follows, of St Edmund's death at the hands of the Danes. Although Gaimar says he will not write at great length about Edmund because more information is available about him elsewhere, he has several details about Edmund's death not found in other sources, such as the name of the man who finally cuts off Edmund's head after he has been shot full of arrows (named by Gaimar as Coran Colbe), and a riddling dialogue between Edmund and the Danes.[31] Even if this material has its roots in the Anglo-Scandinavian society of twelfth-century Lincolnshire, however, the *Estoire* incorporates it into a much larger narrative of English and British history. Gaimar's *Estoire* retells the story of pre-Conquest England for a Norman aristocratic audience who may have seen themselves as the latest in a long line of conquerors, relatively new to England but nonetheless heirs to its history and land.[32] In this text, history, romance and legend blend to such an extent that they become indistinguishable, and together they form a persuasive narrative in which England – and particularly the East Midlands, the home of Gaimar's patrons – emerges as an area which has been contested between many different rulers over the centuries. Within the *Estoire* the Danes, like the Anglo-Saxons and the Normans, can stake their claim to rule on historical precedent and ancestral right.

28. Guy of Warwick fights a dragon (British Library, Yates Thompson MS. 13, f. 14)

THE DANES IN *GUY OF WARWICK*

The idea of a historical Danish right to rule England also appears in the context of an Anglo-Norman retelling of Anglo-Saxon history in the corpus of romance texts which centre on the hero Guy of Warwick. Although Guy's adventures are nominally set in Anglo-Saxon England, in the reign of a king named Æthelstan, Guy cannot be identified with any real figure; his exploits are essentially fictitious, placing a Norman knight within an imagined version of the Anglo-Saxon past. Guy was one of the most celebrated heroes of medieval romance, and his story survives in multiple incarnations.[33] The earliest is an Anglo-Norman verse romance, *Gui de Warewic*, which was written in England in the first decades of the thirteenth century;[34] this may have been composed by a canon of Osney Abbey near Oxford, working under the patronage of the family of the Earls of Warwick.[35] There are also several Middle English versions of the romance surviving in manuscripts of the fourteenth and fifteenth centuries,[36] which differ from each other in various ways, but in general bear a close relationship to the Anglo-Norman poem.[37] As well as the verse romances in Anglo-Norman and English, there are also accounts of the Guy legend in a number of chronicles from the fourteenth century, which find a place for Guy's adventures in the reign of the tenth-century Æthelstan, reconciling the romance with their sources despite the absence of Guy's exploits from any contemporary historical record.[38] Guy was claimed as an ancestor by the Earls of Warwick, who began to name their sons after their supposed tenth-century forebear, and in time the historicity of the romance was reinforced by physical evidence of his existence: 'Guy's Cliff' in Warwick was pointed out as the site of his hermitage, and the axe of his defeated enemy Colbrand could supposedly be seen in Winchester Cathedral in the fourteenth century.[39] The historical veracity of the Guy legend only began to be a subject of doubt in the seventeenth century, by which time Guy had become one of the best-known heroes in English literature.[40]

The basic story of Guy tells of a young knight who tries to win the woman he loves by a series of adventures, then in time repents for his youthful exploits, gives up the knightly life, and becomes a pilgrim and hermit in penance for his sins. Over the course of his lengthy career Guy has many adventures abroad, but we are concerned here with two episodes in the story, from the beginning and the end of Guy's life, which both take place in England. Each involves him fighting on behalf of the English king Æthelstan, in the first case against an Irish dragon which has been terrorising Northumbria, and in the second against an invading Danish army. In this second episode, called back from his life of penance by his country's desperate need, Guy takes on the Danes' champion Colbrand in single combat and repels the invasion.

The two episodes in which Guy fights for Æthelstan – against the dragon and against the Danes – are set apart in several ways from the rest of his exploits. They are instances where the romance takes a particular interest in the pre-Conquest setting of the story, drawing on developing ideas about historical writing in the vernacular, and the first has sometimes been taken as a prefiguring of the second.[41] Although the two English episodes form only a small proportion of Guy's many adventures, they became the most celebrated of his feats: he is named as a famous dragon-slayer in *Beves of Hamtoun* for his victory over the dragon in Northumbria, and subsequent versions of the story singled out his combat against Colbrand for special attention.[42] Because the king in the Guy story is called Æthelstan, these two episodes have often been linked to the reign of the tenth-century king of that name: medieval chroniclers who found a place for Guy in Anglo-Saxon history usually located him in the time of Æthelstan, and both the dragon-fight and the Danish invasion have been interpreted as fictionalised versions of Æthelstan's famous victory at Brunanburh in 937 (although Guy's single combat is actually set in Winchester).[43] One of the combatants at Brunanburh was Olaf Guthfrithson, king of Dublin and York; the name of the leader of Guy's Danish invasion (Anlaf, a version of the Norse name Olaf)[44] and the fact that it is a dragon from Ireland which terrorises Northumbria have both led to speculation that a narrative about Brunanburh lies somewhere behind these two episodes.[45]

It is true that the battle at Brunanburh was the subject of numerous legends – we have seen one of the narratives associated with it in the story of St Oda and the broken sword, and this is only one of several representations of the battle in English and Norse literature.[46] Æthelstan's fame may explain why this name was chosen for the king in the Guy of Warwick legend, but in fact Guy's Æthelstan has very little in common with his Anglo-Saxon namesake. Much like the protagonist of the fourteenth-century romance *Athelston*, this Æthelstan is a fictional character whose name is attributable to contemporary views of the Anglo-Saxon past rather than to any resemblance to the historical king.[47] The presentation of the king and the Danish invasion in the Guy story are in fact both more reminiscent of medieval historians' descriptions of the reign of Æthelred the Unready, with a weak and passive king and an England helpless before the threat of Viking invasion. In the romances the English are presented collectively as craven and feeble, and the king as unable to defend his kingdom. At the Danes' first appearance, Æthelstan's counsellors tell him he will find many brave Englishmen to fight on his behalf, but when the challenge to single combat actually comes, there is no one but Guy. The general impression is of a nation in decline, weakened not only by external attack but by failings and cowardice among the nobility. No one comes forward to answer Æthelstan's request for a champion to fight Colbrand (they all stand around and stare at the ground in embarrassment), and when Guy makes enquiries about the brave knights he knew in England before his pilgrimage abroad, he is told they are absent or dead. As Æthelstan despairingly concludes:

> Full bold be these danys,
> And gret cowardys the Englyssh
> (C 10420–1)

(Very bold are these Danes, and great cowards the English.)

Æthelstan fears losing control of his kingdom, is concerned about being forced to flee the country, and laments that if he had been less stingy to his knights they would have stood by him. It is difficult to recognise the valiant, decisive and generous Æthelstan of William of Malmesbury and other chroniclers in this helpless king;[48] the fictional Æthelstan's acknowledged errors of policy and the sorry state of the English nobility in the face of Danish attack are all more reminiscent of the ways post-Conquest historians (following the *Anglo-Saxon Chronicle*) portrayed the last years of Æthelred's reign. By contrast, the Danes are presented as proud and arrogant: we are given a vivid little picture of the Danes watching the single combat, nudging each other and boasting that England will pay them tribute and for ever be subject to them. This picture of an England helpless in the face of wide-ranging attacks by a Danish army echoes accounts such the *Anglo-Saxon Chronicle*'s description (quoted in Chapter 2) of the arrogant army who defied the threat of Cuckhamsley Barrow in 1006, and there are a number of elements in that entry which provide particularly close parallels with the narrative in *Guy*: the combination of references to both Guy's hometown of Wallingford and the site of his combat at Winchester is particularly striking, and the general fear caused by the invasion and the ineffective results of summoning a defensive English army appear in both narratives. Æthelstan's crisis parliament and the hopeless situation of the nation recall the efforts which attracted the scorn of the chronicler writing about the events of 1006 – and that *Anglo-Saxon Chronicle* entry also contains vainglorious boasting, although there it is on the English side.[49]

Into this context of English weakness and Danish arrogance the romances insert the Norman hero Guy, saviour of the hour. With Æthelstan helpless, the role of national defender is delegated to Guy; in presenting the victory of the English as the single-handed triumph of the Norman knight Guy, the romances reimagine Anglo-Saxon history in a way which must have particularly suited a thirteenth-century Anglo-Norman audience, but which is carried over into the English versions of the story too.[50] It is in this context that the romances introduce the idea of a historical Danish right to rule England. This is first mentioned when Guy is absent abroad, and Æthelstan holds a parliament to discuss the threatened invasion of England by Anlaf of Denmark. It becomes clear that Anlaf's attack is not imagined as a random act of aggression: Æthelstan tells his counsellors that the Danish king is claiming he has a right to rule in England, and asks for reassurance that this claim is not valid. In response, Guy's elderly tutor Heraud, the wisest of Æthelstan's counsellors, describes the history of the Danish king's claim. He acknowledges that while the Danish kings once had a just right to rule the country, they long ago lost it by defeat in battle. He explains:

> Myn eldren seide, ich vnder-stonde,
> Þe Dennisch men hadde riȝt in þis londe,
> Wiþ-outen eni faile…
> & siþþe þai han it lore, y-wis,
> And here folk in bataile.
> (A 17.7–12)

(My elders said, I understand, that the Danish men had a right in this land, without doubt … and afterwards they lost it, indeed, and their men in battle.)

Another version of the romance elaborates a little on this decisive battle:[51]

> And sethen longe tyme a-goone
> Many of hem were here sloone:
> A grete bateyle there they tynte
> Right with strengthe of swerdus dynte;
> Therfor haue thei loste there right:
> Thei were dyscomfyt in that fight.
> (C 8803–9)

(And afterwards, a long time past, many of them were slain here. They fought a great battle there with powerful swords' blows. By that they lost their right; they were defeated in that battle.)

The question of the Danish challenge is presented as a matter of great antiquity: many winters have passed, Æthelstan says, since they first challenged England. Æthelstan asks his barons what their elders have told them about the Danish claim, and Heraud echoes this reference to oral tradition passed down by his ancestors – it is information which only he can give the king in his role here as the aged and wise counsellor. The very antiquity of the claim makes it vague and unspecific: it is not clear what decisive battle the poet may have been thinking of, and it is possible that no specific event is intended to be recognisable here. The romance clearly imagines this battle to have taken place some time before Æthelstan's own reign, and the effect is to place this latest attack within a longer pattern of invasion, defeat and return.

But Guy's victory, of course, will send the Danes away for good. When Guy returns home from pilgrimage he finds that Anlaf, with an army of 15,000 men, has ravaged the land up to the walls of Winchester, capturing and burning towns and castles. Anlaf challenges Æthelstan to find a knight who can defeat his champion, the giant Colbrand, but after another parliament to discuss the crisis the king is unable to find any warrior who will undertake the combat. A dream leads him to Guy, who has come unrecognised to the gates of the city as a pilgrim, and after some persuasion Guy agrees to fight Colbrand. Watched by crowds of Danes and English, he fights and kills the giant, and Anlaf, in accordance with the agreement he has previously made with Æthelstan, concedes defeat. The Danes leave England, promising never to return, and Guy, renouncing the world for the last time, becomes a hermit and dies shortly afterwards.

Some of this seems to reflect the use of information from historical narratives about Danish invasion, with particularly strong parallels to the invasions of Svein and Cnut, and this makes the appearance of the claim of Danish sovereignty in this narrative especially interesting, when compared to the context in which it appears in Gaimar's *Estoire*. There it is Cnut

who describes his ancestral right to England, in the middle of
a single combat which will settle the question for once and all.
Might some version of the story told by Gaimar be the tradition which lies behind Heraud's speech in *Guy of Warwick*?[52]
In the romance, the ultimate motive for Anlaf's attacks on
England is political: the Danes once had a legitimate claim
to rule England which Anlaf is attempting to resurrect. As a
result of this, the invaders are not presented as indiscriminate
raiders but as would-be conquerors with a reason to think
themselves entitled to claim the country. As soon as the battle
is over the Danes at once know themselves to be beaten and
fulfil their promise to leave the country; in doing this they
obey the terms of the oath Anlaf has sworn with Æthelstan,
and the finality of their defeat not only emphasises the glory
of Guy's victory but also underlines the point that this conflict
is a struggle between two nations claiming legitimate rule
over England, not between a landed king and a group of
opportunistic raiders.

Anlaf's invasion is presented as ultimately unjust, but only
because his ancestral right was (Heraud says) overthrown long
ago. There is no mention in Gaimar, as there is in *Guy*, of a
right lost in battle; Cnut clearly considers his claim to be valid
even up to his own day, and Edmund implicitly accepts this by
agreeing to the division of the kingdom. However, a pre-Saxon
setting for Heraud's story fits well with Æthelstan's statement
that the battle took place many years ago, and accords with the
way the idea is put to use in the Guy legend: there the Danes
are to be defeated by Æthelstan's champion, a glorious national
hero, and retreat from England forever. Heraud's version of the
story means that if it were not sufficient that Guy has God on
his side, he has history to support him too; the Danes have not
had a right to rule in England for many years, and Heraud's
story is almost a refutation of the tradition which is voiced by
Gaimar's Cnut.

The appearance of the idea of single combat provides a further
link between the story of Guy and Colbrand and Gaimar's

narrative about Cnut and Edmund in 1016. Margaret Ashdown surveyed a number of examples of single combat in medieval literature, including the Guy–Colbrand and Cnut–Edmund duels, and proposed that many of them could be explained by the existence of a tradition about a single combat fought by Olaf Cuaran, which became linked to the battle of Brunanburh.[53] While this would explain the otherwise obscure connection between the Guy legend and the reign of Æthelstan, the appearance of the Danish sovereignty motif in both the Guy and Cnut stories of single combat suggests the two may be more directly linked. It may be that the composer of the Anglo-Norman romance had access to a source which contained a version of the story of a combat between Cnut and Edmund – not found in the *Anglo-Saxon Chronicle*, but appearing in numerous sources from the mid-eleventh century onwards – which may have formed a more immediate model for the Guy–Colbrand duel than a combat at Brunanburh, particularly if it involved, as Gaimar's version does, a discussion of the idea that the Danes claimed an ancient right to sovereignty in England. The histories of Winchester and Oxford which Gaimar claims to have had access to might well have included such a story; the possible contents of these lost works are especially suggestive in the light of the connections between the Guy legend and Winchester and Osney, near Oxford.[54]

Whatever the precise connection may have been, however, both Gaimar and the Guy story show how stories about Danish rule in England could become part of a longer narrative of England's history, envisaging it as a land which had been conquered many times over. Within this context even Viking invaders could be construed as potentially legitimate conquerors, not merely plunderers, with a claim which can be debated even if it is eventually refuted. This view of the English past may in the first instance have been especially appealing to Anglo-Norman aristocratic audiences, but in the Guy legend it quickly spread beyond this initial context: the reference to the idea of Danish sovereignty appears in both the Anglo-Norman and

Middle English versions of the story, and must have helped to popularise the idea as the legend of Guy became widely known. In this way interpretations of English history which give the Danes a significant role to play could circulate in new and unexpected contexts – and the best example of this is the story of Havelok, the subject of our final chapter.

CHAPTER 5

'OVER THE SALT SEA TO ENGLAND': HAVELOK AND THE DANES

The last story we have to consider is perhaps the most enduringly popular of all the medieval legends about the Vikings in England. It is the tale of Lincolnshire's own Viking hero, the Danish prince Havelok, king of England and Denmark. The story of Havelok is first recorded in the twelfth century and survives in various forms, including Gaimar's *Estoire des Engleis*, an Anglo-Norman *lai*, and a Middle English verse romance from the end of the thirteenth century.[1] There are also a large number of references to Havelok in histories and chronicles in French, English and Latin, suggesting that the legend was widely known, but it is particularly associated with Grimsby, where the orphaned Havelok was said to have been brought up by a fisherman, Grim, who had saved his life.[2] These texts all present different versions of the story, but most share the essential details: the young Danish heir raised in exile, his marriage to an English princess, and the connection with Grimsby.

We can begin by summarising the story as told by the English romance, the most extended of all the versions of the legend. As this poem presents it, it is the story of the parallel, entwined fates of Havelok, son of the king of Denmark, and

Goldburh, daughter of the king of England. Goldburh's father, Athelwold, and Havelok's father, Birkabeyn, both die while their children are still young. They leave their heirs in the care of trusted regents, but both guardians turn out to be traitors, who mistreat the children and usurp their kingdoms. Goldburh is imprisoned by her treacherous guardian Godrich in Dover Castle, deprived of her royal status, and Havelok's fate is even worse: he has to watch his young sisters being murdered by their protector, who then orders a fisherman named Grim to take Havelok and drown him. But Grim, recognising the boy as the rightful heir to Denmark, saves his life and flees with him to England. Grim and his family settle down near the Humber in Lincolnshire, founding what would become the town of Grimsby, and there Havelok grows up. He is a cheerful, good-humoured boy, but he grows so fast that Grim can hardly afford to feed him, so he leaves Grimsby and starts working for his living as a kitchen-boy in Lincoln. There his extraordinary strength and success in a stone-throwing contest bring him to the attention of Godrich, the English usurper. Godrich forces Havelok to marry Goldburh, intending to humiliate her by marrying her to a kitchen-boy, and the pair, initially reluctant to marry, soon fall in love. When Goldburh learns that her husband is in fact of royal birth, she urges him to return to Denmark and regain his kingdom. They travel to Denmark, where Havelok's true identity is revealed by a miraculous beam of light which shines from his mouth as he sleeps – a supernatural token of his royal nature which recurs at key moments in the poem. After winning back his kingdom and avenging the murder of his sisters, Havelok leads an army back to England to conquer it on Goldburh's behalf. The poem ends with Havelok and Goldburh happily married, ruling England and Denmark together in one harmonious union.

Like *Guy of Warwick* and several other medieval romances, *Havelok* is set in a fictionalised version of Anglo-Saxon England, but its recreation of this period is an unusual one: instead of focusing on how English kings and heroes respond to the threat of Danish invasion, *Havelok* presents us with a Danish protagonist who is a lovable and sympathetic hero, an invader who fights for justice, and a popular king of England. The contrast is so striking that early critics of the poem often sought for a Scandinavian origin for the legend, apparently in an effort to account for the unusually positive depiction of Danes and Denmark in this poem. Various historical models have been proposed as the original of Havelok, including Olaf Cuaran, the tenth-century Norse king of Dublin and York (Havelok has the nickname 'Cuaran' in some versions of the story),[3] the Norwegian king Olaf Tryggvason[4] and Cnut.[5] There are, however, no direct parallels between the Havelok legend and the life of any historical figure, and even if there were, this would not really explain why Havelok is presented in such a heroic light; none of these names, except that of Cnut, would have meant much to an English audience by the thirteenth century.

Another method of accounting for the Danish element in *Havelok* was proposed by Edmund Reiss, who sought to identify mythological origins for the legend. He saw the character of Havelok's foster-father Grim as a distant echo of Odin: Grim is recorded as a name for Odin in some Old Norse sources, and Odin sometimes acts as a protector and guide of young warriors (a role which, as we have seen, may perhaps be traced in the prophetic old man of the Siward legend).[6] However, there is little to suggest that any of the medieval writers who tell versions of the Havelok legend were aware of this, and in most of these texts Grim is presented as a kindly, hard-working, but essentially very ordinary fisherman. We will, however, consider some later folklore conceptions of Grim at the end of the chapter.

Whatever the origins of the legend, then, a better way in which to understand the Danish element in the Havelok story is to situate it among the medieval accounts of Viking invasion and settlement which, as we have seen, offer varying interpretations of the Danes' role in English history. Although Havelok cannot be conclusively linked to any historical figure, the story was widely understood to be based on fact: in the earliest version of the story, as presented by Gaimar's *Estoire des Engleis*, Havelok is taken to be part of a long history of Danish rule in England, his reign just one episode among centuries of shared Anglo-Danish history dating back to the time of King Arthur. For Gaimar, Havelok is one among a number of Danish kings to have ruled in England, and his story lends support to the argument for hereditary Danish sovereignty over England discussed in the previous chapter. There are numerous differences between the two main Anglo-Norman versions of the story and the English poem: Gaimar sets the story in the reign of Constantine, nephew of King Arthur, and his version takes place in neighbouring small kingdoms in the East Midlands, rather than presenting England and Denmark as two distinct but eventually unified countries. Other sources fit Havelok into English history in different ways – making Havelok the son of Alfred the Great's opponent Guthrum, for instance, or the father of Cnut.[7] The English poem makes no such attempt to locate Havelok in a dynastic history of England or Denmark – at the end of the poem, it is said that *all* Havelok's 15 sons and daughters became kings and queens, and not one of them is named. However, the name of Goldburh's father Athelwold clearly signals that the poem is set in the Anglo-Saxon past, as does the location of his chief city, Winchester.[8]

The variant strands of the Havelok legend are all, to a greater or lesser degree, engagements with the Anglo-Danish past; at whatever point they situate Havelok in English or British history, all but the very briefest references to the story identify him as a Danish king. They accept significant periods of Danish rule over England, or regions of England, as an established part of pre-Conquest history. One important feature which sets the Middle English romance apart from the other versions, however, is its interest in Danish settlement in England as well as Danish rule. This poem presents Danish settlement as a formative process in both local and national history; in telling the stories of Havelok, Grim and Goldburh, it also tells of the foundation of a new town and a new dynasty. It has been suggested, most influentially by Thorlac Turville-Petre, that this represents an attempt by the poet to integrate the Anglo-Scandinavian heritage of Lincolnshire with a developing conception of national identity, influenced by an awareness of the role Danish settlement played in the region's early history.[9] Turville-Petre argued that the poem should be interpreted in the context of chronicle accounts of Viking raids, and that it offers a self-conscious alternative to the familiar story of the Danes as violent invaders: 'The chronicles tell only of pagan bands raping and pillaging; *Havelok* presents a revisionist view of the Vikings, bringing justice, peace and social integration.'[10] Beyond raping and pillaging, however, we have seen how some traditions of medieval history-writing provided a broader range of narratives about Danish invasion and settlement in England, acknowledging the complexity of the history of Anglo-Danish interaction and telling other kinds of stories about how and why the Danes settled in England. Reading *Havelok* against the background of this wider tradition helps to explain some of the distinctive ways in which this poem tells the story of a Danish prince who becomes king of England.

THE FOUNDING OF GRIMSBY

The chronicler Rauf de Boun, in his *Le Petit Bruit* of 1309, gives a brief summary of the story of Havelok, and comments that fuller information can be found in a text which he refers to as 'l'estorie de Grimesby', the history of Grimsby.[11] By this he probably means the Middle English poem, and his description of it focuses on an important aspect of the story: the link between the Havelok legend and its setting, its place in Lincolnshire history. The poet of *Havelok* clearly knew the area where the poem is set, and carefully, almost lovingly, evokes its specific details. He proudly refers to Lincoln as 'þe gode borw' ('the good city') on several occasions, and identifies sites within the city, such as the green where the traitor Godrich is executed at the end of the poem (2829–30). The busy streets through which Havelok

pushes his way as a kitchen-boy, carrying baskets of fish up to
the castle from the market by the bridge, echo with what
sound like the authentic cries of medieval Lincoln (868–909).[12]
Such details locate the poem in a physical space not bound by
temporal limitations; the world in which Grim and Havelok
live and work can be readily imagined by an audience familiar
with these places, although it may be distant in time.

Grimsby, Havelok's place of refuge, is less closely described
than Lincoln, in part because the poem conceives of it as a new
place – not yet a populous port, but a little settlement for Grim
and his family. The founding of Grimsby is described when
Grim comes to settle in England, after saving the child Havelok
from death at the risk of his own life. Grim and his family flee
Denmark and are driven by a strong wind to the English coast;
the poem lingers on this powerful north wind, perhaps with a
hint that it is an act of providence, a moment of supernatural
intervention driving Havelok and Grim towards their destiny.
With characteristic close attention to detail, the poet describes
the dwelling Grim constructs for his family:

> In Humber Grim bigan to lende,
> In Lindeseye rith at þe north ende.
> Þer sat is ship upon þe sond;
> But Grim it drou up to þe lond,
> And þere he made a litel cote
> To him and to hise flote.
> Bigan he, þere for to erþe,
> A litel hus to maken of erþe,
> So þat he wel þore were
> Of here herboru herborwed þere.
> (734–43)

(In Humber Grim came to land, in Lindsey, right at the
north end. There his ship lay upon the shore, but Grim
drove it up to the land, and there he made a little dwelling
for himself and his companions. In order to live there, he
began to build a little house from earth, so that they were
well protected there by their shelter.)

The repetition of 'litel' emphasises the makeshift, rough-and-ready nature of the dwelling Grim manages to construct – perched on the very edge of England, his family's only shelter against the sea winds. But this temporary lodging, we are told, is the beginning of a town that will last forever:

> And for þat Grim þat place aute
> Þe stede of Grim þe name laute,
> So þat Grimesbi it calle
> Þat þer-offe speken alle;
> And so shulen men callen it ay
> Bituene þis and Domesday.
> (744–9)

(And because Grim owned that place the town took its name from Grim, so that all those who speak of it call it 'Grimsby', and so shall it always be called, from now until Domesday.)

This moment of naming is a proleptic glimpse forwards from the time of the narrative to the present day of the poet and his audience, and on into the future. A combination of the giving of a name and a look towards the future is appropriate for a moment of settlement or invasion, and it is at these moments of first encounter when the nature of the relationship between land and settler is defined. We might think of Siward being addressed by name by the old man who foretells his destiny, or the moment in *Hemings þáttr* where Harald Hardrada and Tostig, landing at Cleveland, discuss the name of Ivar's mound and the significance of landing there.

In *Havelok*, this settlement narrative is also an origin-myth for the town of Grimsby, and the permanence of Grim's new settlement, mentioned at this early point in the poem, fore-shadows the eventual happy union between the English and Danish kingdoms which is brought about by the marriage of Havelok and Goldburh. This account of the founding of Grimsby is followed by a description of how Grim works hard to support his family in the early days after their arrival: the poem devotes nearly 40 lines to telling how Grim builds up his fishing trade, including a list of the fish he catches (sturgeon, herring and many more) and an account of him going around the countryside selling it, exchanging the money he earns for hemp and rope from which to make his nets (750–785). It is hard work which brings Grim – and thereby his namesake town – prosperity and success, and again there seems to be a sense that fortune or providence is on Grim's side: the fruitful sea yields its bounty to him, and he knows how to make the best of it.

This fascination with the details of ordinary working life sets *Havelok* apart from other romances which share the same basic plotline of a dispossessed prince; Havelok is the only hero of medieval romance whose talents include knowing how to skin an eel (919). It is also an indication of how by the thirteenth-century ideas about north-east England's Danish heritage had become bound up with experience of other kinds of contact with Scandinavia, particularly trade. Grimsby, like many other ports on the east coast of England, had strong trading links with Scandinavia throughout the medieval period; the fishing ports of the north-east coast did a thriving trade with Denmark and Norway, and as far away as Iceland.[13] Ships and merchants travelled regularly between England and Scandinavia, and one historian of Grimsby has commented that medieval Lincoln-shire seems to have been 'a kind of remoter suburb of Norway'.[14] The streets of Hull, on the other side of the Humber, were said in the late medieval period to be paved with Icelandic cobblestones, which had been brought there as ballast in ships.[15] All this forms part of the world imagined by *Havelok*, which is as interested in merchants and fishermen as it is in kings: it is Grim's prosperous fishing business which provides the foundation of the town of Grimsby, and Havelok disguises himself as a merchant when he first returns from England to Denmark. The legend of Havelok and Grim is not only an origin-myth for the town, but also an expression of its contemporary commercial identity.

This must be added to the fact that the region around Lincoln, one of the Five Boroughs of the Danelaw, had indeed been an area of extensive Scandinavian settlement in the Viking Age. The name Grimsby really is, as *Havelok* states, place-name evidence of this settlement: it is very likely that Grimsby did take its name from a Scandinavian settler or landowner named Grim (Old Norse *Grímr*).[16] Just as the poet of *Havelok* was conscious of this fact of linguistic history, so too were medieval Norse writers; the thirteenth-century Icelandic historian Snorri Sturluson accurately comments, speaking of the impact of Scandinavian rule in this part of England, that 'Mörg heiti landsins eru þar gefin á norrœna tungu, Grímsbœr ok Hauksfljót ok mörg önnur' ('Many names of places in the country are in the Norse language, such as Grimsby, Hauksfljót and many others').[17]

Although geographically part of England, Grimsby functions in *Havelok* as a kind of no-man's land between England and Denmark – not quite a suburb of Havelok's Danish homeland, but perhaps a colony. Unlike Lincoln, Grimsby is a new place, founded by a Danish man on English soil and inhabited by his Danish family. It is the place where the dual Anglo-Danish identities of Havelok and Grim's family intersect: within this carefully structured and patterned narrative, there are several key moments at which the characters travel between England and Denmark, and these moments always involve journeying through Grimsby. The first, of course, is the original settlement. After this Havelok, fast growing up, travels from Grimsby to Lincoln, and in doing so he is making a journey further into English territory, where a parliament draws people from throughout England and where he can begin to prove his right to be king of two realms. It is at Lincoln that he marries his English wife, but they soon return to Grimsby, and it is there that Havelok begins to assume his identity as a Danish king: in Grimsby Grim's children welcome him as king, Goldburh learns of his royal status, and they embark to regain his kingdom. Unfortunately, the section of the poem which would have dealt with Havelok's return to Denmark is lost, but on his return to England, the decisive battle between the Danes led by Havelok and the English forces of Godrich takes place near Grimsby. In this battle, Havelok's

Danish origins become, for the first time, a source of conflict in
the poem.

HAVELOK AND THE VIKINGS

At this moment, as Havelok is returning from Denmark to
England to regain his wife's inheritance on her behalf, the
English usurper Godrich gives a speech urging his men to fight
against the Danish army. He encourages them by evoking a
familiar stereotype: the Danes as destroyers, hostile to England
and to Christianity. He tells them that Havelok has brought
'uten-laddes' (2581), 'foreign soldiers', who have seized a priory
in Grimsby, and elaborates on the supposed enormities of
these Danish aggressors, claiming they are burning churches,
capturing priests and strangling monks and nuns (2584-5).
This picture of Havelok's men as rapacious Vikings is pure
propaganda, and clearly framed as such in the poem: as the
audience has been told less than 50 lines earlier that Havelok
has in fact founded a priory at Grimsby, to commemorate
Grim, the contrast between this distorted picture of the
Danes and the truth of Havelok's piety is particularly ironic.[18]
None of the characters who travel between Denmark and
England in *Havelok* are actually Viking raiders: they are
merchants, fishermen, settlers and kings.

Godrich's speech, however, suggests that the poem is alert
to the historical resonances of a battle between English and
Danes, and is able to exploit literary tropes associated with the
Danes to produce a moment of heavy narrative irony. Godrich's
speech is a reminder of the poem's setting in the Anglo-Saxon
past, where we would rather expect the defender of the kingdom
against the Danes to be the hero, not the villain, of the story:
Godrich's rhetoric aligns him with a figure like Byrhtnoth in
The Battle of Maldon, yet here he is a traitor whose defeat the
audience is encouraged to enjoy heartily. Our sympathies are
supposed to be entirely with Havelok and the invading Danes
(invading, of course, on Goldburh's behalf): 'daþeit who recke!',

the narrator exclaims when Godrich is finally captured and maimed, 'curse him who cares!' (2757). There is no sympathy for the English earl.

This manipulation of expectations suggests an awareness of how a Danish king like Havelok might be perceived by an English audience, and seems to indicate that the poet knew something of the familiar portrayal of the Vikings in English historical writing. This is also suggested by some of the names given to the Danish characters in this poem, which are not used in the other main versions of the story. As Scott Kleinman has argued in his study of the names in the Havelok legend, the naming strategies in this poem should be understood as drawing not directly on history but on historiography, specifically on what he characterises as a 'chronicle tradition of the twelfth through fourteenth centuries in which writers were engaged in a process of East Anglian history-building, a learned and literate enterprise that attempted to establish an identity for the region'.[19] Like the stereotype of the rampaging Danes conjured up in Godrich's speech, the use of distinctly Scandinavian names suggests an awareness of historiographical traditions about the Anglo-Danish past. The most striking example is the name Ubbe, given to the nobleman who first recognises Havelok's identity after his return to Denmark. The name Ubbe was rare in England,[20] and it seems very likely that the poet of *Havelok* borrowed it from a chronicle or hagiographical source – the role of Ubbe, son of Lothbrok, in the story of St Edmund made him one of the most famous Danes from the Anglo-Saxon period, especially to an audience in the east of England. The use of the name for a leading Danish character in *Havelok* is unlikely to be a coincidence, but it seems an extraordinary choice for a character who plays an important and positive role in the poem: this Ubbe is tough and formidable, but ultimately one of Havelok's most loyal and useful supporters. At the end of the poem Ubbe is appointed regent of Denmark while Havelok rules with Goldburh in England, and so is placed in clear contrast to the two treacherous regents who are the villains of the story.

In English tradition Ubbe appears as a cruel invader – and even a magician – but this poem seems to reject any negative associations with the name.

As we have seen, Ubbe frequently appears alongside a character named Bern, who is either identified as one of his brothers, as in Scandinavian tradition, or as the person responsible for bringing the Danes to England – either by fetching them himself (as in the story of Buern Butsecarl) or by killing their father Lothbrok. In *Havelok*, the second Danish character to appear after Havelok returns to Denmark is named Bernard Brun: Bernard defends Havelok and Goldburh from attack and by his support helps to convince the doubting Ubbe of Havelok's true identity. The name Bernard is, of course, much less rare than Ubbe, but the appearance of the two names together as the most important Danish characters apart from Havelok and Grim is suggestive, given their frequent co-occurrence in the English sources. The Ubbe and Bernard of *Havelok* have little in common with the characters of similar names in the legends about Lothbrok and his sons, but the choice of these names (which do not appear in other versions of the story) suggests that they did not have negative connotations for the poet. They may have been chosen for the characters in *Havelok* to create an air of historicity, evoking associations with other legends which, like the story of Havelok, showed the Danes playing a formative part in the history of the East Midlands.

The Anglo-Danish dynasty established at the end of *Havelok* is similarly underlined by the use of a name which seems to link the Havelok story with later Danish rulers of England: the name of Grim's daughter Gunnild, which appears in association with the Danish royal family in several narratives dealing with the conquest of England by Svein and Cnut. Gunnhild was the name of Svein Forkbeard's sister, who some English sources say was killed with her husband and child in the massacre of St Brice's Day. Svein's invasion in 1013 was, several medieval writers claim, prompted by revenge for the murder of Gunnhild, a beautiful woman who faced death with courage and prophesied that the shedding of her blood would cost England dear.[21] Cnut's daughter was also named Gunnhild, and she too was the subject of a popular legend by the twelfth century. William of Malmesbury tells how this Gunnhild, 'a girl of the greatest beauty for whom many suitors had sighed in her father's time', was married to Henry, emperor of Germany, and he claims that the splendour of her wedding 'even in our own day is still the subject of popular song'. She was wrongly accused of adultery and defended in single combat by a page-boy, keeper of her pet starling, and finally divorced her husband to spend the rest of her life as a nun.[22] The origins of this story (beyond the fact of Gunnhild's marriage, which took place in 1036) are unclear, but it appears in various forms in texts from the twelfth and thirteenth centuries.[23]

By the time *Havelok* was written, therefore, there were two widely recorded legends circulating about a Danish noble-woman named Gunnhild, either of which might have encour-aged the choice of this name for the character. At the end of the poem, Havelok arranges for Gunnild to marry the Earl of Chester, another Anglo-Danish marriage like that between Havelok and Goldburh. At this point the poem refers to her as 'Gunnild of Grimesby' (2866), as if to emphasise her link to the town her father founded. Unlike their brothers, who fight alongside Havelok in battle, Grim's daughters play no role in the poem until the very end; they are not even mentioned by name until Havelok is arranging their marriages.[24] At this point they are substituting for Havelok's own murdered sisters, and they are introduced solely so that their marriages can strengthen the bond between English and Danes. These names may suggest that the poem is deliberately drawing on narratives dealing with Danish rule in England to create a sense of its pre-Conquest setting, perhaps in order to suggest there is historical precedent for the legend of Havelok without tying the story to any particular dynasty or specific moment in English history.

THE LANDSCAPE OF CONQUEST

The double-plot structure of the poem means that in *Havelok*
Denmark and England are presented as twin nations, united at
the end of the poem by marriage. Several critics have argued
that the poem identifies the crucial difference between the two
countries as the superior nature of English law, and that England
has a civilising effect on Havelok and his country;[25] legal procedure aside, however, Denmark is not presented as noticeably
different from England. It is certainly not a pagan country (as
it is in, say, the hagiographical tradition of St Edmund), and
its society essentially mirrors that of England, populated by
knights and merchants, castles and towns. At some moments in
the poem Denmark is even romanticised, as in a tender scene
between Havelok and Goldburh in which Havelok's love for
his kingdom becomes entwined with his relationship with his
new wife. After Godrich has forced them to marry, Havelok and
Goldburh return to Grimsby – they are poor, and have nowhere
else to go. They are welcomed by Grim's children, but Goldburh
continues to grieve, believing she has been wedded unequally.
That night as they lie in bed, Havelok's identity is revealed to her
by miraculous tokens of his royal nature: a light blazing from his
mouth as he sleeps, the birthmark of a cross on his shoulder, and
an angel voice telling her he will be king. She is delighted by this
persuasive cluster of signs, and begins to see there is more to her
new husband than she had first thought. Havelok then wakes
and tells her he has been dreaming a marvellous dream in which
he is seated on a high mound in Denmark:

> Me þouthe Y was in Denemark set,
> But on on þe moste hil
> Þat euere yete kam I til [...]
> Als I sat up-on þat lowe
> I bigan Denemark for to awe,
> Þe borwes and þe castles stronge;
> And mine armes weren so longe

Þat I fadmede al at ones
Denemark with mine longe bones.
And þanne Y wolde mine armes drawe
Til me and hom for to haue,
Al þat euere in Denemark liueden
On mine armes faste clyueden,
And þe stronge castles alle
On knes bigunnen for to falle.
(1287–1303)

(It seemed to me that I was in Denmark, but on one of the
tallest hills which I ever yet came to […] As I sat upon that
mound, I began to possess Denmark, the towns and the
strong castles, and my arms were so long that I embraced
Denmark all at once with my long limbs. And then I wanted
to draw my arms towards me and have them in my keeping,
all who ever lived in Denmark, clasped fast in my arms, and
all the strong castles began to fall to their knees.)

This imagined embrace between Havelok and his kingdom
is not paralleled in the other versions of the story: in the
equivalent scene in Gaimar's *Estoire*, Goldburh has a dream
of a battle between boars, foxes and a savage bear, and of lions
coming out of the forest to pay homage to her husband.[26] Only
in the English poem does this wedding-night dream have an
emphasis on the loving union between the king and his land,
appropriate for the intimate setting of the marital bed. Havelok's
embrace of his kingdom parallels the consummation of his
new, and until this point unwanted, marriage: when Goldburh
is convinced of her husband's royal nature she spontaneously
kisses him, and he addresses her as *lemman* ('darling'), the
first moments of affection between them. Havelok's dream
encompasses not only the towns and castles of Denmark but
also its people, tenderly drawn towards him and clasped in
his arms, and when he describes how in a second dream he flies
across the sea to England to restore the land to Goldburh, he is
accompanied by his people:

> Ich fley ouer þe salte se
> Til Engeland, and al with me
> That euere was in Denemark lyues
> But bondemen and here wiues;
> And þat Ich kom til Engelond –
> Al closede it intil min hond,
> And, Goldeborw, Y gaf [it] þe.
> (1306–12).

(I flew over the salt sea to England, and with me all who ever lived in Denmark, except bondsmen and their wives, and I came to England with it all enclosed within my hand; and, Goldburh, I gave it to you.)

The restoration of Havelok and Goldburh to their proper places is imagined as a dream-world invasion, or migration, from Denmark, and it is stripped of any threat of violence by being figured as a love-gift between husband and wife. The dream inspires a longing for Denmark: Goldburh counsels Havelok to go and regain his country, telling him she will never be happy until she sees Denmark (1340–1).[27] This vision indicates a romantic, even loving, interest in the country of Havelok's birth unparalleled in other versions of the story; where those dreams focus solely on the revelation of Havelok's royal status, this vision links that identity closely to the land and people of Denmark.[28]

There are some features of these dreams which seem to align Havelok's vision with other narrative traditions we have looked at about Danish settlement in England. In his dream Havelok sees himself seated on an area of raised ground, so high that he can look over the whole kingdom, on a mound which is referred to as a 'hil' and a 'lowe'. The latter word, deriving from Old English hlæw,[29] suggests Havelok's hill may be classed with the burial-mounds and barrows which, as we have seen, act as a locus for prophetic knowledge in several narratives about Scandinavian invasion of England. These mounds are specifically connected with conquest, king-making and the ownership of territory – from Cuckhamsley Barrow in the *Anglo-Saxon Chronicle* to the *Historia de Sancto Cuthberto* and the mound where Siward meets the man who prophesies his destiny.[30] It may be that *Havelok* is drawing on this kind of tradition in setting Havelok's dream on an elevated *lowe*. In these narratives such mounds are the sites of prophetic inspiration: what happens there predicts success or failure in an enterprise of conquest such as Havelok is about to undertake. These encounters connect the protagonists to supernatural knowledge about their own future, and grant them power over the land they see (in *Havelok* the rhyme between *lowe* and *owe* 'own' reinforces this connection strikingly). Havelok's vision of himself seated upon a mound seems to participate in this prophetic tradition, and Goldburh interprets it as such: the dream shows that within a year, she says, he will be king of Denmark. In narratives where the mound is the burial-place of a named ruler, the prophetic power of an encounter with the mound must derive in part from the intimate physical connection it represents between the king and his land; interred in the mound, the king continues to exert control over his territory after death. He has given his body and his name to the landscape, and retains the power to determine who shall rule it. Havelok's tender embrace of his land and people, enclosing them first in his arms and then within his hand, seems to engage with a similar kind of union between king and kingdom; in this case the prophetic power of the mound does not warn him away from invasion, but urges him on to return to his country.[31]

THE VENGEANCE OF THE DANES

In the use of this motif and in its treatment of its Danish characters, *Havelok* seems to be drawing on a wider body of narrative material exploring the causes and nature of Danish settlement in England. An awareness of this tradition appears to have influenced *Havelok* in one further respect, which is

more prominent in the English poem than in other versions
of the Havelok story: the role of revenge in Havelok's decision
to reclaim Denmark and invade England. As we have seen,
narratives about the Danish invasions are frequently interested
in providing motives to explain why the Danes came to
England, beyond the simple desire for plunder or violence.
One of the most common motives ascribed to the Danes is
personal vengeance: this features in various forms in English
legends about the sons of Ragnar Lothbrok, and also appears in
the tradition about the murder of Gunnhild on St Brice's Day,
in which Svein is said to have invaded England to avenge his
sister's death. We have seen such explanations for Danish
invasion already being offered in the eleventh century, with
Osbern's story in the *Vita S. Elphegi* that Eadric Streona brought
the Danes to invade England to avenge the death of his brother
at the hands of some Kentish noblemen, and in the idea that
Thorkell raided in England to avenge either his brother (as in
the *Encomium Emmae Reginae*) or his two sisters, said in the
revised version of Herman's *Miracula* to have been killed at
Thetford amid the St Brice's Day slaughter.

Havelok, too, has two sisters to avenge, and the wider context
of these narratives linking invasion to personal vengeance for
the death of a relative may help to explain why *Havelok* lays more
emphasis on the murder of Havelok's sisters than the other
versions of the legend do. The role of the revenge motif in
Havelok is easily overlooked, perhaps because this poem is so
explicitly concerned with institutional law and justice, but it is
fundamental to the movement of the story between England
and Denmark and central to both Havelok's growth to adult
maturity and to his relationship with Goldburh. The subject of
revenge is introduced before Havelok's return to Denmark, when
he prays to God to avenge him on his foe (1364). Havelok lists
the wrongs Godard has done him, and this narrative is repeated
a few lines later, again in Havelok's voice, as he presents the sons
of Grim with his plan to return to Denmark. The recounting of
Havelok's injuries takes up 30 lines, and contains a declaration

of his intent which links his growth to manhood and martial strength with his return to Denmark (1432–40); the emphasis is not placed on the treachery of Godard's seizing the kingdom, or the justice of Havelok's claim to rule Denmark, but the personal injuries against Havelok and his family.[32] Godard's murder of Havelok's sisters does not appear in the Anglo-Norman *lai* or in Gaimar, and is part of a sustained narrative strategy which works to increase the audience's sympathy for Havelok.[33] The multiple later references back to the pathos of their deaths – usually including the formulaic reminder that they were slain 'with a knif' and, in Havelok's speech to Grim's sons, the gruesome detail that they were cut into pieces (1412–15) – add a personal dimension to Havelok's return to Denmark, making it emphatically a quest of family vengeance as well as the regaining of an unjustly seized kingdom.

In the Danish section of the story, the poem separates out the two purposes of Havelok's return: first comes the lengthy episode in which he is recognised by Ubbe (1626–2158), then he is accepted as king (2159–364), and only then does he set out to get revenge on Godard, after swearing a formal oath of vengeance on the book and altar in the presence of all his men (2368–9). This vengeance is not carried out by Havelok himself, since Godard is judged and sentenced by an assembly of Danes drawn from all classes of society, but the emphasis is on his crimes against Havelok's family as much as his treachery: the murder of Havelok's sisters is recorded along with the usurpation of the kingdom in the record of Godard's crimes inscribed above him on the gallows (2483–6). Goldburh, too, is activated by a desire for vengeance, and after Godrich's death she rejoices that she is avenged on her foe (2850). The closing lines of the poem foreground the importance of vengeance, presenting it as one of the strands uniting the twinned stories of Havelok and Goldburh; the poem has told how both were ill-treated and 'hwou he were*n* wreken wel', 'how they were well avenged' (2993). This emphasis on vengeance fits into the wider context of narratives about Danish invasion, which seem to reflect a desire to tell a narrative of military invasion and national conquest in solely personal terms, and in a way which encourages sympathy for the invader.[34]

Before we leave the subject of Havelok, and move beyond the medieval period to look at some later interpretations of the Danes in England, it is worth noting what this legend tells us about the popularity and diversity of narratives about Viking history in medieval England. In their recent edition of the Anglo-Norman *lai*, Burgess and Brook bring together no fewer than 14 short versions of the Havelok story – in addition to the three main versions in French and English – from before the sixteenth century.[35] Some are very brief, but they come from a wide range of chronicle sources, from all over England (as well as one from Scotland). Their details vary considerably, but they all bear witness to some kind of interest in this Danish king who ruled England, considering him a noteworthy part of England's pre-Conquest history. As with the legend of the sons of Lothbrok, scholars have often approached this material only in order to distinguish fact from fiction, to search out the kernel of historical truth which may lie within the elaborations of later legend, but it is important to remember that the legends themselves are widespread, influential, and important in their own right.

For a long time the apparent simplicity of the English poem *Havelok* in narrative and verse form – the folktale quality of its story, and its vigorous short lines – similarly led to its artistic qualities being undervalued, and the assumption long prevailed that this narrative about Danish invasion must simply be an artless reuse of material which had survived in oral tradition from the early days of Scandinavian settlement in Lincolnshire. In recent years, however, studies of the poem have increasingly emphasised the importance of understanding how far its apparent naivety in fact masks a carefully constructed fiction,[36] and this is equally true of its approach to writing about history. It is an imaginative engagement with the Anglo-Danish past, which can be profitably read in the context of a particular tradition of writing about the Danes in England, which aims to explain how and why the Danes came to settle and rule in parts of Anglo-Saxon England and to understand the contribution that Scandinavian settlement made to local and national history. *Havelok* shares with this tradition not only a wish to explore the causes of Danish settlement in England, but also an interest in betrayal and treachery, vengeance and justice, oaths, the treatment of young royal children, and the founding of a new dynasty through marriage and conquest.[37] In drawing on the names, images and motifs of these narratives in telling the story of Havelok, the poem participates in this exploration of the causes and consequences of Scandinavian settlement in England. It imagines the arrival of the Danes as essentially motivated by personal relationships rather than a desire for plunder or even for rule – in the case of *Havelok*, what unites England and Denmark more than anything else is marriage and the bonds of family (including foster-family) affection.

Havelok's positive view of the Danish contribution to English history, in which the Danes bring to England the rule of a just king and families of industrious settlers, is not simply a reflection of the likely sympathies of its Lincolnshire audience but part of a distinctive historiographical tradition, concentrated in but not limited to the East Midlands, incorporating romance and hagiography as well as chronicle-writing.[38] Within this tradition there was space for a variety of ways of understanding the relationship between England and Denmark and the history of Anglo-Danish interaction in the pre-Conquest period. Although we cannot be certain exactly which narratives about Scandinavian settlement and conquest were known to the poet of *Havelok* or his audience, it would seem that the poem, interested in the history of Danish settlement as a foundational myth for Lincolnshire, chooses to situate its Danish hero within a wider context of legendary material about Scandinavians in England. Although *Havelok* does not seek, as other versions of the legend do, to locate the Havelok story within a specific chronology of Danish rule in the Anglo-Saxon period, it creates an allusive sense of historicity by aligning itself with this tradition, echoing and adapting narratives associated with Danish rulers of England from Ubbe to Cnut. The poem imagines a past in which England and Denmark were closely linked, during a formative period in regional identity, and it shapes this imagined history by drawing on some of the many available stories about former Danish rulers of England.

ENGLISH TOWNS AND DANISH FOUNDERS

It is perhaps not surprising that the poem *Havelok* should have been informed by other traditions about the Danes in England, since the Havelok story itself was one of the most popular and best-known legends about the Danes. The chronicler Robert Mannyng, writing in Lincolnshire in the 1330s, provides some valuable evidence for awareness of the story at that date. In his translation of Peter Langtoft's Anglo-Norman *Chronicle*, Mannyng deviates from his source to note that he cannot find the story of Havelok in other histories: neither Bede, Henry of Huntingdon, William of Malmesbury nor Langtoft, he says, tells of King Athelwold and Havelok's rule of England. He contrasts this absence from the most authoritative sources with a number of other forms of evidence for Havelok's existence:

> Bot þat þise lowed men vpon Inglish tellis,
> right story can me not ken þe certeynte what spellis.
> Men sais in Lyncoln castelle ligges ȝit a stone
> þat Hauelok kast wele forbi euerilkone.
> & ȝit þe chapelle standes þer he weddid his wife,
> Goldeburgh, þe kynges douhter, þat saw is ȝit rife,
> & of Gryme, a fisshere, men redes ȝit in ryme,
> þat he bigged Grymesby, Gryme þat ilk tyme.[39]

(But as for what these unlearned men say in English, I cannot be sure of the true story of what is told. It is said that in Lincoln

Castle there still lies a stone which Havelok threw much
further than anyone else; and still the chapel stands where he
wedded his wife, Goldburh, the king's daughter – that is still
widely spoken of. And of Grim, a fisherman, people still read
in rhymes, that he founded Grimsby, Grim at that time.)

Mannyng was originally from Bourne in southern Lincolnshire, but he tells us that he wrote his *Chronicle* at the priory
of Sixhills, which lies about halfway between Lincoln and
Grimsby, in an area repeatedly traversed by the characters in
Havelok. What Mannyng says about Havelok here suggests
he knew a slightly different version of the story from any that
survives today – for instance, the chapel where Havelok and
Goldburh married is not mentioned in any surviving version
of the story – although the 'rhymes' he mentions may be related
to the English poem. His comments provide evidence that the
Havelok legend was not only popular in this area but also an
important strand in the history of the region, important
enough for Mannyng to question why otherwise well-informed
chroniclers fail to include it, and reinforced by the pointing out
of lasting physical reminders of Havelok's historicity. Mannyng
seems to indicate that it was a popular story in both senses of
the word – well-known, but also a tale in oral circulation among
the 'lowed men'.[40]

The story also features on the thirteenth-century seal of the
town of Grimsby, which depicts Grim, Havelok and Goldburh.[41]
All three figures are labelled with their names, and the fact that
Havelok's queen is here named Goldburh (rather than Argentille,
as she is called in the Anglo-Norman versions) suggests a closer
connection to the English strand of the story than to Gaimar
and the *Lai*. Goldburh and Havelok are shown with crowns, and
Goldburh has a royal sceptre, Havelok a ring and an axe. It is
Grim, however, who is the most prominent figure: he is placed
in the centre, armed with sword and shield, and considerably
larger than the other two. This is an interesting detail, as it again
suggests a different interpretation of the story from any of the

surviving medieval texts. There is no sign in the Anglo-Norman and English poems of Grim ever fighting a battle, and this image seems to hint at a different conception of Grim from the medieval poems' peaceful (and at times even slightly cowardly) fisherman. Havelok too is presented in a distinctive way. On the seal, the small figure of Havelok shelters under Grim's protecting arm; while Grim does save the young Havelok's life in the medieval texts, Havelok's unusual height and strength are so often emphasised there that it is remarkable to find him appearing as such a diminutive figure on the seal. It would seem that in medieval Grimsby – perhaps naturally enough – it was the town's founder and namesake who was the most important and dynamic character in the story.

There are also some alternative versions of the legend surviving from Grimsby, from a much later date, a testament to enduring interest in the story in the town which Grim had supposedly founded. In the seventeenth century, the Grimsby-born antiquarian Gervase Holles recorded several accounts of the Havelok legend which he claims came from inhabitants of the town.[42] These legends too differ in noteworthy ways from the medieval sources, suggesting that the tradition was continuing to develop and change, and they deserve some close attention. Holles is prompted to record them by his objection to William Camden's sceptical reference to the legend in his *Britannia*: Camden had said the story was only fit for lovers of old wives' tales, but Holles cites in Grimsby's defence various local traditions and landmarks, as well as the town's seal.[43] He notes – accurately – that the etymology of the name 'Grimsby' suggests it was named after a Scandinavian settler, 'ye termination *By* signifying in ye Danish tongue *habitatio*, a dwelling',[44] and observes that there was a large stone in Grimsby known as 'Havelok's stone', which recalls Robert Mannyng's comments about the stone in Lincoln Castle. (A later local legend about this stone, which can still be seen in Grimsby, said that it was brought by the Danes from their own country, and that it was formed of an indestructible material.[45])

One of the traditions Holles records says that Grim was a poor fisherman who put out to sea in the Humber and found the child Havelok drifting in an otherwise empty boat. This is a common motif (Moses is an obvious parallel), but in this context it particularly recalls the legend of the Danish king Scyld Scefing: at the beginning of *Beowulf*, Scyld is found as a baby by the Danes alone in a boat, and he grows up to be the progenitor of the Danish royal house, the Scyldings.[46] After this point, other elements in the story are consistent with the medieval sources: Havelok comes to public notice by his great strength and thereby marries the daughter of the king of England, finally discovering his true identity as the son of the king of Denmark. The happy conclusion of the legend is the foundation of Grimsby: Havelok 'exceedingly aduanced and enriched his Foster-father Grime, who thus enriched, builded a fayre Towne neare the place where Hauelocke was founde, & named it Grimesby'.[47]

Holles goes to observe that tellings of the story differ; in another, Grim is not a fisherman but a merchant, and Havelok spends time working in the king's kitchen as a scullion. For Holles, the differences of the stories are immaterial: 'they all agree in ye consequence, as concerning ye Towne's foundation, to which (sayth ye Story) Hauelocke ye Danish prince, afterward graunted many immunityes'.[48] This explains, he says, why in his day Grimsby still had particular trading privileges and immunities in Denmark. The story is therefore closely linked to Grimsby's commercial identity as a trading and fishing port, and for Holles at least it is the role of the town which is the most important factor in the legend.

Stories about Grim seem to have endured in local folklore in Grimsby even after this date. In his 1828 edition of *Havelok*, Frederick Madden records (with disdain) a story communicated to him by George Oliver, the author of a book on the history of Grimsby, which was apparently 'preserved among the lower classes at Grimsby' in the early nineteenth century.[49] This tradition says that the church at Grimsby originally had four turrets, but 'Old Grime' kicked three of them down from the tower to

defend his ships from attack at sea. The first turret flew out to
sea, and fell among the enemy's ships; the second, kicked as
his strength was diminishing, fell in Wellowgate, and became
'Havelock's stone'; the third only fell into the churchyard, and
the fourth he could not move at all. Oliver, Madden and Skeat
(who calls this tale 'absurd'[50]) are all scornful of this local story,
but it offers an intriguing picture of a gigantic Grim, closer to
the image on the medieval seal than to any of the earlier texts
about Grim and Havelok. The 'Old Grime' of this story is comparable to the use of the name 'Grim' in English folklore to refer
to landscape features said to have been formed by giants or
the devil, such as Grime's Graves in Norfolk.[51] The attribute of
superhuman strength which in the medieval romance is attached
to Havelok – demonstrated through his ability at stone-casting –
is here ascribed to Grim, in a way which aligns him with a
widespread folklore motif.

The legend of Grim and Havelok is the best-recorded example of an English town claiming to have a Scandinavian founder,
but it may not have been the only one. Robert Mannyng makes
reference to a man named Skardying or Scarthe, who was said
to be the founder of Scarborough, and his brother Flayn.[52] This
Scarthe may be identified with a character in the Old Norse
Kormaks saga, the hero's brother Thorgils, who has the nickname
Skarði; Kormakr and Thorgils/Skarði are said in the saga to have
established Scarborough while raiding in Britain.[53] Mannyng
attributes his information to two otherwise unknown authors,
'Thomas of Kendale' and 'Master Edmond', who both tell the
story of Scarthe and Flayn. These lost narratives may have been
in chronicle form or, since Mannyng calls the work of Thomas
of Kendale a 'tale', they may have been closer to a verse narrative
like *Havelok*.[54] Mannyng does not recognise the Scandinavian
connection, since he associates Scarthe and Flayn with the
earlier Anglo-Saxon settlement of England (linking them to
another onomastic story involving the hero Engle, namesake
of the English). However, the parallel with the pair of brothers
in *Kormaks saga* suggests that other northern towns besides

Grimsby may have looked back to Scandinavian settlement as a local myth of origins. Later writers like Gervase Holles were able to deduce the possibility of Scandinavian founders from etymology: Holles compares his theory on the origin of Grimsby to some other Lincolnshire examples, saying confidently 'I know noe reason, why Grimsby should not import ye dwelling of Grime, & receaue this denomination from him, as well as *Ormes-by* from Orme, and *Ketels-by* from Ketell, two Danish captaines under Canute, in the dayes of King Ethelred'.[55] By the time Holles was writing in the seventeenth century, folklore, medieval legend and antiquarian speculation about England's Danish history had become very difficult to disentangle – and this brings us to the subject of the epilogue.

The Danes in English Folklore

The stories we have been looking at offer a variety of perspectives on the Vikings and their relationship with England. In these narratives, Danish characters of the Viking Age feature not just as foreign invaders, conquerors and settlers, but as individuals with names, families and motivations of their own, which go beyond the stereotypical idea of Viking greed and love of violence. These narratives explore a range of interpretations to explain how people of Danish birth came to settle in England: whether they are in search of vengeance, or seeking to claim their birthright, or led by divine providence, or merely hoping to pursue their trade in peace, like Grim and his family in *Havelok*, their behaviour is motivated and satisfactorily explained within the world of the narrative. In their own way, these stories propose answers to some of the questions about the Vikings which have occupied historians for centuries: why did the Vikings come to England, and what impact did their presence have?

In these stories the Danes have a complex and ongoing relationship with England, especially with the regions around its eastern coast. It is not surprising that this area should feature so prominently in these narratives: to the inhabitants of eastern England in the Middle Ages, Denmark was geographically closer and easier to reach than some parts of England, a near neighbour and trading partner, and when the characters in these stories freely cross and recross the sea between England and Denmark they are perhaps reflecting how the audience of these texts conceptualised their North Sea world. No wonder they could imagine many ways in which Danes might have crossed the sea to settle in the Viking Age, as merchants and traders as well as invaders.

However, these narratives are unusual, in part because they are so specific. They tell the stories of particular Viking warriors or Danish settlers, mostly localised to certain places or to specific moments in the Viking Age. However far away from historical reality these legends may have developed, Lothbrok and his sons belong to East Anglia in the time of St Edmund, Siward and Waltheof to Huntingdon and Northumbria in the time of Edward the Confessor, Havelok and Grim to Grimsby and a romance version of Anglo-Saxon England – although exactly where they fit into pre-Conquest history varies between different interpretations of the story. The fact that they are so closely tied to particular places, to specific towns and land-scapes, is a huge part of their power: nothing illustrates this better than the story of Havelok, which is so firmly rooted in the real world of Lincoln and Grimsby, melding with the more distantly imagined worlds of Anglo-Saxon England and Viking Age Denmark. However, this focus on named individuals – though not the link to specific places – is part of what makes these stories distinctive.

It is far more common for English writers, in the medieval period and afterwards, to see the Danes in much more gener-alised and hostile terms. Particularly interesting is the wide-spread role played by the Danes in English folklore, where they typically feature as a vague and undifferentiated enemy force, nameless but powerful despoilers and destroyers. Traditions from all over the country, collected by local historians and antiquarian scholars after the end of the medieval period, attri-bute many kinds of activities to 'the Danes'; legends abound linking them to local customs, place-names and landmarks, ranging from battlefields, earthworks and stone circles to barrows and caves.[1] It has been said that 'more references to the Danes occur in popular lore of the [early modern] period than to any other invading host, from the Romans to the Normans'.[2] The very widely distributed nature of these traditions suggests that some of these stories may have originally been popular legends, but many also arose as learned attempts by scholars to account for ancient landscape features at a time when knowledge of prehistory was rudimentary: in the absence of reliable ways of dating such features of the landscape, anything from Neolithic monuments to Roman earthworks came to be attributed to 'the Danes'. As Jennifer Westwood and Jacqueline Simpson put it, early antiquaries 'solved most dating problems connected with ancient sites by reference to Romans and Danes, and so, it seems, did locals'.[3]

These inquiries into the history of the English landscape also came at a time when there was a burgeoning scholarly interest in the Viking Age in both Britain and Scandinavia.[4] In the sixteenth and seventeenth centuries, Old Norse and Old English texts and the work of medieval historians like Saxo Grammaticus began to be rediscovered, and were studied for the evidence they might provide into the early history of the Germanic peoples, their culture, language, customs and myths. Scholars attempted to investigate the shared ancestors of the Anglo-Saxons and Scandinavians – usually understood to be the 'Goths' and other northern European peoples – and to explain the relationship between the Norse gods described in medieval sources and the much more scantily attested belief system of the pre-Christian Anglo-Saxons. Scandinavian and Icelandic scholars corresponded with British antiquarians, sharing ideas, texts and linguistic expertise. This was valuable and pioneering work, although sometimes they misunderstood their medieval sources in ways which invented new and pervasive legends about the Vikings: the idea (still sometimes encountered today) that the Vikings drank from the skulls of their enemies arose from a misinterpretation of a poem about

Ragnar Lothbrok by the Danish scholar Ole Worm in his *Literatura Runica* of 1636.[5]

In this context, it is not surprising that antiquarian sources of the period are full of speculation about 'the Danes' and what they did in England. Many of the traditions they cite are ascribed to popular legends associated with particular places or landmarks, but – as we saw with Gervase Holles' speculations about the Danish history of Grimsby – it is difficult to know how far scholarly theorising and popular tradition have become entwined. The boundaries between learned and popular interpretations of England's early history were very porous, and we have already seen how medieval historians like Henry of Huntingdon or Gaimar incorporated what may at the time have been oral legends about figures like Siward or Havelok into larger narratives of English and British history. The role of archetypal foreign enemy, attributed to 'the Danes' in later popular and antiquarian tradition, was one they had already begun to fill in the medieval period: by the twelfth century it was already common to attribute any rupture or unexplained gap in the early history of a particular church or community to an attack by the Vikings.[6] They performed a convenient historiographical function, aided of course by the fact that Viking activity in the Anglo-Saxon period was indeed widespread, destructive, and well-attested by early sources. Even so, it seems highly unlikely that the Danes were to blame for every atrocity attributed to them by medieval historians, and still less likely that they can have been responsible for most of the activities ascribed to them in post-medieval tradition. It is debatable to what extent this should be thought of as a continuation of the medieval narratives about the Danes which have been the subject of this book, rather than a distinct phenomenon originating towards the end of the fifteenth century.[7] There are, however, some particularly striking examples which are comparable with the medieval sources, and which are worth exploring here. What the plentiful and various appearances of 'the Danes' in English folklore indicate more than anything, though, is how the idea of England's Viking history continued to capture the popular imagination, far outside areas of former Scandinavian settlement and long after the end of the medieval period.

DANES IN THE LANDSCAPE

Many of these stories about the Danes in post-medieval sources are aetiological: that is, they purport to explain the origin of place-names and landscape features as the sites of Danish war-camps, battlefields, or burial-places of slaughtered Viking armies. Any place with a name that sounded or looked anything like 'Dane' was fertile ground for nurturing stories about a link to the Danes. Examples include Danes Moor and Daventry in Northamptonshire, Danesborough in Somerset, and Danbury in Essex, all said to be the sites of Danish camps or battles against the Danes; similarly Bloodsdale, at Drayton near Norwich, and Bloodmere Hill, in Pakefield, Suffolk, were said to have got their names from the blood spilled in battle against the Danes there.[8] The fifteenth-century chronicle of Crowland Abbey provides a good example of this kind of folk etymology in its explanation of the name of the village of Threekingham, near Sleaford in Lincolnshire. The name Threekingham (sometimes found as Threckingham) is of Anglo-Saxon origin, and probably means something like 'the homestead of the family of Tric',[9] but the Crowland chronicle explains that it came about because three Danish kings were buried near the village after a great battle in 870. The chronicle says the village had previously been called Laundon, but was then renamed 'Trekyngham', that is, 'the village of the three kings'.[10] Whatever the source of this belief, it was an enduring legend. Threekingham held a yearly fair which was believed to commemorate the killing of the kings, and was held on an area of ground said to have been the battlefield; three stone coffins in the church, and also various tumuli around the village, were claimed as the burial-places of the three kings.[11] By the nineteenth century, the name of the neighbouring village of Folkingham was being attributed to the same origins: in this case it was said to derive from *fall-king-ham*, because the kings fell there.[12]

Such explanations almost always involve warfare, battles and other kinds of conflict against the Danes, rather than any more peaceful kind of interaction. They are reminiscent of the medieval references to the death of Ivar at Hungerford (explaining the name as *Hyngarford*) and Beorn at Frindsbury, although the Danes in question are not usually identified as specifically as this. Other traditions surround barrows, earthworks and monuments said to be the burial-sites of the Danes, although in fact they are often much older than the Viking Age. From Sussex comes a legend linked to Kingley Vale, near Chichester, where a group of Bronze Age barrows known as the Kings' Graves are said to be the burial-place of Danish warriors killed in battle there. Some modern versions of the story say that the Danes lie buried beneath the roots of a nearby grove of ancient yew trees, and that at night the trees are haunted by the ghosts of Viking warriors.[13]

Stone circles were also sometimes linked to the Danes, including in the medieval sources; in one fifteenth-century chronicle, Havelok is said to have been buried at Stonehenge.[14] The Rollright Stones, on the border between Oxfordshire and Warwickshire, have a particularly interesting legend linking them to Danish invasion. The Rollright Stones, a complex of Neolithic and Bronze Age monuments, comprise one of the most important megalithic monuments in Britain. They include three distinct elements: a burial chamber constructed of huge standing stones, known as the Whispering Knights, a single monolith called the King Stone, and a circle of 77 closely spaced stones, 'the King's Men'. The names given to the stones derive from a local legend, first recorded in the sixteenth century, which explained the origin of these monuments by saying they were an army of men who had been turned into stone. A warrior and his army were riding towards Long Compton – the next village to the Rollright Stones, over the border in Warwickshire – because it had been prophesied that if he came within sight of Long Compton, he would be king of England. Before the army could reach Long Compton, however, they were all turned into stone. There was a local rhyme recording the prophecy:

> If Long Compton thou canst see,
> King of England thou shalt be.[15]

Some antiquarians linked this petrified king to the invading Danes. Camden speculated that the place-name *Rollright* indicated a connection with Rollo, the Viking warrior who was credited as the founder of Normandy.[16] Jennifer Westwood has compared the Rollright Stones legend to a number of other stories and folktales linking particular landmarks to prophecies about invasion and conquest, some of which we have already encountered in the context of medieval legends about Danish invasion.[17] The general idea of the story, as she says, is 'pass such-and-such a point and such-and-such will follow', and these traditions are often expressed in rhyming prophecies. A similar tradition and rhyme to that found at Rollright is recorded of Edgcote in Northamptonshire; there it is linked with a place called Danesmoor, which was, of course, said to be the site of a battle against the Danes.[18] The earliest recorded instance of this prophecy tradition appears to be the *Anglo-Saxon*

29. The Rollright Stones (Jason Ballard)

Chronicle's entry for the year 1006, when Svein Forkbeard and his army were overrunning Wessex, and defied the local boast (or prophecy) which said that 'if they reached Cuckhamsley Barrow they would never get to the sea'; Cuckhamsley Barrow is about 35 miles from the Rollright Stones, to the south of Oxford. The boast recorded in the *Chronicle* appears to be part of the wider legendary tradition surrounding the supernatural power of burial-mounds and their influence on kingship, accession and invasion, and the story attached to the Rollright Stones may be, as Westwood suggests, a later folklore version of this motif, linked (as in the *Anglo-Saxon Chronicle*) to an ancient landmark which pre-dates the Danish invasions by many years.

Danes' skins and Danes' blood

One particularly gruesome and surprisingly common tradition about the Danes is the story of 'Danes' skins'. A number of English churches preserve a legend telling how a Danish warrior attempted to rob the church, but was caught by the local people and flayed alive, and his tanned skin was then nailed to the church door as a warning to other would-be pillagers. This tradition is remarkably widely distributed, recorded from Kent to Yorkshire: Samuel Pepys was told of this legend when he visited Rochester Cathedral in 1661, and it is also recorded from Westminster Abbey, Stillingfleet in Yorkshire, Stogursey and Mark in Somerset, and the Essex churches of Copford, Hadstock and East Thurrock.[19]

It seems unlikely, to say the least, that all or indeed any of these doors were actually covered with the remains of captured Danish pirates. Most of the doors in question date from after the end of the Anglo-Saxon period, and it is probable that some of these 'skins' were simply animal leather, as it was fairly common in the Middle Ages for wooden doors to be protected in this way. However, some surviving fragments from various churches have been analysed, first in the nineteenth century and again in the 1970s, and while most turned out to be animal leather, the samples from Hadstock and Copford were judged to be probably human skin.[20] Rather than being the skins of Viking pirates, it seems likely that these were the much later remains of executed criminals who were flayed after death. The practice of flaying was rare in medieval England, although it does appear in some medieval sources as a punishment for treason (not sacrilege): at the end of *Havelok*, the treacherous Danish usurper Godard is flayed as a punishment for his betrayal and murder of the royal children he had sworn to protect (*Havelok*, 2430–511).[21] Even this fictional example is, however, imagined very differently from the kind of vigilante justice referenced in the 'Danes' skin' legends: the romance describes Godard's humiliating punishment with characteristic relish, but it is enacted through a formal judicial procedure, laid down by a parliament of Danes convened by the king.

The idea of 'Danes' skins' is also found in other contexts in folklore. In Sussex, 'Dane's skin' was a term for light, freckled skin, while in the south-west of England Danish blood was instead associated with red hair: in Somerset, red-haired people

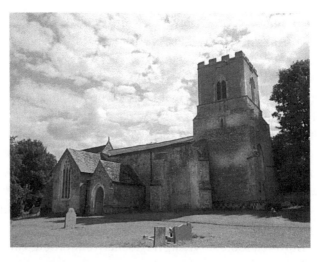

30. St Botolph's, Hadstock, in Essex, a possible site of the church built by Cnut in commemoration of the 1016 Battle of Assandun

were once said to be 'a bit touched with the Danes', while in Wiltshire they were 'crossed with the Danes'.[22] Red hair generally has negative associations in folklore, so these comments were presumably not intended to be complimentary, and it suggests a broader application of the phrase than the 'skins' on the church doors. Even if there is no plausible historical basis for the legend of these 'skins', however, the fact that these were identified as *Danes'* skins suggests how the idea of the Danes had captured the popular imagination. Rather than reflecting any real continuity of tradition from the early medieval period, this kind of story demonstrates the later medieval and early modern tendency to identify the Viking Age as a formative period of national conflict.

But there may also be particular local resonances to this widespread tradition, since some of the churches where it appears are in fact associated with the Danes in one way or another. The existence of this tradition in seventeenth-century Rochester is noteworthy, since we have seen that one medieval story about the death of Beorn, son of Lothbrok, claimed he was swallowed up by the earth near Rochester; it is not clear where this idea originated, but there may have been some kind of imagined link between Beorn and Rochester in the later Middle Ages. Hadstock is even more interesting. This church is close to one of the possible sites for the Battle of Assandun, the last battle fought between Cnut and Edmund Ironside, which took place on 18 October 1016. This was the battle at which Cnut 'won for himself all the English nation', as the *Anglo-Saxon Chronicle* puts it, but its location has never been identified. The most likely sites are either Ashdon, close to Hadstock in north-west Essex, or Ashingdon, in the south-east of the county. A few years after becoming king, Cnut founded a minster church near the site of the battle to commemorate his victory, and St Botolph's in Hadstock has been suggested as a likely candidate for this church, which would have been an important and impressive building.[23] If Hadstock is Cnut's church, the presence of a 'Dane's skin' legend here is intriguing. The door of this church has been dated

31. The eleventh-century door of St Botolph's, Hadstock, said to
have once been covered by a 'Dane's skin'

to the mid-eleventh century (a little later than Cnut's foundation
of 1020) – is it possible that some local awareness persisted here
of a connection between this church and the Danes?

This is not the only piece of folklore from the area around
Hadstock which is linked to the Danes and the Battle of
Assandun. Local tradition, of uncertain date, claims that the
battle was believed to have been fought at a certain Red Field –
'red' indicating that blood had been shed there – and that
weapons had been dug up in the area.[24] Hadstock and Ashdon
are close to the Bartlow Hills, a Roman cemetery of round
barrows long popularly associated with a battle between the
English and Danes.[25] These hills are the largest Roman barrows
in Britain; there were originally seven, of which three remain.[26]
Their name has sometimes been recorded as the 'Battle Hills',
and Camden noted that local lore said they were built to bury a
slain Danish army:

> The country people say that they were reared after a field
> there fought against the Danes. For, *Dane-wort* which with
> bloud-red berries, commeth up heere plenteously, they still
> call by no other name than *Danes-bloud*, of the number of
> Danes that were there slaine, verily beleeving that it blometh
> from their bloud.[27]

'Dane-wort' and 'Danes-blood' are part of another widely
distributed tradition, the idea that certain plants grew on
battlefields where the blood of Viking armies had been shed.[28]
The same story and similar names are attached in different parts
of the country to the pasque flower, the snake's head fritillary
and the clustered bell-flower, all of which bear purple or reddish
flowers reminiscent of the colour of blood. 'Dane-wort' usually
refers to the dwarf elder, which has stems and leaves which turn
red in September and fruit which when ripe yields a purple-red
juice. The berries are poisonous, and Somerset tradition
said this was because it grew from the bodies of slaughtered
Danes.[29] It grows in churchyards and in disturbed soil, so may
indeed have flourished around tumuli and battlegrounds, and
been associated with the dead. These names are not recorded
before the sixteenth century, but the Anglo-Saxons called
the dwarf-elder *wealhwyrt*, in which the first element may
mean either 'foreigner' (*wealh*) or 'slaughter' (*wæl*), and either
interpretation seems to indicate that a connection between this
plant and blood shed in battle against a foreign army goes back
a long way.[30] A parallel tradition is also recorded from Sweden,
where the names *Danskablod* and *mannablod* were used for the
dwarf elder, believed to have sprung from the blood of Danes
fallen in battle.[31]

The folklore association between battlefields and the blood-
red flowers which grow upon them is a very common one,
found across the world, and it is an idea still familiar in modern
Britain from the Remembrance Day poppy. The prevalence of
the 'Danes' blood' idea, though, like the 'Danes' skins', illustrates
how the Danes had come to take on the role of archetypal

enemies: any despoiler of a church must have been a Dane, any battle and bloodshed must have had conflict with Danes at the root.

RESISTANCE AGAINST THE DANES

As 'the Danes' had become such a convenient national enemy, those who had fought against them were celebrated as national heroes. The popularity of Guy of Warwick, defender of England against a Viking invasion, endured well into the eighteenth century; enthusiasts of this hero could visit 'Guy's Cliff' in Warwick, which was said to be the place where Guy had spent his last pious days as a hermit. Although Warwick claimed Guy as its own, other towns also made a play for him: in the sixteenth century, Coventry rivalled nearby Warwick by displaying a bone of the giant boar supposedly slain by Guy.[32] He was remembered too in Winchester, the supposed site of his single combat against the Danish champion Colbrand: in the fourteenth century visitors could marvel at the vanquished Colbrand's axe, hanging in Winchester Cathedral.[33] Guy's legend is perhaps one of the best examples of how traditions about the Danes could endure and evolve from their medieval beginnings: from his origins in the family myth of an Anglo-Norman aristocratic dynasty and his chivalric adventures in the medieval romances, Guy became a hero who fulfilled the role of giant-killer and even the slayer of a monstrous cow.[34]

Similarly, Wiltshire tradition celebrated a local man named John Rattlebone, who had supposedly fought for Edmund Ironside against the Danes at the Battle of Sherston in 1016. This story is first recorded in the seventeenth century by John Aubrey, who says that a small carved figure in Sherston church was believed to represent Rattlebone; in the battle Rattlebone was mortally wounded, but staunched the flow of blood by pressing a stone tile to his wound, and fought to the bitter end.[35] Just as folk etymology provided a variety of battlefields and burial-sites belonging to 'the Danes', so celebration of the

resistance could also be developed out of place-names: Camden
records that the inhabitants of Manchester believed that their
town derived its name from the valiant way their ancestors
had fought against the Danes, and in honour of their manly
endeavours, they had been rewarded with the name Manchester,
'city of men'. (Camden politely notes his own doubts about
this etymology, since the name, as he knew, long pre-dated the
Danish invasions.)[36]

In the late medieval period, victory over the Danes was
also linked with the customs of Hocktide, a festival celebrated
on the second Monday and Tuesday after Easter.[37] The chief
activity associated with Hocktide involved groups of women
capturing men and binding them with ropes until they paid a
small ransom to be freed. This was apparently a kind of post-
Easter festival of misrule, but the origins of these Hocktide
customs – and even the name of the festival – are very obscure.
It was first recorded in London in 1406 and became popular
over the course of the fifteenth and sixteenth centuries, mostly
within a fairly restricted area in the south of England. The late
emergence of the custom notwithstanding, however, Hocktide
was retrospectively explained as a celebration of Anglo-Saxon
victory over the Danes: it was variously said to commemorate the St Brice's Day massacre in 1002, the death of the last
Danish king, Harthacnut, in 1042, or an unspecified occasion
when a group of Saxon women outwitted and captured some
invading Danes.[38] (It is probably worth noting that St Brice's
Day is in November, and Harthacnut died in June; neither
date was connected in any way to Easter.) In Coventry the
townspeople re-enacted their ancestors' supposed triumph
over the Danes with a yearly Hock Tuesday play; although
suppressed in the sixteenth century, it was revived and
performed before Queen Elizabeth in 1575.[39] Hocktide had
almost entirely died out by the end of the seventeenth century.
The only place which still celebrates a version of the festival is
Hungerford in Berkshire, but – despite the medieval legend
that the town took its name from the Danish warrior Ivar –

the Danes do not feature in modern Hungerford's Hocktide festivities.

In this group of stories we might also include the legends which proliferated about Alfred the Great's battles against the Danes, which usually involve a mixture of antiquarian investigation of the Anglo-Saxon sources mingled with a great deal of imagination. Alfred was already a larger-than-life figure in historical writing by the end of the Anglo-Saxon period, and the growth of legends around him only accelerated after the Norman Conquest as he became idealised as 'England's darling', wise ruler and defender of his kingdom against invasion. Some of the most well-known traditions about his resistance to the Danes are, however, of much later date: for instance, the idea that Alfred cut or restored the White Horse of Uffington to celebrate his victory over the Danes was first put forward in 1738, and became popular with Alfred's many Victorian admirers.[40]

Not all the Danish links produced by folk etymology and antiquarian speculation cast Danes as the enemy, although most did. The town of Knutsford in Cheshire, which presumably took its name from a Scandinavian settler or landowner named Cnut (Old Norse *Knútr*), claimed that this Cnut was in fact the eleventh-century king of England. (Cnut was a fairly common name, and there is no particular reason to think the king was the town's namesake.) Local legend explains that the name arose when Cnut, with his army, forded the river that runs through the town. After crossing the river he sat down to shake the sand from his shoes, just at the moment when a wedding party happened to be passing by. He wished the couple joy, and as many children as there were grains of sand in his shoe. This was said to be the origin of the town's custom of 'sanding', decorating the street in front of a bride's house with elaborate patterns drawn in coloured sand.[41]

It is unusual, but not unique, to find Cnut featuring in local folklore as a benevolent fairytale king. He was remembered in a similarly positive light at Ely, as early as the twelfth century,[42] and in the area around Ramsey and Peterborough. It was said that Cnut had a fishing-box at Bodsey, near Ramsey, and that his children would travel by boat between Peterborough and Ramsey on their way to school. One day a storm blew up as they were crossing Whittlesey Mere, and two of Cnut's sons were drowned. They were buried at Bodsey, and local tradition claimed their tombstone could once be seen in the dining room of Bodsey House. To prevent any more such tragedies, the story goes, Cnut had a ditch cut on the border between Huntingdonshire and Cambridgeshire, which was known as 'Knouts-delf' or 'Kings-delf'.[43]

And, of course, a number of towns in England proudly claim to be the place where Cnut tried to hold back the tide. This is today perhaps the most genuinely popular piece of folklore about Cnut, still commonly cited (and commonly misunderstood)

32. A modern memorial to Cnut at Shaftesbury Abbey, showing the king demonstrating that he could not command the waves as a warning against arrogance or the foolishness of trying to command what is beyond one's control. The story dates back to the first half of the twelfth century, when it was first told by Henry of Huntingdon and Gaimar; they both regard it as an illustration of Cnut's wisdom and piety, demonstrating how Cnut, as a Christian Viking king, knew better than anyone that only God can control the sea.[44] Gaimar says that the incident took place on the banks of the Thames at Westminster, while Henry does not specify a location. Over the years, however, it has been variously claimed to have taken place at Southampton, Bosham in Sussex, Canewdon in Essex (another argument from folk etymology, deriving the name 'Canewdon' from 'Canute'), and Gainsborough in Lincolnshire. These towns vigorously defend their claims to be the place where Cnut really tried to hold back the sea (or the tide of the River Trent, in Gainsborough's case). As the event is unlikely to have happened at all, unfortunately none of these claims can be substantiated, but it is an example of how enduring some of the medieval legends about the Danes have been – there are still places keen to celebrate a link with the most successful of all Viking kings.

Some of this has taken us a long way from the medieval texts, but there are elements of these more recent traditions which resonate with some of the earlier narratives – particularly the sense that Viking invasion can serve as an explanation for the characteristics, landscape or customs of certain English places. Today many parts of England are proud of their Viking heritage, and look to it as an explanation for some of the ways in which the former Danelaw differs from the rest of England. York is full of memorials to its Viking history (though not to Siward, who is known today, if he is known at all, from his role in *Macbeth*), while Grimsby still remembers Grim and Havelok. The medieval stories we have been looking at suggest that some of the inhabitants of these regions in the medieval period were no less interested in why the Vikings came to England, what they did there, and what legacy they might have left to their descendants. It is striking how often these stories focus on ancestry and heredity, from St Oda, growing from his Danish origins 'like a rose among thorns', to the fathers and sons of the Edmund/Lothbrok legends, the lines of paternal descent traced in the story of Siward (with the tell-tale ears of a bear), and Havelok, who comes into the care of a succession of adoptive fathers, good and bad, but in the end proves himself his Danish father's son. Part of this is what happens as history becomes legend, as national conflicts are reimagined as personal struggles driven by private motives such as vengeance or love, and it reflects, too, the place of these stories in the family mythology of prominent aristocratic dynasties, both Anglo-Scandinavian and Anglo-Norman, who preserved and promoted legends about their distinguished ancestors. The family relationships which proliferate at the end of *Havelok* – a happy ending driven by marriages between English and Danish characters, adopted siblings, and the promise of many future children – draw attention to the recurring interest in these narratives in bonds of kinship as well as kingship. Perhaps this derives from a sense that for medieval writers and audiences in the former Danelaw, exploring the history of the Vikings in England was an opportunity not only to consider an important and formative moment in regional and national history, but also to tell stories of their ancestors.

NOTES

INTRODUCTION

1 'Daci ... terram undique creberrime diutissime insilientes et assilientes, eam non optinere sed predari studebant, et omnia destruere non dominari cupiebant' [Henry of Huntingdon, *Historia Anglorum*, ed. Diana Greenway (Oxford, 1996), pp. 272–3]. For discussion of Henry's view see R. I. Page, '*A Most Vile People': Early English Historians on the Vikings* (London, 1987), pp. 14–17.

2 'Þæt wæron þa ærestan scipu deniscra monna þe Angelcynnes lond gesohton' [Janet Bately (ed.), *The Anglo-Saxon Chronicle, MS. A* (Cambridge, 1986), p. 39]. Translations from the *Anglo-Saxon Chronicle* are my own unless otherwise stated. The date was actually 789; for the different versions of this event, see *The Anglo-Saxon Chronicles*, trans. Michael Swanton (London, 2000), pp. 54–5.

3 *The Anglo-Saxon Chronicles*, trans. Swanton, pp. 54–7.

4 For overviews of the history of the Vikings in England, see Katherine Holman, *The Northern Conquest: Vikings in Britain and Ireland* (Oxford, 2007), and Simon Keynes, 'The Vikings in England, *c.*790–1016', in Peter Sawyer (ed.), *The Oxford Illustrated History of the Vikings* (Oxford, 1997), pp. 48–82.

5 'mycel hæðen here' [Susan Irvine (ed.), *The Anglo-Saxon Chronicle, MS. E* (Cambridge, 2004), p. 48].

6 'ergende wæron 7 hiera tilgende' [Bately (ed.), *The Anglo-Saxon Chronicle MS. A*, p. 50].

7 On this period of Scandinavian settlement in England, see D. M. Hadley, *The Vikings in England: Settlement, Society and Culture* (Manchester, 2006); D. M. Hadley and J. D. Richards (eds), *Cultures in Contact: Scandinavian Settlement in England in the Ninth and Tenth Centuries* (Turnhout, 2000); Matthew Townend, *Viking Age Yorkshire* (Pickering, 2014).

8 For varying assessments of the nature and scale of the settlement, see F. M. Stenton, 'The Danes in England', *Proceedings of the British Academy* XIII (Oxford, 1927); H. R. Loyn, *The Vikings in Britain* (London, 1977); P. H. Sawyer, *The Age of the Vikings* (London, 1971); D. M. Hadley, '"And they proceeded to plough and support themselves": the Scandinavian

settlement of England', *Anglo-Norman Studies* 19 (1997), pp. 69–96; Hadley, "'Cockles amongst the wheat": the Scandinavian settlement of England', in William O. Frazer and Andrew Tyrrell (eds), *Social Identity in Early Medieval Britain* (London and New York, 2000), pp. 111–35.

9 For discussion of the value of place-name evidence in understanding the Scandinavian settlement, see L. Abrams and D. N. Parsons, 'Place-names and the history of Scandinavian settlement in England', in J. Hines, A. Lane and M. Redknap (eds), *Land, Sea and Home* (Leeds, 2004), pp. 379–431; see also Margaret Gelling, *Signposts to the Past* (Chichester, 1988), pp. 215–36; Gillian Fellows Jensen, 'Scandinavian influence on the place-names of England', in P. S. Ureland and G. Broderick (eds), *Language Contact in the British Isles* (Tübingen, 1991), pp. 337–54. On Old Norse personal names in England see Gillian Fellows Jensen, *Scandinavian Personal Names in Lincolnshire and Yorkshire* (Copenhagen, 1968), *The Vikings and Their Victims: The Verdict of the Names* (London, 1995), and also Cecily Clark, 'Onomastics', in Richard M. Hogg (ed.), *The Cambridge History of the English Language, Volume 1* (Cambridge, 1992), pp. 452–89 (465–7).

10 On language contact between Norse and English speakers and the influence of the Old Norse language on English see J. Hines, 'Scandinavian English: a creole in context', in Ureland and Broderick (eds), *Language Contact in the British Isles*, pp. 403–27; P. Bibire, 'North Sea language contacts in the Early Middle Ages: English and Norse', in T. R. Liszka and L. E. M. Walker (eds), *The North Sea World in the Middle Ages* (Dublin, 2001), pp. 88–107; Matthew Townend, *Language and History in Viking Age England* (Turnhout, 2002); Richard Dance, *Words Derived from Old Norse in Early Middle English: Studies in the Vocabulary of the South-West Midlands Texts* (Tempe, 2003).

11 For an overview see Hadley, *The Vikings in England*, and the bibliography at pp. 282–9.

12 Judith Jesch, 'Skaldic verse in Scandinavian England', in James Graham-Campbell, Michael Hall, Judith Jesch and David N. Parsons (eds), *Vikings and the Danelaw* (Oxford, 2001), pp. 313–25; Matthew Townend, 'Whatever happened to York Viking poetry? Memory, tradition and the transmission of skaldic verse', *Saga-Book of the Viking Society* XXVII (2003), pp. 48–90; John McKinnell, 'The context of *Völundarkviða*', *Saga-Book of the Viking Society* XXIII (1990–3), pp. 1–27.

13 Richard Bailey, *Viking Age Sculpture in Northern England* (London, 1980); David M. Wilson and Ole Klindt-Jensen, *Viking Art* (London, 1980), pp. 103–8; Sue Margeson, 'The Völsung legend in medieval art', in Flemming G. Andersen et al. (eds), *Medieval Iconography and Narrative: A Symposium* (Odense, 1980), pp. 183–211; John McKinnell, 'Eddic poetry in Anglo-Scandinavian northern England', in Graham-Campbell et al. (eds), *Vikings and the Danelaw*, pp. 327–44.

14 For discussion of the relationship between English and Old Norse literature in the Anglo-Saxon period, see Richard Dance, 'North Sea currents:

Old English–Old Norse relations, literary and linguistic', *Literature Compass* 1 (2004), pp. 1–10; Robert E. Bjork, 'Scandinavian relations', in P. Pulsiano and E. Treharne (eds), *A Companion to Anglo-Saxon Literature* (Oxford, 2001), pp. 388–99; Heather O'Donoghue, *Old Norse-Icelandic Literature: A Short Introduction* (Oxford, 2004), pp. 136–48; Roberta Frank, 'Anglo-Scandinavian poetic relations', *ANQ* 3/2 (1990), pp. 74–9. For attempts to trace Scandinavian influence in Middle English literature, see Rory McTurk, *Chaucer and the Norse and Celtic Worlds* (Aldershot, 2005), and Paul Beekman Taylor, *Sharing Story: Medieval Norse-English Literary Relationships* (New York, 1998).

15 See for instance Hadley, 'And they proceeded to plough and support themselves', pp. 82–93, and 'Cockles amongst the wheat', pp. 111–35, and also Simon Trafford, 'Ethnicity, migration theory, and the historiography of the Scandinavian settlement of England', in Hadley and Richards (eds), *Cultures in Contact*, pp. 17–39.

16 Holman, *The Northern Conquest*, pp. 186–7.

17 On this period, see Alfred P. Smyth, *Scandinavian York and Dublin* (Dublin, 1975–9); Clare Downham, *Viking Kings of Britain and Ireland* (Edinburgh, 2007); Townend, *Viking Age Yorkshire*, pp. 25–84; Holman, *The Northern Conquest*, pp. 95–103.

18 On this battle and its context, see Michael Livingston (ed.), *The Battle of Brunanburh: A Casebook* (Exeter, 2011).

19 *The Anglo-Saxon Chronicles*, trans. Swanton, p. 110; Cyril Hart, *The Danelaw* (London, 1992), pp. 6–20; Matthew Innes, 'Danelaw identities: ethnicity, regionalism and political allegiance', in Hadley and Richards (eds), *Cultures in Contact*, pp. 65–88.

20 On this period, see Ian Howard, *Swein Forkbeard's Invasions and the Danish Conquest of England 991–1017* (Woodbridge, 2003); Angelo Forte, Richard Oram and Frederik Pedersen, *Viking Empires* (Cambridge, 2005), pp. 184–92.

21 *The Anglo-Saxon Chronicles*, trans. Swanton, pp. 143–4; Howard, *Swein Forkbeard's Invasions*, pp. 99–119.

22 On Cnut's reign see Elaine Treharne, *Living Through Conquest: The Politics of Early English, 1020–1220* (Oxford, 2012); M. K. Lawson, *Cnut: England's Viking King, 1016–1035* (Stroud, 2011); Timothy Bolton, *The Empire of Cnut the Great: Conquest and the Consolidation of Power in Northern Europe in the Early Eleventh Century* (Leiden, 2009); Bolton, *Cnut the Great* (New Haven, 2017).

23 Holman, *The Northern Conquest*, pp. 181–94; Paul Gazzoli, 'Anglo-Danish relations in the later eleventh century' (unpublished DPhil thesis, University of Cambridge, 2010).

24 Henry Goddard Leach, *Angevin Britain and Scandinavia* (London, 1921), pp. 25–72, remains a useful summary; see also David Bates and Robert Liddiard (eds), *East Anglia and its North Sea World in the Middle Ages* (Woodbridge, 2015).

25 Lesley Abrams, 'The Anglo-Saxons and the Christianization of Scandinavia', *Anglo-Saxon England* 24 (1995), pp. 213–49; Goddard Leach, *Angevin Britain and Scandinavia*, pp. 73–113.

26 James Campbell, 'Some twelfth-century views of the Anglo-Saxon past', in *Essays in Anglo-Saxon History* (London, 1986), pp. 209–28; Richard Southern, 'Aspects of the European tradition of historical writing: 4, The sense of the past', *Transactions of the Royal Historical Society* 23 (1973), pp. 243–63; Andrew Galloway, 'Writing history in England', in David Wallace (ed.), *The Cambridge History of Medieval English Literature* (Cambridge, 1999), pp. 255–83; Judith Weiss, 'Insular beginnings: Anglo-Norman romance', in Corinne Saunders (ed.), *A Companion to Romance: From Classical to Contemporary* (Oxford, 2004), pp. 26–44; Martin Brett and David A. Woodman (eds), *The Long Twelfth-Century View of the Anglo-Saxon Past* (London, 2016).

27 Today 'Viking' is often used in this sense, but the word does not occur with this meaning in medieval English texts; for discussion see Christine Fell, 'Old English *wicing*: a question of semantics', *Proceedings of the British Academy* 72 (1986), pp. 295–316. For a summary of the language used to describe these Scandinavian peoples in medieval sources and in modern scholarship, see Downham, *Viking Kings of Britain and Ireland*, pp. xv–xx.

28 For examples, see Magnús Fjalldal, *Anglo-Saxon England in Icelandic Medieval Texts* (Toronto, 2005); Elizabeth Ashman Rowe, 'Helpful Danes and pagan Irishmen: saga fantasies of the Viking Age in the British Isles', *Viking and Medieval Scandinavia* 5 (2009), pp. 1–21.

29 Fjalldal, *Anglo-Saxon England in Icelandic Medieval Texts*, p. 27; see for instance the use of the term in *Knýtlinga saga*, in Bjarni Guðnason (ed.), *Danakonunga sögur* (Reykjavík, 1982), pp. 91–321 (124).

30 P. G. Foote (ed.), *Gunnlaugs saga Ormstungu* (London, 1957), p. 15.

31 On continuity as well as rupture after 1066, see especially Treharne, *Living Through Conquest*; Laura Ashe, *Fiction and History in England, 1066–1200* (Cambridge, 2007); John Gillingham, *The English in the Twelfth Century: Imperialism, National Identity, and Political Values* (Woodbridge, 2000); Hugh Thomas, *The English and the Normans: Ethnic Hostility, Assimilation, and Identity 1066–c.1220* (Oxford, 2003).

CHAPTER 1: 'FROM THE NORTH COMES ALL THAT IS EVIL': VIKINGS, KINGS AND SAINTS, C.985–1100

1 On the poem and its context see Janet Cooper (ed.), *The Battle of Maldon: Fiction and Fact* (London, 2003); Donald Scragg (ed.), *The Battle of Maldon AD 991* (Oxford, 1991); Simon Keynes, 'Apocalypse then: England A.D. 1000', in Przemysław Urbańczyk (ed.), *Europe Around the Year 1000* (Warsaw, 2001), pp. 247–70.

2 D. G. Scragg (ed.), *The Battle of Maldon* (Manchester, 1981).

3   For an alternative view, see Leonard Niedorf, '*II Æthelred* and the politics
     of *The Battle of Maldon*', *Journal of English and Germanic Philology* 111
     (2012), pp. 451–73. On the possible composition and leaders of the Viking
     army at Maldon, see Donald Scragg, *The Return of the Vikings: The Battle
     of Maldon 991* (Stroud, 2006), pp. 63–9.

4   For recent assessments of Æthelred's reign see Ryan Lavelle, *Æthelred II:
     King of the English, 978–1016* (Stroud, 2002); Ann Williams, *Æthelred the
     Unready: The Ill-Counselled King* (London, 2003); Levi Roach, *Æthelred
     the Unready* (New Haven, 2016); and on his later reputation, Simon
     Keynes, 'The declining reputation of King Æthelred the Unready', in
     D. A. E. Pelteret (ed.), *Anglo-Saxon History: Basic Readings* (New York,
     2000), pp. 157–90.

5   *The Anglo-Saxon Chronicles*, trans. Swanton, pp. 126–44.

6   Williams, *Æthelred the Unready*, pp. 52–4.

7   The *Passio* is edited by Michael Winterbottom in *Three Lives of English
     Saints* (Toronto, 1972), pp. 67–87, and translated in Lord Francis Hervey
     (ed.), *Corolla Sancti Eadmundi* (London, 1907), pp. 6–59; for discussion
     see Rebecca Pinner, *The Cult of St Edmund in Medieval East Anglia*
     (Woodbridge, 2015), pp. 33–47.

8   Ælfric, *Lives of Saints*, ed. Walter W. Skeat (London, 1881–1900), vol. 2,
     pp. 314–35 (314).

9   On the use of eyewitness testimony in medieval history-writing, see
     Elisabeth van Houts, 'Genre aspects of the use of oral information in
     medieval historiography', in B. Frank, T. Haye and D. Tophinke (eds),
     Gattungen mittelalterlicher Schriftlichkeit (Tübingen, 1997), pp. 297–311,
     and on the plausibility of Abbo's claim, van Houts, *Memory and Gender in
     Medieval Europe, 900–1200* (Basingstoke, 2009), pp. 47–8.

10   On Æthelstan's reputation see Michael Wood, 'The making of King
     Aethelstan's empire: an English Charlemagne?' in Patrick Wormald,
     Donald A. Bullough and Roger Collins (eds), *Ideal and Reality in Frankish
     and Anglo-Saxon Society* (Oxford, 1983), pp. 250–72; Elaine M. Treharne,
     'Romanticizing the past in the Middle English *Athelston*', *Review of English
     Studies* 50 (1999), pp. 1–21.

11   Adelard of Ghent, 'Lectiones in Depositione S. Dunstani', in Michael
     Winterbottom and Michael Lapidge (eds), *The Early Lives of St Dunstan*
     (Oxford, 2012), pp. 142–3; see C. Cubitt, 'Archbishop Dunstan: a prophet
     in politics?' in Julia Barrow and Andrew Wareham (eds), *Myth, Rulership,
     Church and Charters: Essays in Honour of Nicholas Brooks* (Aldershot,
     2008), pp. 145–66.

12   Hervey (ed.), *Corolla Sancti Eadmundi*, pp. 18–19.

13   Alcuin quotes the same passage in reference to the attack on Lindisfarne;
     on this and other examples see Simon Coupland, 'The rod of God's wrath
     or the people of God's wrath? The Carolingian theology of the Viking
     invasions', *Journal of Ecclesiastical History* 42/4 (1991), pp. 535–54 (538). On
     the apocalyptic overtones of such language, see James Palmer, 'Apocalyptic
     outsiders and their uses in the early medieval West', in W. Brandes,

F. Schmieder and R. Voß (eds), *Peoples of the Apocalypse: Eschatological Beliefs and Political Scenarios* (Berlin and Boston, 2016), pp. 307–20.

14 Hervey (ed.), *Corolla Sancti Eadmundi*, p. 21.

15 On the development of the cult of St Edmund see Pinner, *Cult of St Edmund*; Simon Yarrow, *Saints and Their Communities: Miracle Stories in Twelfth-Century England* (Oxford, 2006), pp. 24–62; Anthony Bale (ed.), *St Edmund, King and Martyr: Changing Images of a Medieval Saint* (Woodbridge, 2009); Grant Loomis, 'The growth of the Saint Edmund legend', *Harvard Studies and Notes in Philology and Literature* 14 (1932), pp. 83–115; Dorothy Whitelock, 'Fact and fiction in the legend of St Edmund', *Proceedings of the Suffolk Institute of Archaeology* 31 (1969), pp. 217–33.

16 Support for Edmund's cult by the West Saxon kings, including Æthelstan and Æthelred, has been interpreted as a means of easing the assimilation of East Anglia – until Edmund's death an independent kingdom – into the kingdom of England; see Susan J. Ridyard, *The Royal Saints of Anglo-Saxon England: A Study of West Saxon and East Anglian Cults* (Cambridge, 1988), pp. 224–6.

17 Ælfric, *Lives of Saints*, vol. 2, p. 316. On Ælfric's *Life* see Carl Phelpstead, 'King, martyr and virgin: *Imitatio Christi* in Ælfric's *Life of St Edmund*', in Bale (ed.), *St Edmund, King and Martyr*, pp. 27–44.

18 Byrhtferth of Ramsey, *The Lives of St Oswald and St Ecgwine*, ed. Michael Lapidge (Oxford, 2009); on the dating of Byrhtferth's works, see pp. xxviii–xxix.

19 'Dicunt quidam quod ex ipsis Danis pater eius esset qui cum classica cohorte cum Huba et Hinuuar ueniebant: ideo pater non penitus Christo seruire studuit' (Byrhtferth, *Life of St Oswald*, pp. 16–17).

20 Andrew Wareham, 'Saint Oswald's family and kin', in Nicholas Brooks and Catherine Cubitt (eds), *St Oswald of Worcester: Life and Influence* (London and New York, 1996), pp. 46–63; Dorothy Whitelock, 'The conversion of the Eastern Danelaw', *Saga-Book of the Viking Society* XII (1937–45), pp. 159–76; Nicholas Brooks, *The Early History of the Church of Canterbury: Christ Church from 597 to 1066* (Leicester, 1984), pp. 223–4.

21 Lesley Abrams, 'The conversion of the Danelaw', in Graham-Campbell et al. (eds), *Vikings and the Danelaw*, pp. 31–44; Abrams, 'Conversion and assimilation', in Hadley and Richards (eds), *Cultures in Contact*, pp. 135–53; Hadley, *The Vikings in England*, pp. 192–236.

22 See Byrhtferth, *Life of St Oswald*, p. 16, n. 52.

23 Antonia Gransden, *Legends, Tradition and History in Medieval England* (London, 1992), pp. 49, 83–4.

24 Cyril Hart, 'The East Anglian Chronicle', *Journal of Medieval History* 7 (1981), pp. 249–82.

25 'inedicibiliter est repleta et mercatorum gazis locupletata, qui undique adueniunt, maxime ex Danorum gente' (Byrhtferth, *Life of St Oswald*, pp. 150–1).

26 Townend, *Viking Age Yorkshire*, pp. 183–5, and Dorothy Whitelock, 'The dealings of the kings of England with Northumbria in the tenth and eleventh centuries', in Peter Clemoes (ed.), *The Anglo-Saxons: Studies in Some Aspects of their History and Culture Presented to Bruce Dickins* (London, 1959), pp. 70–88.

27 'nefandi Dani'; the quotation from Jeremiah occurs in his account of the Battle of Maldon, which follows immediately on from the chapter which describes the Danish presence in York (Byrhtferth, *Life of St Oswald*, pp. 154–9).

28 The best accounts of Cnut's reign are Lawson, *Cnut*, and Bolton, *The Empire of Cnut the Great*.

29 On Cnut's use of the English language see Treharne, *Living Through Conquest*, pp. 16–43; M. K. Lawson, 'Archbishop Wulfstan and the homiletic element in the laws of Æthelred II and Cnut', in Alexander Rumble (ed.), *The Reign of Cnut: King of England, Denmark and Norway* (London, 1994), pp. 141–64.

30 Jan Gerchow, 'Prayers for King Cnut: the liturgical commemoration of a conqueror', in Carola Hicks (ed.), *England in the Eleventh Century* (Stamford, 1992), pp. 219–38; T. A. Heslop, 'The production of *de luxe* manuscripts and the patronage of King Cnut and Queen Emma', *Anglo-Saxon England* 19 (1990), pp. 151–95; Lawson, *Cnut*, pp. 111–47; Bolton, *The Empire of Cnut*, pp. 77–106; Nicole Marafioti, *The King's Body: Burial and Succession in Late Anglo-Saxon England* (Toronto, 2014), pp. 192–229; Ridyard, *Royal Saints of Anglo-Saxon England*, pp. 150–4, 194–6, 224–6.

31 See Roberta Frank, 'King Cnut in the verse of his skalds', in Rumble (ed.), *The Reign of Cnut*, pp. 106–24; Judith Jesch, 'Knútr in poetry and history', in Michael Dallapiazza et al. (eds), *International Scandinavian and Medieval Studies in Memory of Gerd Wolfgang Weber* (Trieste, 2000), pp. 243–56; Jesch, 'Skaldic verse in Scandinavian England', pp. 313–25; R. G. Poole, *Viking Poems on War and Peace: A Study in Skaldic Narrative* (Toronto, 1991), pp. 86–90; Matthew Townend, 'Contextualizing the *Knútsdrápur*: skaldic praise-poetry at the court of Cnut', *Anglo-Saxon England* 30 (2001), pp. 145–79.

32 Townend, 'Contextualizing the *Knútsdrápur*', pp. 175–6.

33 Dietrich Hofmann, *Nordisch-englische Lehnbeziehungen der Wikingerzeit* (Copenhagen, 1955), pp. 75–9, 88–93; Russell Poole, 'Skaldic verse and Anglo-Saxon history: some aspects of the period 1009–1016', *Speculum* 62 (1987), pp. 265–98; Frank, 'King Cnut in the verse of his skalds', pp. 108–9.

34 Judith Jesch, 'Scandinavians and "cultural paganism" in late Anglo-Saxon England', in Paul Cavill (ed.), *The Christian Tradition in Anglo-Saxon England* (Cambridge, 2004), pp. 55–67; Frank, 'King Cnut in the verse of his skalds', pp. 115–24.

35 Óttarr svarti, *Knútsdrápa*, ed. and trans. Matthew Townend, in Diana Whaley (ed.), *Poetry from the Kings' Sagas 1: From Mythical Times to c.1035*

(Turnhout, 2012), Part 2, pp. 767–83; see Poole, 'Skaldic verse and Anglo-Saxon history', pp. 265–98.

36 Óttarr svarti, *Knútsdrápa*, in Whaley (ed.), *Poetry from the Kings' Sagas 1*, Part 2, p. 771.

37 Poole, *Viking Poems on War and Peace*, pp. 99–107; Bolton, *Cnut the Great*, pp. 76–8.

38 Frank, 'King Cnut in the verse of his skalds', pp. 110–13.

39 Sigvatr Þórðarson, *Knútsdrápa*, ed. and trans. Matthew Townend, in Whaley (ed.), *Poetry from the Kings' Sagas 1*, Part 2, pp. 649–63 (651); see Roberta Frank, 'Viking atrocity and skaldic verse: the rite of the blood-eagle', *English Historical Review* 99 (1984), pp. 332–43.

40 On Ælla and his later reputation, see Neil McGuigan, 'Ælla and the descendants of Ivar: politics and legend in the Viking Age', *Northern History* 52 (2015), pp. 20–34. The name Ælla appears in later skaldic verse as the defining element in a kenning for England or the English (Matthew Townend, '*Ella*: an Old English name in Old Norse poetry', *Nomina* 20 (1997), pp. 23–35).

41 Frank, 'King Cnut in the verse of his skalds', p. 111.

42 Roberta Frank, 'Skaldic verse and the date of *Beowulf*', in Colin Chase (ed.), *The Dating of Beowulf* (Toronto, 1981), pp. 123–39 (126–9); see also Frank, 'King Cnut in the verse of his skalds', pp. 111–12.

43 Ted Johnson South (ed.), *Historia de Sancto Cuthberto: A History of Saint Cuthbert and a Record of his Patrimony* (Cambridge, 2002), pp. 48–51. This text dates to the tenth or eleventh century; for discussion of its date see pp. 25–36.

44 In Óttarr's *Knútsdrápa*, Edmund Ironside is referred to as the 'descendant of Edmund', which might refer to either St Edmund or Edmund, brother of Æthelstan, king of England between 939 and 946 – or indeed both [Whaley (ed.), *Poetry from the Kings' Sagas 1*, Part 2, pp. 775–6].

45 Alistair Campbell (ed.), *Encomium Emmae Reginae*, reprinted with an introduction by Simon Keynes (Cambridge, 1998). On the context of the *Encomium*, see Eric John, 'The *Encomium Emmae Reginae*: a riddle and a solution', *Bulletin of the John Rylands University Library of Manchester* 63 (1980), pp. 58–94; Andy Orchard, 'Literary background to the *Encomium Emmae Reginae*', *Journal of Medieval Latin* 11 (2001), pp. 157–84.

46 On Emma's life see Pauline Stafford, *Queen Emma and Queen Edith: Queenship and Women's Power in Eleventh-Century England* (Oxford, 2001).

47 Elizabeth M. Tyler, 'Talking about history in eleventh-century England: the *Encomium Emmae Reginae* and the court of Harthacnut', *Early Medieval Europe* 13 (2005), pp. 359–83, and Eleanor Parker, 'So very memorable a matter: Anglo-Danish history and the *Encomium Emmae Reginae*', in Ian Giles et al. (eds), *Beyond Borealism: New Perspectives on the North* (London, 2016), pp. 41–53.

48 See Elizabeth M. Tyler, 'Fictions of family: The *Encomium Emmae Reginae* and Virgil's *Aeneid*', *Viator* 36 (2005), pp. 149–79.

49 Campbell (ed.), *Encomium*, pp. 9–11.

50 'Cui dum multa de regni gubernaculo multaque hortaretur de Christianitatis studio, Deo gratias illi uirorum dignissimo sceptrum commisit regale' (ibid., pp. 14–15).

51 See Peter Sawyer, 'Swein Forkbeard and the historians', in Ian Wood and G. A. Loud (eds), *Church and Chronicle in the Middle Ages: Essays Presented to John Taylor* (London, 1991), pp. 26–40.

52 Campbell (ed.), *Encomium*, pp. 24–5.

53 'þe hi ræfen heton' [Katherine O'Brien O'Keeffe (ed.), *The Anglo-Saxon Chronicle, MS. C* (Cambridge, 2001), p. 62].

54 See David Dumville and Michael Lapidge (eds), *Annals of St Neots* (Cambridge, 1985), p. 78. For a description of the relevant sources, see N. Lukman, 'The raven banner and the changing ravens: a Viking miracle from Carolingian court poetry to saga and Arthurian romance', *Classica et Medievalia* 19 (1958), pp. 133–51.

55 Matthew Townend, 'Cnut's poets: an Old Norse literary community in eleventh-century England', in E. M. Tyler (ed.), *Conceptualising Multilingualism in Medieval England, 800–1250* (Turnhout, 2011), pp. 197–215 (208–11).

56 *The Anglo-Saxon Chronicles*, trans. Swanton, p. 152.

57 Óttarr svarti, *Knútsdrápa*, in Whaley (ed.), *Poetry from the Kings' Sagas 1*, Part 2, p. 779.

58 Frank Barlow, *The Godwins: The Rise and Fall of a Noble Dynasty* (London, 2003); Emma Mason, *The House of Godwine: The History of a Dynasty* (London, 2004).

59 Matthew Townend, 'Knútr and the cult of St Óláfr: poetry and patronage in eleventh-century Norway and England', *Viking and Medieval Scandinavia* 1 (2005), pp. 251–79.

60 Dominic Tweddle et al. (eds), *Corpus of Anglo-Saxon Stone Sculpture Volume IV: South-East England* (Oxford, 1995), pp. 314–22; for other evidence for a Scandinavian presence in Winchester see Barbara Yorke, *Wessex in the Early Middle Ages* (London, 1995), pp. 143–5; Birthe Kjølbye-Biddle and R. I. Page, 'A Scandinavian rune-stone from Winchester', *The Antiquaries Journal* 55/2 (1975), pp. 389–94; Martin Biddle, 'Excavations at Winchester 1965: fourth interim report', *The Antiquaries Journal* 46/2 (1966), pp. 308–32; Signe Horn Fuglesang, *Some Aspects of the Ringerike Style: A Phase of 11th-Century Scandinavian Art* (Odense, 1980), pp. 47–69.

61 Martin Biddle and Birthe Kjølbye-Biddle, 'Danish royal burials in Winchester: Cnut and his family', in Ryan Lavelle and Simon Roffey (eds), *Danes in Wessex: The Scandinavian Impact on Southern England, c.800–c.1100* (Oxford, 2016), pp. 212–49.

62 Lene Demidoff, 'The death of Sven Forkbeard – in reality and later tradition', *Medieval Scandinavia* 11 (1978–9), pp. 30–47.

63 Herman the Archdeacon and Goscelin of Saint-Bertin, *Miracles of St Edmund*, ed. Tom Licence and Lynda Lockyer (Oxford, 2014). This part

of the text may have been written at an earlier stage, perhaps in the 1070s; on the date, see pp. liv–lix. On Herman and the abbey of Bury St Edmunds in this period, see Tom Licence, 'History and hagiography in the late eleventh century: the life and work of Herman the Archdeacon, monk of Bury St Edmunds', *English Historical Review* 124/508 (2009), pp. 516–44; Licence (ed.), *Bury St Edmunds and the Norman Conquest* (Woodbridge, 2014).

64 John of Worcester, *The Chronicle of John of Worcester*, ed. R. R. Darlington, P. McGurk and J. Bray (Oxford, 1995), vol. 2, pp. 476–7.

65 Herman, *Miracles of St Edmund*, pp. lxxviii–lxxix.

66 'ubique ponit tributum, quod infortunium hodieque luit Anglia multum, felix, diues, ac dulcis nimium, si non forent tributa suorum regum' (ibid., pp. 14–15).

67 E. O. Blake (ed.), *Liber Eliensis* (London, 1962), pp. 212–13.

68 Herman, *Miracles of St Edmund*, p. 37.

69 Ibid., pp. 56–9.

70 See Licence's comments in Herman, *Miracles of St Edmund*, pp. xxxvii–xxxviii.

71 Lawson, *Cnut*, pp. 132–3; Marafioti, *The King's Body*, pp. 206–12.

72 'nequaquam lupum sicut putatur tam magnum fore' (Herman, *Miracles of St Edmund*, pp. 40–1).

73 Ibid., p. 42.

74 The name corresponds to ON *Ásbjörn*; see John Frankis, 'Sidelights on post-Conquest Canterbury: towards a context for an Old Norse runic charm ("DR" 419)', *Nottingham Medieval Studies* 44 (2000), pp. 1–27 (17–19). Frankis also discusses the evidence for a small Scandinavian presence at Christ Church, Canterbury, in the years after the Norman Conquest. On Osbern's life, see Jay Rubenstein, 'The life and writings of Osbern of Canterbury', in R. Eales and R. Sharpe (eds), *Canterbury and the Norman Conquest* (London, 1995), pp. 27–40.

75 On the context for Osbern's work at Canterbury, see Jay Rubenstein, 'Liturgy against history: the competing visions of Lanfranc and Eadmer of Canterbury', *Speculum* 74 (1999), pp. 279–309; R. W. Southern, *Saint Anselm and his Biographer: A Study of Monastic Life and Thought 1059–c.1130* (Cambridge, 1963), pp. 246–53; J. Hobson, 'National-ethnic narratives in eleventh-century literary representations of Cnut', *Anglo-Saxon England* 43 (2014), pp. 267–95.

76 'quousque regnum tuum transferatur in regnum alienum cujus ritum et linguam gens cui praesides non novit' [Osbern, *Vita Sancti Dunstani*, in William Stubbs (ed.), *Memorials of Saint Dunstan Archbishop of Canterbury* (London, 1874), pp. 69–128 (115), my translation].

77 Simon Keynes, 'The burial of King Æthelred the Unready at St Paul's', in David Roffe (ed.), *The English and Their Legacy, 900–1200: Essays in Honour of Ann Williams* (Woodbridge, 2012), pp. 129–48.

78 For the *Vita*, see Osbern, *Vita S. Elphegi*, in Henry Wharton (ed.), *Anglia Sacra* (London, 1691), vol. 2, pp. 122–42, and *Osbern's Life of Alfege*, trans. Frances Shaw (London, 1999). The *Translatio* is edited and translated by

Rosemary Morris and Alexander Rumble as an appendix in Rumble (ed.), *The Reign of Cnut*, pp. 283–315.

79 'Jacet itaque terra prædonum furori obnoxia ... Rex namque Anglorum Ethelredus imbellis quia imbecillis, Monachum potius quam militem actione prætendebat' (Osbern, *Vita S. Elphegi*, p. 131; *Life of Alfege*, p. 51).

80 Campbell (ed.), *Encomium*, pp. 10–11; for discussion of the story see Campbell's comments at pp. 73–4; Simon Keynes, 'Cnut's earls', in Rumble (ed.), *The Reign of Cnut*, pp. 43–88 (54–60); John, 'The *Encomium Emmae Reginae*', pp. 68–70. A story about Thorkell's revenge also appears in Scandinavian sources, where Thorkell's brother Heming is said to have been killed in London during an uprising against the Danes after the death of Svein (see *Encomium*, pp. 92–3). Adam of Bremen provides another example of such a story from the eleventh century: he says that Svein came to England to avenge his brother Hiring, who ruled part of Northumbria but was betrayed and killed by the Northumbrians (Lawson, *Cnut*, pp. 29–30).

81 Herman, *Miracles of St Edmund*, pp. 158–9.

82 'Sufficeret namque ad communem regni perniciem aut sola pontificis injuria, aut funesta urbis excidia, ne dum utroque Anglia decore privata, esset nunquam deinceps ad priorem statum reformanda' (Osbern, *Vita S. Elphegi*, p. 136; *Life of Alfege*, p. 63).

83 Osbern, *Life of Alfege*, p. 76; the Latin verb used is *radicare*.

84 The ceremony is described in MS. D of the *Anglo-Saxon Chronicle* [G. P. Cubbin (ed.), *The Anglo-Saxon Chronicle, MS. D* (Cambridge, 1996), p. 64].

85 Lawson, *Cnut*, pp. 130–2; Bolton, *The Empire of Cnut*, pp. 79–81; Marafioti, *The King's Body*, pp. 192–7.

86 It is possible that the date was not known at Canterbury; it is recorded in the *Annals of Lindisfarne*, but the date given in *Anglo-Saxon Chronicle* D and E is the erroneous 8 January (*The Anglo-Saxon Chronicles*, trans. Swanton, p. 57). The archbishop who arranged for the translation, Æthelnoth, had been consecrated on a similarly resonant anniversary of Anglo-Danish conflict: St Brice's Day, 13 November. Æthelnoth was a loyal supporter of the Danish regime, and according to Osbern had consecrated Cnut as king (Osbern, *Translatio Sancti Ælfegi*, p. 301).

87 'consilium sequitur diuinæ propitiationis declaratio. Non post multos etenim dies Cnut pacem obtinuit, post pacem regni dimidium, post dimidium totum' (Osbern, *Translatio Sancti Ælfegi*, pp. 300–1).

88 Ibid., pp. 306–7.

89 'regia nauis aureis rostrata draconibus' (ibid., pp. 308–9).

90 'quos lingua Danorum huscarles uocant' (ibid., pp. 302–3). On Osbern's use of *huscarl* see Townend, *Language and History in Viking Age England*, pp. 185–6.

91 'ab omnipotenti Deo terribiliter occiso' (Osbern, *Vita S. Elphegi*, p. 131; *Life of Alfege*, p. 50); for comment see Herman, *Miracles of St Edmund*, p. 22, n. 98.

92   Herman, *Miracles of St Edmund*, pp. 152–3.
93   'aurum ... divinae sapientiae' (Osbern, *Vita S. Elphegi*, p. 140).
94   Eadmer of Canterbury, *Lives and Miracles of Saints Oda, Dunstan and Oswald*, ed. Andrew J. Turner and Bernard J. Muir (Oxford, 2006), pp. xxxv–xliv.
95   Ibid., pp. 4–5.
96   Ibid., pp. 12–15.
97   On other versions of the story, which sometimes attribute the miracle of the sword to St Aldhelm instead of Oda, see Eadmer, *Lives*, pp. xliii–xliv.
98   Ibid., pp. xliv–liii.

CHAPTER 2: THE SONS OF RAGNAR LOTHBROK

1   Heather O'Donoghue, *English Poetry and Old Norse Myth: A History* (Oxford, 2014), pp. 40–6.
2   Elizabeth Ashman Rowe, *Vikings in the West: The Legend of Ragnarr Loðbrók and His Sons* (Wien, 2012); Rory McTurk, *Studies in Ragnars saga Loðbrókar and its Major Scandinavian Analogues* (Oxford, 1991); Alfred Smyth, *Scandinavian Kings in the British Isles 850–880* (Oxford, 1977); Niels Lukman, 'Ragnarr Lothbrok, Sigifrid, and the saints of Flanders', *Medieval Scandinavia* 9 (1976), pp. 7–50; Downham, *Viking Kings of Britain and Ireland*; Jan de Vries, 'Die Entwicklung der Sage von den Lodbrokssöhnen in den historischen Quellen', *Arkiv för nordisk filologi* 44 (1928), pp. 117–63.
3   For this argument and discussion of the English narratives see Ashman Rowe, *Vikings in the West*, pp. 107–9; Smyth, *Scandinavian Kings*, pp. 54–67; McTurk, *Studies in Ragnars saga Loðbrókar*; C. E. Wright, *The Cultivation of Saga in Anglo-Saxon England* (Edinburgh, 1939), pp. 107–44.
4   Ashman Rowe, *Vikings in the West*, pp. 178–80.
5   His dying speech is the subject of the Old Norse poem *Krákumál*; see McTurk, *Studies in Ragnars saga Loðbrókar*, pp. 125–33.
6   For a full survey of texts which refer to Ragnar and his sons, see Ashman Rowe, *Vikings in the West*, pp. 13–109. For *Ragnars saga* see Magnus Olsen (ed.), *Völsunga saga ok Ragnars saga Loðbrókar* (Copenhagen, 1906–8); Elizabeth Ashman Rowe, '*Ragnars saga loðbrókar, Ragnarssona þáttr*, and the political world of Haukr Erlendsson', in Agneta Ney, Ármann Jakobsson and Annette Lassen (eds), *Fornaldarsagaerne: Myter og virkelighed* (Copenhagen, 2009), pp. 347–60. Saxo's narrative of Ragnar and his sons is told in Book IX of the *Gesta Danorum*: Saxo Grammaticus, *Gesta Danorum: The History of the Danes*, ed. Karsten Friis-Jensen and Peter Fisher (Oxford, 2015), vol. 1, pp. 628–69. For the date see vol. 1, pp. xxxiii–xxxv.
7   Ashman Rowe, *Vikings in the West*, pp. 111–64; Smyth, *Scandinavian Kings*; Downham, *Viking Kings of Britain and Ireland*.

8   'Bier Costae ferreae' [William of Jumièges, *The Gesta Normannorum Ducum of William of Jumièges, Orderic Vitalis, and Robert of Torigni*, ed. Elisabeth M. C. van Houts (Oxford, 1992–5), vol. 1, pp. 10–27].

9   Elisabeth van Houts, 'Scandinavian influence in Norman literature of the eleventh century', *Anglo-Norman Studies* 6 (1983), pp. 107–21; for an alternative view see Ashman Rowe, *Vikings in the West*, pp. 166–9.

10 Adam of Bremen, *Gesta Hammaburgensis Ecclesiae Pontificum*, ed. Georg Waitz (Hanover, 1876), p. 28; *History of the Archbishops of Hamburg-Bremen*, trans. Francis J. Tschan (New York, 1959), p. 37.

11 Ari Þorgilsson, *Íslendingabók and Kristni Saga*, trans. Siân Grønlie (London, 2006), p. 3 and note; see Ashman Rowe, *Vikings in the West*, pp. 168–71.

12 Dumville and Lapidge (eds), *The Annals of St Neots*, p. 78.

13 Ibid., pp. xv–xvi.

14 For discussion see Hart, 'The East Anglian Chronicle'; Eric John, 'The Annals of St Neots and the defeat of the Vikings', in R. Evans (ed.), *Lordship and Learning: Studies in Memory of Trevor Aston* (Woodbridge, 2004), pp. 51–62.

15 On such statements in medieval chronicles see van Houts, 'Genre aspects of the use of oral information', pp. 303–5.

16 See Ashman Rowe, *Vikings in the West*, pp. 82–4.

17 Judith Jesch, 'England and *Orkneyinga saga*' in C. Batey, J. Jesch and C. Morris (eds), *The Viking Age in Caithness, Orkney and the North Atlantic* (Edinburgh, 1993), pp. 222–39 (232–5).

18 Charlotte D'Evelyn and Anna J. Mill (eds), *The South English Legendary* (London, 1956), vol. 2, p. 512.

19 John Frankis, 'Views of Anglo-Saxon England in post-Conquest vernacular writing', in Herbert Pilch (ed.), *Orality and Literacy in Early Middle English* (Tübingen, 1996), pp. 227–47 (235); see also Page, 'A Most Vile People'.

20 Ridyard, *Royal Saints of Anglo-Saxon England*, p. 217.

21 Hervey (ed.), *Corolla Sancti Eadmundi*, pp. 134–61. On Geoffrey's *De Infantia* see Rodney M. Thomson, 'Geoffrey of Wells, De Infantia Sancti Edmundi (BHL 2393)', *Analecta Bollandiana* 95 (1977), pp. 25–42; Pinner, *Cult of St Edmund*, pp. 75–9; Paul Anthony Hayward, 'Geoffrey of Wells' *Liber de infantia sancti Edmundi* and the "Anarchy" of King Stephen's reign', in Bale (ed.), *St Edmund, King and Martyr*, pp. 63–86.

22 Wells in Somerset has also been suggested as his place of origin, but Norfolk seems more likely, especially given the interest he displays in his text in the north Norfolk coast.

23 Hervey (ed.), *Corolla Sancti Eadmundi*, pp. 134–5.

24 Geoffrey points out that this was not the more famous Offa of Mercia, nor the devout Offa of Essex mentioned by Bede, but the last king of the East Angles before the time of St Edmund [Hervey (ed.), *Corolla Sancti Eadmundi*, pp. 144–5].

25 Hervey (ed.), *Corolla Sancti Eadmundi*, pp. 150–1.

26 Ibid., pp. 156–7.

27 For a summary of the various theories, see McTurk, *Studies in Ragnars saga Loðbrókar*, pp. 6–39.

28 See for example William of Jumièges, *Gesta Normannorum Ducum*, vol. 1, pp. 12–17.

29 Hervey (ed.), *Corolla Sancti Eadmundi*, pp. 156–7.

30 Wright, *Cultivation of Saga*, pp. 123–6.

31 Hervey (ed.), *Corolla Sancti Eadmundi*, pp. 158–9.

32 The idea that Edmund was originally from Saxony seems to arise from his interpretation of a comment by Abbo about Edmund's descent *ex antiquorum Saxonum*, 'from the Old Saxons'; it is likely that by this Abbo meant no more than that Edmund came from the ancient line of East Anglian kings, but it became a common understanding of Edmund's origins (Whitelock, 'Fact and fiction in the legend of St Edmund', p. 219).

33 On the relation of this aspect of the *De Infantia* to contemporary concerns about royal inheritance in the light of the civil war which followed Henry I's death in 1135, see Hayward, 'Geoffrey of Wells' *Liber de infantia sancti Edmundi*'.

34 It is tempting to suggest that Geoffrey's emphasis on this particular image might relate to his own origins: when he names himself *Galfridus de Fontibus*, he translates his surname (presumably the town of his birth), identifying himself as Geoffrey of 'wells' or 'springs'.

35 'gnydia mundu nu grisir, ef þeir visse, hvat enn gamle þyldi' [Olsen (ed.), *Völsunga saga ok Ragnars saga Loðbrókar*, p. 158].

36 Saxo Grammaticus, *Gesta Danorum*, ed. Friis-Jensen and Fisher, vol. 1, pp. 660–5; Olsen (ed.), *Völsunga saga ok Ragnars saga Loðbrókar*, pp. 161–2.

37 Roger of Wendover, *Chronica, sive Flores Historiarum*, ed. H. O. Coxe (London, 1841), vol. 1, pp. 303–15. Roger died in 1236, and he was probably working on his chronicle from *c*.1220 to his death.

38 'probetur, si illum Deus velit a periculo liberare' (Roger of Wendover, *Chronica*, vol. 1, p. 306).

39 On this manuscript, Oxford, Bodleian Library, MS. Bodley 240, see Pinner, *Cult of St Edmund*, pp. 86–8.

40 John Lydgate, *Lives of Ss Edmund and Fremund and the Extra Miracles of St Edmund*, ed. Anthony Bale and A. S. G. Edwards (Heidelberg, 2009), pp. 64–71. On the context of Lydgate's poem, see Pinner, *Cult of St Edmund*, pp. 89–111; Cynthia Turner Camp, *Anglo-Saxon Saints' Lives as History-Writing in Late Medieval England* (Cambridge, 2015), pp. 173–209.

41 Lydgate, *Lives of Ss Edmund and Fremund*, p. 12. This manuscript is now London, British Library, Harley MS. 2278.

42 Ibid., p. 64.

43 Ibid., pp. 11–18.

44 Thomas Elmham, *Historia Monasterii S. Augustini Cantuariensis*, ed. Charles Hardwick (London, 1858), p. 221.

45 Hervey (ed.), *Corolla Sancti Eadmundi*, p. xxxi.

46 Phelpstead, 'King, martyr and virgin', pp. 42–4.

47 See Timothy Bolton, 'Was the family of Earl Siward and Earl Waltheof a
    lost line of the ancestors of the Danish royal family?', *Nottingham Medieval
    Studies* 51 (2007), pp. 41–71 (67).

48 The text is printed in Carl Horstmann (ed.), *Nova Legenda Anglie* (Oxford,
    1901), vol. 2, pp. 727–31, and translated in R. M. Serjeantson, 'A mediæval
    legend of St Peter's, Northampton', *Associated Architectural Societies'
    Reports and Papers* 29 (1907), pp. 113–20.

49 This manuscript (London, British Library, Additional MS. 38817) was
    made in the second half of the twelfth century, but the Ragner text is a
    somewhat later addition; see Bertram Colgrave and R. A. B. Mynors (eds),
    Bede's Ecclesiastical History of the English People (Oxford, 1991), p. liv.

50 For a description of this manuscript, now Dublin, Trinity College
    MS. 172 (B. 2. 7), see M. L. Colker, *Trinity College Library, Dublin:
    Descriptive Catalogue of Medieval and Renaissance Latin Manuscripts*
    (Dublin, 1991), vol. 1, pp. 310–20, and Goscelin of Saint-Bertin, *The
    Hagiography of the Female Saints of Ely*, ed. Rosalind C. Love (Oxford,
    2004), pp. lv–lvi.

51 'Norweganum genere, mire simplicitatis et pacientie uirum' (Horstmann,
    Nova Legenda Anglie, vol. 2, p. 728).

52 Hugh Candidus, *The Chronicle of Hugh Candidus*, ed. W. T. Mellows
    (London, 1949), p. 60; see David Rollason, 'Lists of saints' resting-places
    in Anglo-Saxon England', *Anglo-Saxon England* 7 (1978), pp. 61–93 (71).

53 John H. Williams, 'From "palace" to "town": Northampton and urban
    origins', *Anglo-Saxon England* 13 (1984), pp. 113–36 (126–7). See also
    L. Whitbread, 'St Ragner of Northampton', *Notes and Queries* CXCV
    (November 1950), pp. 511–12.

54 The date of St Ragner's feast was added to the calendar of a Missal which
    probably belonged to St Peter's in the fifteenth century; on this manuscript
    (Oxford, Bodleian Library MS. Lat. liturg. b. 4) see F. Madan and H. H.
    E. Craster (eds), *A Summary Catalogue of Western Manuscripts in the
    Bodleian Library at Oxford* (Oxford, 1924), vol. 6, p. 187 (SC 32703).

55 On Fremund see Pinner, *Cult of St Edmund*, pp. 105–11; in the Dublin
    manuscript, the *Inventio* is followed by an account of the passion of St
    Fremund. For Eadwold, see Tom Licence, 'Goscelin of St. Bertin and
    the Life of St. Eadwold of Cerne', *Journal of Medieval Latin* 16 (2006),
    pp. 182–207.

56 There was an English cognate, *dryhten*, which was also used to refer to
    God in Middle English poetry, although it was becoming increasingly rare;
    however, this text explicitly identifies *drotin* as a Norse word.

57 Ron Baxter, 'St Peter, Northampton', *The Corpus of Romanesque Sculpture
    in Britain and Ireland*. Available at http://www.crsbi.ac.uk/site/248/
    (accessed 2 June 2017).

58 Ivar probably died in Ireland in 873 (Smyth, *Scandinavian Kings*,
    pp. 234–6).

59 The manuscript is Cambridge, Pembroke College MS. 82, and these notes
    are reproduced in M. R. James, *A Descriptive Catalogue of the Manuscripts*

in the Library of Pembroke College, Cambridge (Cambridge, 1905), p. 71. See also Kari Anne Rand, *The Index of Middle English Prose, Handlist XVIII: Manuscripts in the Library of Pembroke College, Cambridge, and the Fitzwilliam Museum* (Cambridge, 2006), p. 1; N. R. Ker, *Catalogue of Manuscripts Containing Anglo-Saxon* (Oxford, 1957), p. 124.

60 On the idea of Tostig as founder or re-founder of Tynemouth, see Paul Anthony Hayward, 'Sanctity and lordship in twelfth-century England: Saint Albans, Durham, and the cult of Saint Oswine, king and martyr', *Viator* 30 (1999), pp. 105–44 (128–31).

61 Roger of Howden, *Chronica Magistri Rogeri de Houedene*, ed. William Stubbs (London, 1868), vol. 1, pp. lxxx–lxxxii and 39.

62 Edward Edwards (ed.), *Liber Monasterii de Hyda* (London, 1866), p. 10; R. M. Wilson, *The Lost Literature of Medieval England* (London, 1952), p. 43. The manuscript is London, British Library, Additional MS. 82931, a collection of charters, annals and other documents relating to Hyde Abbey, made in the late fourteenth or early fifteenth century.

63 Geffrei Gaimar, *Estoire des Engleis: History of the English*, ed. Ian Short (Oxford, 2009), pp. 172–3.

64 Margaret Gelling and Ann Cole, *The Landscape of Place-Names* (Stamford, 2000), pp. 178–80.

65 Charles Plummer (ed.), *Two of the Saxon Chronicles Parallel* (Oxford, 1899), vol. 2, p. 93.

66 Olsen (ed.), *Völsunga saga ok Ragnars saga Loðbrókar*, p. 169.

67 On this text and its sources, see Gillian Fellows Jensen (ed.), *Hemings þáttr Áslákssonar* (Copenhagen, 1962); *Hemings þáttr*, trans. Anthony Faulkes (Dundee, 2016), pp. 6–8; Margaret Ashdown, 'An Icelandic account of the survival of Harold Godwinson', in Clemoes (ed.), *The Anglo-Saxons*, pp. 122–36.

68 Fellows Jensen (ed.), *Hemings þáttr*, p. 46.

69 Hilda Roderick Ellis, *The Road to Hel: A Study of the Conception of the Dead in Old Norse Literature* (New York, 1968), pp. 30–9, 100–20.

70 Sarah Semple, 'A fear of the past: the place of the prehistoric burial mound in the ideology of Middle and Later Anglo-Saxon England', *World Archaeology* 30/1 (1998), pp. 109–26; Howard Williams, *Death and Memory in Early Medieval Britain* (Cambridge, 2006), pp. 198–211; Hilda R. Ellis Davidson, 'The hill of the dragon: Anglo-Saxon burial mounds in literature and archaeology', *Folklore* 61/4 (1950), pp. 169–85.

71 Michael Swanton (ed.), *Beowulf* (Manchester, 1997), lines 2802–8 and 3156–62.

72 On Beowulf's burial-mound see Fred C. Robinson, 'The tomb of Beowulf', in *'The Tomb of Beowulf' and Other Essays on Old English* (Oxford, 1993), pp. 3–19; Williams, *Death and Memory*, pp. 200–4. For different (sometimes very mundane) reasons cited in Norse literary sources for burial on a headland, see Ellis, *The Road to Hel*, p. 37.

73 Stefan Brink, 'Law and legal customs in Viking Age Scandinavia', in Judith Jesch (ed.), *The Scandinavians from the Vendel Period to the Tenth Century:*

An Ethnographic Perspective (Woodbridge, 2012), pp. 87–127 (100–2); for examples from Norse, Irish and Welsh tradition, see Ellis, *The Road to Hel*, pp. 105–11.

74 McTurk, *Studies in Ragnars saga Loðbrókar*, p. 247, and see Lukman, 'Ragnarr Lothbrok, Sigifrid, and the saints of Flanders', pp. 39–40. McTurk also notes a possible Orkney connection, observing that the Maeshowe inscription which names Lothbrok is in a burial-mound. For an alternative view, see Ashman Rowe, *Vikings in the West*, pp. 239–41.

75 Johnson South (ed.), *Historia de Sancto Cuthberto*, pp. 50–3.

76 'duc eum cum toto exercitu super montem qui uocatur Oswigesdune et ibi pone in brachio eius dextero armillam auream, et sic eum omnes regem constituant' (ibid., pp. 52–3).

77 David Rollason, *Northumbria, 500–1100: Creation and Destruction of a Kingdom* (Cambridge, 2003), pp. 245–6; William M. Aird, *St Cuthbert and the Normans: The Church of Durham, 1071–1153* (Woodbridge, 1998), pp. 29–32.

78 Smyth, *Scandinavian York and Dublin*, vol. 2, pp. 267–8.

79 For instance in Symeon of Durham, *Libellus de Exordio atque Procursu istius hoc est Dunhelmensis Ecclesie*, ed. David Rollason (Oxford, 2000), pp. 122–3.

80 O'Brien O'Keeffe (ed.), *The Anglo-Saxon Chronicle MS. C*, pp. 91–2.

81 Alexandra Sanmark and Sarah Semple, 'Places of assembly: new discoveries in Sweden and England', *Fornvännen* 103 (2008), pp. 245–59; Howard M. R. Williams, 'Placing the dead: investigating the location of wealthy barrow burials in seventh-century England', in Martin Rundkvist (ed.), *Grave Matters: Eight Studies of First Millennium AD Burials in Crimea, England, and Southern Scandinavia* (Oxford, 1999), pp. 57–86; Sarah Semple, *Perceptions of the Prehistoric in Anglo-Saxon England: Religion, Ritual, and Rulership in the Landscape* (Oxford, 2013), pp. 1–2, 87.

82 Margaret Gelling, *The Place-Names of Berkshire* (Cambridge, 1974), Part 2, pp. 481–2.

83 Williams, *Death and Memory*, pp. 207–11.

84 John Blair, *Anglo-Saxon Oxfordshire* (Oxford, 1998), pp. 35–41; Williams, *Death and Memory*, p. 211.

85 On the language here see Page, 'A Most Vile People', pp. 27–8, and on the significance of the choice of site, Guy Halsall, *Warfare and Society in the Barbarian West, 450–900* (London, 2003), p. 157.

86 'Per mandata ducis rex hic Heralde quiescis, / Ut custos maneas littoris et pelagi' [Frank Barlow (ed.), *The Carmen de Hastingae Proelio of Guy, Bishop of Amiens* (Oxford, 1999), pp. 34–5].

87 William of Poitiers, *The Gesta Guillelmi of William of Poitiers*, ed. R. H. C. Davis (Oxford, 1998), pp. 140–1.

88 Laura Ashe, 'Harold Godwineson', in Neil Cartlidge (ed.), *Heroes and Anti-Heroes in Medieval Romance* (Cambridge, 2012), pp. 59–80; Barlow, *The Godwins*, pp. 156–60; Marafioti, *The King's Body*, pp. 230–47.

89 Gillian Fellows-Jensen, 'The myth of Harold II's survival in the Scandinavian sources', in Gale R. Owen-Crocker (ed.), *King Harold II and the Bayeux Tapestry* (Woodbridge, 2005), pp. 53–64.

90 van Houts, 'Scandinavian influence in Norman literature', pp. 111–12.

91 Barlow, *The Godwins*, pp. 160–70.

92 Holman, *The Northern Conquest*, pp. 181–9.

93 Smyth, *Scandinavian Kings*, p. 54.

94 On the promotion of Edmund as a national saint, see Bale (ed.), *St Edmund, King and Martyr*, pp. 15–17.

CHAPTER 3: THE STORY OF SIWARD

1 'Tradunt relaciones antiquorum quod vir quidam nobilis, quem Dominus permisit, contra solitum ordinem humane propaginis, ex quodam albo urso patre, muliere generosa matre, procreari, Ursus genuit Spratlingum; Spratlingus Ulsium; Ulsius Beorn, cognomento Beresune, hoc est *filius ursi*. Hic Beorn Dacus fuit natione, comes egregius et miles illustris. In signum autem illius diversitatis speciei ex parte generantium, produxerat ei natura paternas auriculas, sive ursi. In aliis autem speciei materne assimilabatur. Hic autem, post multas virtutis ac milicie experiencias, filium genuit fortitudinis et milicie paterne probum imitatorem. Nomen autem huic Siuuardus' [Francisque Michel (ed.), *Chroniques anglo-normandes* (Rouen, 1836–40), vol. 2, pp. 99–142 (104–5); my translation].

2 On the manuscript, now Douai, Bibliothèque municipale, MS. 852, see Chrétien Dehaisnes, *Manuscrits de la bibliothèque de Douai* (Paris, 1878), and Bertram Colgrave (ed.), *Felix's Life of Saint Guthlac* (Cambridge, 1956), pp. 39–42.

3 For discussion of the text see Wright, *Cultivation of Saga*, pp. 127–35; Axel Olrik, 'Siward Digri of Northumbria: a Viking saga of the Danes in England', *Saga-Book of the Viking Society* VI (1908–9), pp. 212–37; A. H. Smith, 'The early literary relations of England and Scandinavia', *Saga-Book of the Viking Society* XI (1928–1936), pp. 215–32; Wilson, *Lost Literature of Medieval England*, pp. 56–7; Christine Rauer, *Beowulf and the Dragon: Parallels and Analogues* (Cambridge, 2000), pp. 125–33; Bolton, 'Family of Earl Siward and Earl Waltheof'; Eleanor Parker, 'Siward the dragon-slayer: mythmaking in Anglo-Scandinavian England', *Neophilologus* 98 (2014), pp. 481–93.

4 On Siward's career, see William Kapelle, *The Norman Conquest of the North* (London, 1979), pp. 27–49; Keynes, 'Cnut's earls', pp. 65–6; Whitelock, 'The dealings of the kings of England with Northumbria', pp. 83–5.

5 Keynes, 'Cnut's earls', pp. 57–8.

6 For discussion see Bolton, 'Family of Earl Siward and Earl Waltheof'.

7 Symeon of Durham, *Libellus de Exordio*, pp. 168–71.

8 Kapelle, *Norman Conquest of the North*, pp. 28–9. In Siward's time this earldom included the shires of Huntingdon and Northampton, and

probably also Rutland, Bedfordshire and Cambridgeshire; see Forrest Scott, 'Earl Waltheof of Northumbria', *Archaeologia Aeliana* 30 (1952), pp. 149–215 (157–63).

9   Kapelle, *Norman Conquest of the North*, pp. 31–3.

10   Cubbin (ed.), *The Anglo-Saxon Chronicle, MS. D*, p. 74.

11   Christopher Morris, *Marriage and Murder in Eleventh-Century Northumbria: A Study of 'De Obsessione Dunelmi'* (York, 1992), p. 25.

12   Cubbin (ed.), *The Anglo-Saxon Chronicle, MS. D*, p. 74.

13   See Bruce Dickins, 'The cult of S. Olave in the British Isles', *Saga-Book of the Viking Society* XII (1937–45), pp. 53–80 (55); Edvard Bull, 'The cultus of Norwegian saints in England and Scotland', *Saga-Book of the Viking Society* VIII (1913–14), pp. 135–48; Townend, 'Knútr and the cult of St Óláfr'.

14   Townend, *Viking Age Yorkshire*, p. 196.

15   John of Worcester, *Chronicle*, vol. 2, p. 574.

16   For other instances of *digri* (from ON *digr* 'big, fat'), see Gösta Tengvik, *Old English Bynames* (Uppsala, 1938), p. 310.

17   'Siwardus, dux Northumbrorum, Dan[ic]a lingua "Digara", hoc est fortis, nuncupatus' [Frank Barlow (ed.), *The Life of King Edward who rests at Westminster* (Oxford, 1992), p. 34]. The byname also appears in William of Malmesbury's *Gesta Regum*, where Siward's son Waltheof is described as 'filius Siwardi magnificentissimi comitis, quem Digera Danico uocabulo, id est fortem, cognominabant' ('son of Siward, the very grand earl called *Digera* in Danish, which means "the Mighty"', vol. 1, pp. 468–9), and it is included as a marginal note in the *Gesta antecessorum* (in the Douai MS, but not the Delapré text), perhaps copied from William of Malmesbury.

18   Kapelle, *Norman Conquest of the North*, pp. 30–1. The name Waltheof is an anglicisation of Old Norse *Valþjófr*, but it is not recorded in Siward's native Denmark until the sixteenth century; see Fellows Jensen, *Scandinavian Personal Names in Lincolnshire and Yorkshire*, pp. 330–1.

19   David Bates, *William the Conqueror* (New Haven, 2016), pp. 209–10.

20   On the sources for Waltheof's life, see Scott, 'Earl Waltheof of Northumbria', pp. 149–215; Ann Williams, *The English and the Norman Conquest* (Woodbridge, 1995), pp. 63–5, 146–7.

21   For discussion see Bates, *William the Conqueror*, p. 350.

22   On the development of the cult see Carl Watkins, 'The cult of Earl Waltheof at Crowland', *Hagiographica* III (1996), pp. 95–111.

23   Jesch, 'Skaldic verse in Scandinavian England', p. 322.

24   Thorkell Skallason, *Valþjófsflokkr*, ed. and trans. Kari Ellen Gade, in Gade (ed.), *Poetry from the Kings' Sagas 2: From c.1035 to c.1300* (Turnhout, 2009), Part 1, pp. 382–4.

25   Forrest Scott, 'Valþjófr jarl: an English earl in Icelandic sources', *Saga-Book of the Viking Society* XIV (1953–7), pp. 78–94.

26   Orderic Vitalis, *The Ecclesiastical History of Orderic Vitalis*, ed. Marjorie Chibnall (Oxford, 1969–80), vol. 2, pp. xxv–xxix, 322–51.

27   Ibid., vol. 2, pp. 344–5.

28   Ibid., vol. 2, p. 348.

29 William of Malmesbury, *Gesta Regum*, vol. 1, pp. 468–9.

30 'Anglorum astipulationi diuinitas assentiri uidetur, miracula multa et ea permaxima ad tumbam illius ostendens' [William of Malmesbury, *Gesta Pontificum Anglorum*, ed. Michael Winterbottom and R. M. Thomson (Oxford, 2007), vol. 1, pp. 488–9].

31 Watkins, 'The cult of Earl Waltheof at Crowland', p. 102. For a variety of views on the uses of Waltheof's cult in the twelfth century see Williams, *The English and the Norman Conquest*, pp. 146–7; Joanna Huntington, 'The taming of the laity: writing Waltheof and rebellion in the twelfth century', *Anglo-Norman Studies* 32 (2009), pp. 79–95; Emma Cownie, *Religious Patronage in Anglo-Norman England 1066–1135* (Woodbridge, 1998), pp. 119–21.

32 Watkins, 'The cult of Earl Waltheof', pp. 97–8.

33 Michel (ed.), *Chroniques anglo-normandes*, vol. 2, pp. 123–31.

34 This survives only in a seventeenth-century transcript of a manuscript from Delapré, now Oxford, Bodleian Library, MS Dugdale 18; see N. Denholm-Young, 'An early thirteenth-century Anglo-Norman MS', *The Bodleian Quarterly Record* 6 (1931), pp. 225–30; John Spence, *Reimagining History in Anglo-Norman Prose Chronicles* (Woodbridge, 2013), pp. 147–52.

35 See for instance John Spence, 'Genealogies of noble families in Anglo-Norman', in Raluca L. Radulescu and Edward Donald Kennedy (eds), *Broken Lines: Genealogical Literature in Late-Medieval Britain and France* (Turnhout, 2008), pp. 63–77 (70). It might also conceivably refer not to the language in which the book was written but to a chronicle *about* the English, such as Henry of Huntingdon's *Historia Anglorum*, which contains two stories about Siward.

36 Denholm-Young, 'An early thirteenth-century Anglo-Norman MS'; Spence, 'Genealogies of noble families in Anglo-Norman'.

37 The text is printed by Michel (ed.), *Chroniques anglo-normandes*, vol. 2, pp. 104–11, and most of it is translated in Wright, *Cultivation of Saga*, pp. 129–33.

38 This was first suggested by Edward A. Freeman, *The History of the Norman Conquest of England* (Oxford, 1870–6), vol. 1, pp. 791–2.

39 We might compare the dispute on the bridge to a comment by Gaimar that under the Danish kings, the English were expected to give the Danes precedence when they met at a bridge-crossing; Gaimar claims that the English would be punished if they did not give way, and that this was the cause of great resentment against the Danes (*Estoire des Engleis*, pp. 259–61). Perhaps Gaimar had heard a story like that told of Siward and Tostig in the *Gesta antecessorum*, or the author of the *Gesta* had read Gaimar, although for the purposes of the *Gesta* both men are Danish.

40 Henry of Huntingdon, *Historia Anglorum*, pp. 376–9.

41 Bjarni Einarsson (ed.), *Egils saga* (London, 2003), pp. 31–2.

42 Olrik, 'Siward Digri', p. 226.

43 William Shakespeare, *Macbeth*, ed. Sandra Clark and Pamela Mason (London, 2015), p. 298 (Act 5, Scene 9).

44 Henry of Huntingdon, *Historia Anglorum*, pp. 378–81.

45 Wright, *Cultivation of Saga*, pp. 128–9; Olrik, 'Siward Digri', pp. 212–37 (226).

46 Heather O'Donoghue, *From Asgard to Valhalla: The Remarkable History of the Norse Myths* (London, 2007), pp. 51–4.

47 R. G. Finch (ed.), *Völsunga saga* (London, 1965), pp. 2–3. For more examples, see Ellis, *The Road to Hel*, pp. 105–11.

48 Finnbogi Guðmundsson (ed.), *Orkneyinga saga* (Reykjavík, 1965), pp. 24–7.

49 E. H. Lind, *Norsk-isländska personbinamn från medeltiden* (Uppsala, 1920–5), cols. 60–1.

50 Jesch, 'England and *Orkneyinga saga*', pp. 231–2.

51 Wright, *Cultivation of Saga*, pp. 126–7.

52 *Haralds saga Sigurðarsonar*, ch. 22, in Snorri Sturluson, *Heimskringla*, ed. Bjarni Aðalbjarnarson (Reykjavík, 1941–51), vol. 3, p. 96.

53 Finnur Jónsson (ed.), *Morkinskinna* (Copenhagen, 1932), pp. 272–9, and Finnur Jónsson (ed.), *Fagrskinna* (Copenhagen, 1902–03), pp. 287, 292–4; for translations see *Morkinskinna: The Earliest Icelandic Chronicle of the Norwegian Kings (1030–1157)*, trans. T. M. Andersson and K. E. Gade (Ithaca and London, 2000), pp. 268–73, and *Fagrskinna, a Catalogue of the Kings of Norway*, trans. Alison Finlay (Leiden, 2004), pp. 225–31.

54 William of Malmesbury, *Gesta Regum*, vol. 1, pp. 479–81; see R. I. Page, *Chronicles of the Vikings* (London, 1995), pp. 100–4.

55 See Scott, 'Valþjófr jarl'.

56 Saxo Grammaticus, *Gesta Danorum*, ed. Friis-Jensen and Fisher, vol. 1, pp. 664–5.

57 The historical Sigurðr was active in northern France from *c*.880 until his death in 887; see Lukman, 'Ragnarr Lothbrok, Sigifrid, and the Saints of Flanders', p. 9.

58 Smyth, *Scandinavian Kings*, pp. 40–50; McTurk, *Studies in Ragnars saga Loðbrókar*, pp. 96–8.

59 For discussion of the name, see Saxo Grammaticus, *The History of the Danes*, ed. Peter Fisher and Hilda Ellis Davidson (Cambridge, 1979–80), vol. 2, p. 155.

60 Saxo Grammaticus, *Gesta Danorum*, ed. Friis-Jensen and Fisher, vol. 1, pp. 638–41. Lukman argues that this story originates from Flemish hagiography surrounding the healing sand of the grave of St Arnulf; see 'Ragnarr Lothbrok, Sigifrid, and the saints of Flanders', p. 24.

61 Rauer, *Beowulf and the Dragon*, pp. 42–4.

62 By contrast, a twelfth-century text added to a manuscript of John of Worcester's *Chronicle* does record Waltheof's Northumbrian maternal ancestry, and makes him a descendant of Ælla; see McGuigan, 'Ælla and the descendants of Ivar'.

63 On this element of the Siward narrative see Bolton, 'Family of Earl Siward and Earl Waltheof'.

64 For examples and discussion see J. Michael Stitt, *Beowulf and the Bear's Son: Epic, Saga, and Fairytale in Northern Germanic Tradition* (New York

and London, 1992); Gwyn Jones, *Kings, Beasts and Heroes* (London, 1972), pp. 129–43; John McKinnell, *Meeting the Other in Norse Myth and Legend* (Cambridge, 2005), pp. 126–46.

65 Saxo Grammaticus, *Gesta Danorum*, ed. Friis-Jensen and Fisher, vol. 1, pp. 734–7 (737).

66 John of Worcester, *Chronicle*, vol. 2, p. 549. Plummer examines the differences between the accounts of Beorn's death in John of Worcester's chronicle and *Anglo-Saxon Chronicle* C, D and E in *Two of the Saxon Chronicles Parallel*, vol. 2, pp. 229–31. John of Worcester is the only one to provide a genealogy for Beorn in his narrative of the events of 1049.

67 Bolton, 'Family of Earl Siward and Earl Waltheof'.

68 See Dorothy Whitelock, 'Scandinavian personal names in the *Liber Vitae* of Thorney Abbey', *Saga-Book of the Viking Society* XII (1937–45), 127–53 (134–5), and Keynes, 'Cnut's earls', pp. 62–4; see also Campbell (ed.), *Encomium*, pp. 82–7. The story of his death is told in *Óláfs saga helga*, ch. 152–3, where Ulf's family connection with Godwine is mentioned (Snorri, *Heimskringla*, vol. 2, pp. 283–6).

69 Adam of Bremen, *Gesta Hammaburgensis Ecclesiae Pontificum*, p. 104; *History of the Archbishops*, pp. 124–5. See Freeman, *The Norman Conquest*, vol. 2, pp. 60–5.

70 Barlow, *The Godwins*, pp. 47–55.

71 Three of Svein's sons also took part; John of Worcester names two of them as Harold and Cnut, and Gaimar names a third son, 'Buern Leriz' (Gaimar, *Estoire des Engleis*, p. 294).

72 John of Worcester, *Chronicle*, vol. 3, pp. 8–14, William of Malmesbury, *Gesta Regum*, vol. 1, p. 480, and Cecily Clark (ed.), *The Peterborough Chronicle 1070–1154* (Oxford, 1970), p. 5.

73 Walter Map, *De nugis curialium*, ed. M. R. James, revised by C. N. L. Brooke and R. A. B. Mynors (Oxford, 1983), pp. 432–7; Saxo Grammaticus, *Gesta Danorum*, ed. Friis-Jensen and Fisher, vol. 1, pp. 740–3. The composition of *De nugis curialium* is usually dated to *c.*1181–2.

74 Godwine probably did go to Denmark on Cnut's orders, perhaps in 1022–3; the evidence for his expedition is discussed by Keynes, 'Cnut's earls', pp. 70–4.

75 Walter de Gray Birch (ed.), *Vita Haroldi, The Romance of the Life of Harold, King of England* (London, 1885), pp. 13–15.

76 See Wright, *Cultivation of Saga*, pp. 224–9; G. N. Garmonsway, *Canute and his Empire* (London, 1964), pp. 8–9; Saxo Grammaticus, *Gesta Danorum*, ed. Friis-Jensen and Fisher, vol. 1, pp. 182–221.

77 The numerous stories about Godwine are collected by Wright, *Cultivation of Saga*, pp. 213–36; see also Barlow, *The Godwins*, pp. 31–3; Mason, *The House of Godwine*, pp. 31–3.

78 Bjarni Guðnason (ed.), *Danakonunga sögur*, pp. 109–11.

79 Walter Map, *De nugis curialium*, pp. 412–37.

80 Barlow, *The Godwins*, pp. 23–4.

81 For discussion of how such information may have become known at
    Worcester, see A. S. Napier and W. H. Stevenson (eds), *The Crawford
    Collection of Early Charters and Documents now in the Bodleian Library*
    (Oxford, 1895), pp. 143–4, and Keynes, 'Cnut's earls', pp. 46–7.

82 John of Worcester, *Chronicle*, vol. 2, p. 549.

83 For the text see the appendix in T. D. Hardy and C. T. Martin (eds), *Lestorie
    des Engles solum la translacion Maistre Geffrei Gaimar* (London, 1888–9),
    vol. 1, pp. 339–404; for a translation see 'The Life of Hereward the Wake',
    trans. Michael Swanton, in T. Ohlgren (ed.), *Medieval Outlaws: Ten Tales
    in Modern English* (Stroud, 1998), pp. 12–60.

84 J. D. Martin, *The Cartularies and Registers of Peterborough Abbey*
    (Peterborough, 1978), pp. 7–12; N. R. Ker (ed.), *Medieval Manuscripts in
    British Libraries* (Oxford, 1969–2002), vol. 4, pp. 162–4.

85 Blake (ed.), *Liber Eliensis*, pp. xxxiv–xxxvi.

86 On the historical evidence for Hereward's life, see J. Hayward, 'Hereward
    the outlaw', *Journal of Medieval History* 14 (1988), pp. 293–304, and Hart,
    The Danelaw, pp. 625–48; for the plundering of Peterborough see Clark
    (ed.), *The Peterborough Chronicle*, pp. 2–4. According to the twelfth-
    century Peterborough writer Hugh Candidus, Hereward's actions caused
    particular outrage because he was a tenant of the monastery, a statement
    confirmed by Domesday Book (Hugh Candidus, *Chronicle*, pp. 77–82).
    On Hereward's Domesday holdings, see C. W. Foster and Thomas Longley
    (eds), *The Lincolnshire Domesday and the Lindsey Survey* (Horncastle,
    1924), p. 58.

87 On Hereward and Robin Hood see J. C. Holt, *Robin Hood* (London, 1982),
    pp. 64–75; Maurice Keen, *The Outlaws of Medieval Legend* (London,
    2000), pp. 10–38.

88 For discussion of the episode, see Elisabeth van Houts, 'Hereward and
    Flanders', *Anglo-Saxon England* 22 (1999), pp. 201–23 (215–7); P. G.
    Schmidt, 'Biblisches und hagiographisches Kolorit in den *Gesta Herwardi*',
    in Katherine Walsh and Diana Wood (eds), *The Bible in the Medieval
    World: Essays in Memory of Beryl Smalley* (Oxford, 1985), pp. 85–95;
    Axel Olrik, *The Heroic Legends of Denmark* (New York, 1919), pp. 374–5.

89 'Fabula Danorum' is an emendation of the manuscript's *fabula davorum*;
    see Hardy and Martin (eds), *Lestorie des Engles*, vol. 1, p. 343.

90 Ibid., vol. 1, p. 339.

91 Clark (ed.), *The Peterborough Chronicle*, pp. 2–4.

92 A. J. Holden (ed.), *Le Roman de Waldef* (Cologny-Genève, 1984); see
    Rosalind Field, '*Waldef* and the matter of/with England', in Judith Weiss,
    Jennifer Fellows and Morgan Dickson (eds), *Medieval Insular Romance:
    Translation and Innovation* (Cambridge, 2000), pp. 25–39.

93 Holden (ed.), *Le Roman de Waldef*, lines 11821–12518.

94 Waldef, like Hereward, saves a woman from a forced marriage by arriving
    at the wedding feast in Dublin, where she recognises him by means of a
    ring. Both may have borrowed the episode from an early version of another

romance; see Judith Weiss, 'Thomas and the Earl: literary and historical contexts for the *Romance of Horn*' in Rosalind Field (ed.), *Tradition and Transformation in Medieval Romance* (Cambridge, 1999), pp. 1–13.

95 In a number of Old Norse sagas, a fight against a bear, a berserkr, or a man named Björn features as part of the hero's initiation into manhood; see Mary Danielli, 'Initiation ceremonial from Old Norse literature', *Folklore* 56/2 (1945), pp. 229–45.

96 The Crowland Chronicle purports to be the work of Abbot Ingulf (1085–1108) with continuations by later writers, and is therefore often known as 'the chronicle of Pseudo-Ingulf'; see Walter de Gray Birch (ed.), *The Chronicle of Croyland Abbey by Ingulph* (Wisbech, 1883) and *Ingulph's Chronicle of the Abbey of Croyland, with the continuations by Peter of Blois and Anonymous Writers*, trans. Henry T. Riley (London, 1854), pp. 134–43.

97 Field, '*Waldef* and the matter of/with England', pp. 29–31.

CHAPTER 4: DANISH SOVEREIGNTY
AND THE RIGHT TO RULE

1 For examples and discussion see Robert Allen Rouse, *The Idea of Anglo-Saxon England in Middle English Romance* (Cambridge, 2005) and Frankis, 'Views of Anglo-Saxon England'.

2 For discussion of the date and context of Gaimar's work, see Ian Short, 'Patrons and polyglots: French literature in twelfth-century England', *Anglo-Norman Studies* 14 (1992), pp. 229–49; Gaimar, *Estoire des Engleis*, pp. ix–xvi; Paul Dalton, 'The date of Geoffrey Gaimar's *Estoire des Engleis*, the connections of his patrons, and the politics of Stephen's reign', *The Chaucer Review* 42 (2007), pp. 23–47.

3 Gaimar, *Estoire des Engleis*, p. ix; see also Short, 'Patrons and polyglots', pp. 243–4.

4 Alexander Bell, 'Gaimar's early "Danish" kings', *PMLA* 65/4 (1950), pp. 601–40; Elizabeth Freeman, 'Geffrei Gaimar, vernacular historiography, and the assertion of authority', *Studies in Philology* 93 (1996), pp. 188–206.

5 Gaimar, *Estoire des Engleis*, pp. 50–3.

6 For the treatment of this incident in other chronicles, see Page, '*A Most Vile People*', pp. 21–5.

7 This is probably a reference to Adelbriht, the king Gaimar names as Havelok's father-in-law and a Danish king of Norfolk; see *Estoire des Engleis*, pp. 4–7.

8 Gaimar, *Estoire des Engleis*, pp. 114–15.

9 Ibid., pp. 234–7.

10 Margaret Ashdown discusses the meeting and the traditions surrounding it in 'The single combat in certain cycles of English and Scandinavian tradition and romance', *The Modern Language Review* 17 (1922), pp. 113–30; see also Wright, *Cultivation of Saga*, pp. 191–5.

11 O'Brien O'Keeffe (ed.), *Anglo-Saxon Chronicle MS. C*, p. 103.

12 Campbell (ed.), *Encomium*, pp. 24–31.

13 William of Malmesbury, *Gesta Regum*, vol. 1, pp. 316–9.

14 Henry of Huntingdon, *Historia Anglorum*, pp. 360–1.

15 Walter Map, *De nugis curialium*, pp. 424–7.

16 Roger of Wendover, *Chronica*, vol. 1, pp. 457–9; for comment on this episode see Phillip Pulsiano, ' "Danish men's words are worse than murder": Viking guile and *The Battle of Maldon*', *Journal of English and German Philology* 96 (1997), pp. 13–25 (21–2).

17 Gaimar, *Estoire des Engleis*, pp. 236–7.

18 See for instance William of Malmesbury, *Gesta Regum*, vol. 1, p. 319.

19 Geoffrey of Monmouth, *The History of the Kings of Britain*, ed. Michael D. Reeve and Neil Wright (Woodbridge, 2007), pp. 248–51.

20 For a list, see Saxo Grammaticus, *The History of the Danes*, ed. Fisher and Davidson, vol. 2, pp. 25–6. The etymology comes ultimately from Isidore of Seville, and is mentioned by several Norman historians; Orderic Vitalis, in tracing the descent of the Normans from Troy, comments that the Danes took their name from Danus, son of Antenor, who settled in the north after escaping from the sack of Troy (*Ecclesiastical History*, vol. 5, pp. 24–5).

21 Saxo Grammaticus, *Gesta Danorum*, ed. Friis-Jensen and Fisher, vol. 1, pp. 18–25.

22 M. C. Gertz (ed.), *Scriptores Minores Historiæ Danicæ Medii Ævi* (Copenhagen, 1917–18), vol. 1, p. 43. Saxo used this text as one of his sources, but he gives Dan a different father and origin and places him 20 generations further back in history; see Saxo Grammaticus, *Gesta Danorum*, ed. Friis-Jensen and Fisher, vol. 1, p. 19, n. 1.

23 Snorri, *Heimskringla*, vol. 1, pp. 4–5, 35.

24 It is tempting to connect Saxo's 'Angul' with the warrior 'Engle' from whom Robert Mannyng says the English took their name, but both names could be derived independently from etymological speculation [Robert Mannyng, *The Chronicle*, ed. Idelle Sullens (Binghamton, NY, 1996), pp. 440–2].

25 On the belief, found in this saga and others, in the myth of a pre-Cnut Viking empire which included the British Isles, see Ashman Rowe, 'Helpful Danes and pagan Irishmen'.

26 See Gillingham, *The English in the Twelfth Century*, p. 119; Scott Kleinman, 'The legend of Havelok the Dane and the historiography of East Anglia', *Studies in Philology* 100 (2003), pp. 245–77 (263); Spence, *Reimagining History in Anglo-Norman Prose Chronicles*, pp. 89–90. This right is also mentioned in William of Newburgh's *Historia Regum Anglicarum*, in Richard Howlett (ed.), *Chronicles of the Reigns of Stephen, Henry II, and Richard I* (London, 1884), vol. 1, p. 368.

27 Gaimar, *Estoire des Engleis*, pp. 140–55; see Alexander Bell, 'Buern Bucecarle in "Gaimar"', *Modern Language Review*, 27 (1932), pp. 168–74.

28 For discussion of this story see Bell, 'Buern Bucecarle in "Gaimar"', and McTurk, *Studies in Ragnars saga Loðbrókar*, pp. 210–35. McTurk compares

a thirteenth-century story about Ælla, the *Narratio de uxore Aernulfi ab Ella rege Deirorum violate*. See also Wright, *Cultivation of Saga*, pp. 107–16.

29 Jane Zatta, 'Gaimar's rebels: outlaw heroes and the creation of authority in twelfth-century England', *Essays in Medieval Studies* 16 (1999), pp. 27–40.

30 Gaimar, *Estoire des Engleis*, pp. 411–12.

31 Ibid., pp. 156–61.

32 On the developing English identity of the Anglo-Norman aristocracy in the twelfth century, see Ashe, *Fiction and History*.

33 For a description of the many incarnations of the legend from the twelfth century to the present day, see Velma Bourgeois Richmond, *The Legend of Guy of Warwick* (New York, 1996); Ronald S. Crane, 'The vogue of Guy of Warwick from the close of the Middle Ages to the Romantic revival', *PMLA* 30 (1915), pp. 125–94.

34 Alfred Ewert (ed.), *Gui de Warewic: roman du XIIIe siècle* (Paris, 1932–3); Judith Weiss (ed.), *Boeve de Haumtone and Gui de Warewic: Two Anglo-Norman Romances* (Tempe, 2008). For discussion of the Anglo-Norman poem, see Marianne Ailes, '*Gui de Warewic* in its manuscript context', in Alison Wiggins and Rosalind Field (eds), *Guy of Warwick: Icon and Ancestor* (Cambridge, 2007), pp. 12–26.

35 Emma Mason, 'Legends of the Beauchamps' ancestors: the use of baronial propaganda in medieval England', *Journal of Medieval History* 10 (1984), pp. 25–40.

36 See Alison Wiggins, 'The manuscripts and texts of the Middle English *Guy of Warwick*', in Wiggins and Field (eds), *Guy of Warwick: Icon and Ancestor*, pp. 61–80. Two of the Middle English versions are edited by J. Zupitza in *The Romance of Guy of Warwick, edited from the Auchinleck MS. in the Advocates' Library, Edinburgh and from MS. 107 in Caius College, Cambridge* (London, 1883–91; reprinted as one volume, 1966). Quotations are taken from this edition; as Zupitza prints the Auchinleck and Caius texts in parallel, the version referred to will be identified as A and C respectively. The fifteenth-century version in Cambridge University Library, MS. Ff.2.38 is edited by Zupitza as *The Romance of Guy of Warwick: the second or 15th-century version* (London, 1875–6; repr. 1966).

37 Rosalind Field, 'From *Gui* to *Guy*: the fashioning of a popular romance', in Wiggins and Field (eds), *Guy of Warwick: Icon and Ancestor*, pp. 44–60; Maldwyn Mills, 'Techniques of translation in the Middle English versions of *Guy of Warwick*', in Roger Ellis (ed.), *The Medieval Translator II* (London, 1991), pp. 209–29.

38 Richmond, *The Legend of Guy of Warwick*, pp. 65–76.

39 Mason, 'Legends of the Beauchamps' ancestors', pp. 33–4; Richmond, *The Legend of Guy of Warwick*, pp. 68–70.

40 Crane, 'The vogue of Guy of Warwick', p. 191.

41 For an overview of the relationship between the *Guy* romances and historiography, see Judith Weiss, '*Gui de Warewic* at home and abroad:

a hero for Europe', in Wiggins and Field (eds), *Guy of Warwick: Icon and Ancestor*, pp. 1–11. On structural parallels between the two episodes see Carol Fewster, *Traditionality and Genre in Middle English Romance* (Cambridge, 1987), pp. 83–4.

42 Eugen Kölbing (ed.), *The Romance of Sir Beues of Hamtoun* (London, 1885, 1886, 1894), pp. 122–3; see Laura A. Hibbard, *Mediæval Romance in England: A Study of the Sources and Analogues of the Non-Cyclic Metrical Romances* (New York, 1960), pp. 127–39.

43 See for instance Rouse, *The Idea of Anglo-Saxon England*, pp. 62–3.

44 The Middle English versions give the Danes only one leader, but the Anglo-Norman poem mentions two, Anlaf and Gunlaf; for discussion see Ashdown, 'The single combat', p. 119. The giant Colbrand also has a Norse name, an anglicisation of *Kolbrandr*; for occurrences of the name in England see Jón Stefansson, 'The oldest known list of Scandinavian names', *Saga-Book of the Viking Society* IV (1905–6), pp. 296–311 (302); Fellows Jensen, *Scandinavian Personal Names in Lincolnshire and Yorkshire*, pp. 177–8.

45 See Ashdown, 'The single combat', p. 123, n. 2.

46 For surveys of references to the battle, see Alistair Campbell (ed.), *The Battle of Brunanburh* (London, 1938), pp. 147–60; Livingston (ed.), *The Battle of Brunanburh: A Casebook*. On later traditions, see Patrizia Lendinara, 'The Battle of Brunanburh in later histories and romances', *Anglia* 117 (1999), pp. 201–35; Campbell, *Skaldic Verse and Anglo-Saxon History*, pp. 5–7; C. W. Whistler, 'Brunanburh and Vinheith in Ingulf's Chronicle and Egil's Saga', *Saga-Book of the Viking Society* VI (1908–9), pp. 59–67.

47 See Treharne, 'Romanticizing the past in the Middle English *Athelston*'. On the king and the nation in *Guy*, see Susan Crane, *Insular Romance: Politics, Faith and Culture in Anglo-Norman and Middle English Literature* (Berkeley, 1986), pp. 65–6.

48 See William of Malmesbury, *Gesta Regum*, vol. 2, pp. 116–20; Wood, 'The making of King Aethelstan's empire', pp. 265–7.

49 For discussion of the English boasting in the *Anglo-Saxon Chronicle* see Page, '*A Most Vile People*', pp. 27–8.

50 Rouse, *The Idea of Anglo-Saxon England*, pp. 60–3.

51 The equivalent passage in the Anglo-Norman is lines 9135–9142 (Ewert (ed.), *Gui de Warewic*, pp. 73–4).

52 Perhaps coincidentally, the earl who speaks up against Heraud at Æthelstan's parliament in the Anglo-Norman poem is named Modred (*Medyok* in Auchinleck and *Moderyse* in Caius); in Cnut's speech in Gaimar, Mordred is said to have granted the English king Cerdic his right to rule.

53 Ashdown, 'The single combat'.

54 Gaimar mentions a 'book of Oxford', a history of Winchester, and 'an English book at Washingborough' (*Estoire des Engleis*, pp. 348–51); see Wilson, *Lost Literature of Medieval England*, p. 79.

CHAPTER 5: 'OVER THE SALT SEA TO ENGLAND':
HAVELOK AND THE DANES

1   For these three versions see Gaimar, *Estoire des Engleis*, pp. 4–47; Glyn
    S. Burgess and Leslie C. Brook (eds), *The Anglo-Norman Lay of Havelok*
    (Cambridge, 2015); G. V. Smithers (ed.), *Havelok* (Oxford, 1987).
    Quotations from *Havelok* are from Smithers' edition, by line number. On
    the manuscript context of *Havelok*, see Kimberly K. Bell and Julie Nelson
    Couch (eds), *The Texts and Contexts of Oxford, Bodleian Library, MS Laud
    Misc. 108: The Shaping of English Vernacular Narrative* (Boston, 2011).
2   For a survey of references to Havelok with extracts from the texts, see
    Burgess and Brook (eds), *The Anglo-Norman Lay of Havelok*, pp. 151–210.
3   This was first suggested by Gustav Storm, 'Havelok the Dane and the
    Norse king Olaf Kuaran', *Englische Studien* III (1880), pp. 533–5; see also
    Charles W. Dunn, '*Havelok* and Anlaf Cuaran', in J. B. Bessinger and R. P.
    Creed (eds), *Medieval and Linguistic Studies in Honour of Francis Peabody
    Magoun, Jr* (London, 1965), pp. 244–9.
4   See Alexander Bugge, 'Havelok and Olaf Tryggvason: a contribution
    towards the further understanding of the kings' sagas', *Saga-Book of the
    Viking Society* VI (1910), pp. 257–95.
5   Smithers (ed.), *Havelok*, p. lvii.
6   Edmund Reiss, '*Havelok the Dane* and Norse mythology', *Modern Language
    Quarterly* 27 (1966), pp. 115–24.
7   See for instance the references to Havelok in the chronicles of Peter Langtoft
    [Burgess and Brook (eds), *The Anglo-Norman Lay of Havelok*, pp. 164–5],
    and Henry Knighton, *Chronicon Henrici Knighton vel Cnitthon, Monachi
    Leycestrensis*, ed. J. R. Lumby (London, 1889), vol. 1, pp. 18–27.
8   On the use of the Anglo-Saxon past in Middle English romance see
    Rouse, *The Idea of Anglo-Saxon England*; Rosalind Field, 'Romance as
    history, history as romance', in Maldwyn Mills, Jennifer Fellows and
    Carol M. Meale (eds), *Romance in Medieval England* (Cambridge, 1991),
    pp. 163–73.
9   Thorlac Turville-Petre, *England the Nation: Language, Literature and
    National Identity, 1290–1340* (Oxford, 1996), pp. 142–55; see also Turville-
    Petre, '*Havelok* and the history of the nation', in Carol M. Meale (ed.),
    Readings in Medieval English Romance (Cambridge, 1994), pp. 121–34;
    Turville-Petre, 'Representations of the Danelaw in Middle English
    literature', in Graham-Campbell et al. (eds), *Vikings and the Danelaw*,
    pp. 345–55.
10 Turville-Petre, *England the Nation*, p. 152. For discussion of this argument,
    see Rouse, *The Idea of Anglo-Saxon England*, pp. 102–5; Raluca L.
    Radulescu, 'Genealogy in insular romance', in Radulescu and Kennedy
    (eds), *Broken Lines*, pp. 7–25; Helen Cooper, 'When romance comes true',
    in Neil Cartlidge (ed.), *Boundaries in Medieval Romance* (Woodbridge,
    2008), pp. 13–27.

11 Burgess and Brook (eds), *The Anglo-Norman Lay of Havelok*, p. 155.

12 Smithers (ed.), *Havelok*, p. 109.

13 See Edward Gillett, *A History of Grimsby* (London, 1970), pp. 6–9; Goddard Leach, *Angevin Britain and Scandinavia*, pp. 40–2.

14 Gillett, *A History of Grimsby*, p. 8.

15 K. J. Allison, *A History of the County of York East Riding: Volume 1, the City of Kingston Upon Hull* (London, 1969), pp. 371–86.

16 Kenneth Cameron and John Insley, *A Dictionary of Lincolnshire Place-Names* (Nottingham, 1998), p. 54.

17 *Hákonar saga góða*, ch. 3, in Snorri, *Heimskringla*, vol. 1, p. 153. Hauksfljót has not been identified.

18 See Turville-Petre, 'Representations of the Danelaw', pp. 352–3. It may be significant that of the six uses of the word 'Denshe' in the poem, three occur within the context of Godrich's resistance to Havelok's army (lines 2575, 2689 and 2693).

19 Kleinman, 'The legend of Havelok the Dane and the historiography of East Anglia', p. 249.

20 Fellows Jensen, *Scandinavian Personal Names in Lincolnshire and Yorkshire*, pp. 319–30.

21 William of Malmesbury, *Gesta Regum*, vol. 1, pp. 300–1. William is the first source for this story, but it was repeated by later writers; for discussion see Simon Keynes, *The Diplomas of King Æthelred 'the Unready' 978–1016: A Study in their Use as Historical Evidence* (Cambridge, 1980), p. 214; Keynes, 'The massacre of St Brice's Day (13 November 1002)', in N. Lund (ed.), *Beretning fra seksogtyvende tværfaglige vikingesymposium* (Aarhus, 2007), pp. 32–67; Williams, *Æthelred the Unready*, pp. 53–4.

22 William of Malmesbury, *Gesta Regum*, vol. 1, 339.

23 The story appears with varying details in Ralph of Diceto, *The Historical Works*, ed. William Stubbs (London, 1876), p. 174, and Matthew Paris, *Chronica Majora*, ed. H. R. Luard (London, 1872), vol. 1, pp. 514–15; see Wilson, *Lost Literature of Medieval England*, p. 55.

24 Smithers suggested that the poet of *Havelok* found the name Gunnhild, along with other names used in the poem, in the twelfth-century *Life and Miracles of William of Norwich* [Smithers (ed.), *Havelok*, pp. lxix–lxx]. Even if this is the case, the associations of Gunnhild with Svein and Cnut may have made it seem a particularly appropriate choice.

25 See Rouse, *The Idea of Anglo-Saxon England*, pp. 103–5; Larissa Tracy, *Torture and Brutality in Medieval Literature: Negotiations of National Identity* (Cambridge, 2012), pp. 140–55; W. R. J. Barron, 'The penalties for treason in medieval life and literature', *Journal of Medieval History* 7 (1981), pp. 187–202.

26 Gaimar, *Estoire des Engleis*, pp. 12–15.

27 For a discussion of Goldburh's role as counsellor in this episode, see Alexandra H. Olsen, 'The valkyrie reflex in Havelok the Dane', in Loren C. Gruber (ed.), *Essays on Old, Middle, Modern English and Old Icelandic* (Lewiston, NY, 2000), pp. 317–35.

28 For another interpretation of this dream, see Diane Speed, 'The construction of the nation in medieval English romance', in Meale (ed.), *Readings in Medieval English Romance*, pp. 135–57.

29 Gelling and Cole, *The Landscape of Place-Names*, pp. 178–80.

30 For comparable examples in Norse, Irish and Welsh literature see Ellis, *The Road to Hel*, pp. 105–11.

31 Intriguingly, there are records of at least two significant earthworks (now destroyed) in Grimsby in the form of mounds, named Toote Hill and Cun Hu Hill; Barrie Cox suggests that the first name derives from OE *tōt-hyll*, 'a look-out hill' and the latter from Old Norse *konungr* and *haugr* [Cox, 'Yarboroughs in Lindsey', *Journal of the English Place-Name Society*, 28 (1995–6), pp. 50–60]. Possibly this feature of the local landscape is connected in some way to Havelok's dream.

32 See also 2395–8 and 2453–60.

33 For discussion of this point see R. M. Liuzza, 'Representation and readership in the Middle English *Havelok*', *Journal of English and Germanic Philology* 93 (1994), pp. 504–19; Julie Nelson Couch, 'The vulnerable hero: Havelok and the revision of romance', *Chaucer Review* 42 (2008), pp. 330–52.

34 See further Eleanor Parker, 'Havelok and the Danes in England: history, legend, and romance', *Review of English Studies* 67 (2016), pp. 428–47.

35 Burgess and Brook (eds), *The Anglo-Norman Lay of Havelok*, pp. 151–210.

36 See especially Ananya J. Kabir, 'Forging an oral style? *Havelok* and the fiction of orality', *Studies in Philology* 98 (2001), pp. 18–48.

37 For instance, some contemporary narratives of Cnut's reign involve detailed and emotive stories of the Danish king's treatment of his rival's young children [Robert of Gloucester, *The Metrical Chronicle of Robert of Gloucester*, ed. William Aldis Wright (London, 1887), vol. 1, pp. 466–9].

38 On the relationship between *Havelok* and the hagiographical context of its only surviving manuscript, see Bell and Nelson Couch (eds), *Texts and Contexts*.

39 Robert Mannyng, *Chronicle*, pp. 499–500. A later revision of Mannyng's *Chronicle* in the Lambeth MS. omits the quoted passage and substitutes an interpolation summarising the story of Havelok, following the version of the story represented by Gaimar and the *Lai*; see W. W. Skeat (ed.), *The Lay of Havelok the Dane*, revised by K. Sisam (Oxford, 1915; repr. 1967), pp. xvii–xix.

40 Nancy Mason Bradbury, 'The traditional origins of *Havelok the Dane*', *Studies in Philology* 90 (1993), pp. 115–42.

41 Ibid., pp. 124–5.

42 Holles' comments are printed in Frederick Madden (ed.), *The Ancient English Romance of Havelok the Dane* (London, 1828), pp. xxxix–xl.

43 For Camden's remarks see Burgess and Brook (eds), *The Anglo-Norman Lay of Havelok*, pp. 207–8.

44 Skeat (ed.), *The Ancient English Romance of Havelok the Dane*, p. xl.

45 Katherine M. Briggs (ed.), *A Dictionary of British Folk-Tales in the English Language* (London, 1971), Part B, vol. 2, p. 223.

46 G. N. Garmonsway and Jacqueline Simpson, *Beowulf and Its Analogues* (London, 1980), pp. 118–23. A related story also appears in the twelfth century in William of Malmesbury's *Gesta Regum*, vol. 1, pp. 176–7.

47 Madden (ed.), *The Ancient English Romance of Havelok the Dane*, p. xxxix.

48 Ibid., p. xl.

49 Ibid., pp. xli–xlii.

50 Skeat (ed.), *The Lay of Havelok the Dane*, p. liv.

51 Jennifer Westwood, *Albion: A Guide to Legendary Britain* (London, 1987), pp. 84–7.

52 Robert Mannyng, *Chronicle*, pp. 440–1.

53 T. Möbius (ed.), *Kormaks saga* (Halle, 1886), p. 54.

54 See Wilson, *Lost Literature of Medieval England*, pp. 44–5.

55 Madden (ed.), *The Ancient English Romance of Havelok the Dane*, p. xl.

EPILOGUE: THE DANES IN ENGLISH FOLKLORE

1   See Daniel Woolf, 'Of Danes and giants: popular beliefs about the past in early modern England', *Dalhousie Review* 71 (1991), pp. 166–209, and *The Social Circulation of the Past: English Historical Culture, 1500–1730* (Oxford, 2003), pp. 345–9; Adam Fox, *Oral and Literate Culture in England, 1500–1700* (Oxford, 2000), pp. 243–8; Jennifer Westwood and Jacqueline Simpson, *The Lore of the Land: A Guide to England's Legends, from Spring-Heeled Jack to the Witches of Warboys* (London, 2005), pp. 530–1.

2   Woolf, 'Of Danes and giants', p. 193.

3   Westwood and Simpson, *Lore of the Land*, p. 530.

4   For an overview see O'Donoghue, *English Poetry and Old Norse Myth*, pp. 28–64.

5   Ibid., pp. 38–41.

6   Julia Barrow, 'Danish ferocity and abandoned monasteries: the twelfth-century view', in Brett and Woodman (eds), *The Long Twelfth-Century View of the Anglo-Saxon Past*, pp. 77–93.

7   See Woolf, *The Social Circulation of the Past*, p. 345.

8   Westwood and Simpson, *Lore of the Land*, pp. 255, 528, 530–1.

9   Cameron and Insley, *A Dictionary of Lincolnshire Place-Names*, p. 127.

10 *Ingulph's Chronicle of the Abbey of Croyland*, trans. Riley, p. 42.

11 E. Gutch and Mabel Peacock, *Examples of Printed Folk-Lore Concerning Lincolnshire*, County Folk-Lore 5 (London, 1908), p. 315.

12 Ibid., p. 436.

13 Jacqueline Simpson, *Folklore of Sussex* (Stroud, 2013), p. 45.

14 The *Eulogium historiarum sive temporis*, on which see Burgess and Brook (eds), *The Anglo-Norman Lay of Havelok*, pp. 198–202.

15 On various legends attached to the stones, see L. V. Grinsell, *The Rollright Stones and their Folklore* (St Peter Port, 1977).

16 William Camden, *Britain, or A chorographicall description of the most flourishing kingdomes, England, Scotland, and Ireland, and the ilands adioyning, out of the depth of antiquitie*, trans. Philemon Holland (London, 1610), p. 374.

17 Jennifer Westwood, 'The Rollright Stones, Part 1: The Danes', *3rd Stone* 38 (2000), pp. 6–10.

18 Westwood and Simpson, *Lore of the Land*, pp. 535–6.

19 See H. St George Gray, 'Notes on "Danes' skins"', *Saga-Book of the Viking Society* V (1907–8), pp. 218–29; M. J. Swanton, '"Dane-skins": excoriation in early England', *Folklore* 87/1 (1976), pp. 21–8; Westwood and Simpson, *Lore of the Land*, p. 258.

20 Swanton, 'Dane-skins', p. 26.

21 Ibid.

22 Gray, 'Notes on "Danes' skins"', p. 229.

23 Warwick Rodwell, 'The Battle of *Assandun* and its memorial church', in Cooper (ed.), *The Battle of Maldon: Fiction and Fact*, pp. 127–58.

24 Patricia Croxton-Smith, 'The site of the Battle of Assandun, 1016', *Saffron Walden Historical Journal* 3 (2002).

25 Westwood and Simpson, *Lore of the Land*, pp. 250–1.

26 Hella Eckardt et al., 'The Bartlow Hills in context', *Proceedings of the Cambridge Antiquarian Society* XCVIII (2009), pp. 47–64.

27 Camden, *Britain*, trans. Holland, p. 452.

28 See Donald Watts, *Dictionary of Plant Lore* (Boston, 2007), p. 101; Westwood and Simpson, *Lore of the Land*, p. 251.

29 Watts, *Dictionary of Plant Lore*, p. 123.

30 Westwood and Simpson, *Lore of the Land*, p. 251.

31 Ibid., p. 531.

32 Woolf, 'Of Danes and giants', p. 177.

33 Girardus Cornubiensis, *De Gestis Regum Westsaxonum*, quoted in Edwards (ed.), *Liber Monasterii de Hyda*, pp. 118–23; see Richmond, *The Legend of Guy of Warwick*, pp. 68–70.

34 Richmond, *The Legend of Guy of Warwick*, p. 98.

35 Westwood and Simpson, *Lore of the Land*, pp. 794–5.

36 Woolf, 'Of Danes and giants', p. 173.

37 Ronald Hutton, *The Stations of the Sun: A History of the Ritual Year in Britain* (Oxford, 1996), pp. 207–13.

38 There may be a link to the idea found in some medieval Anglo-Norman chronicles that an army of English men and women rebelled against Harthacnut and drove the Danes out of England; this group was called the *hounhere*, which seems to mean something like 'shame-army' [Burgess and Brook (eds), *The Anglo-Norman Lay of Havelok*, pp. 165–6; Spence, *Reimagining History in Anglo-Norman Prose Chronicles*, pp. 89–91].

39 Woolf, 'Of Danes and giants', p. 194.

40 Westwood and Simpson, *Lore of the Land*, p. 26; Joanne Parker, *England's Darling: The Victorian Cult of Alfred the Great* (Manchester, 2007).

41 Westwood and Simpson, *Lore of the Land*, pp. 81–4.

42 The *Liber Eliensis* tells two stories about Cnut, one describing how the king composed a song in honour of the monks' singing, the other telling how Cnut rewarded a local man named Brihtmær Budde for helping him cross the frozen fen to Ely [Blake (ed.), *Liber Eliensis*, pp. 153–4]. For a twentieth-century tradition about Cnut as benefactor to a local man, oddly reminiscent of the medieval stories, see W. H. Barrett, *Tales from the Fens* (London, 1963).

43 John Wise and W. Mackreth Noble, *Ramsey Abbey, Its Rise and Fall* (Huntingdon, 1882), pp. 95–6, 204–5.

44 Eleanor Parker, 'Pilgrim and patron: Cnut in post-Conquest historical writing', *The Medieval Chronicle* 9 (2014), pp. 271–95.

BIBLIOGRAPHY

Works are divided into editions of primary texts and secondary sources. Medieval texts with no known author are listed under the names of their editors. Most of the medieval and all the Icelandic authors are listed under their first name.

PRIMARY SOURCES

Adam of Bremen, *Gesta Hammaburgensis Ecclesiae Pontificum*, ed. Georg Waitz (Hanover, 1876).

—— *History of the Archbishops of Hamburg-Bremen*, trans. Francis J. Tschan (New York, 1959).

Adelard of Ghent, 'Lectiones in Depositione S. Dunstani', in Michael Winterbottom and Michael Lapidge (eds), *The Early Lives of St Dunstan* (Oxford, 2012), pp. 111–45.

Ælfric, *Lives of Saints*, ed. Walter W. Skeat, Early English Text Society Original Series 76, 82, 94, 111 (London, 1881–1900), 2 vols.

Andersson, T. M. and K. E. Gade (trans.), *Morkinskinna: The Earliest Icelandic Chronicle of the Norwegian Kings (1030–1157)* (Ithaca and London, 2000).

Ari Þorgilsson, *Íslendingabók and Kristni Saga*, trans. Siân Grønlie (London, 2006).

Barlow, Frank (ed.), *The Life of King Edward who Rests at Westminster* (Oxford, 1992).

—— (ed.), *The Carmen de Hastingae Proelio of Guy, Bishop of Amiens* (Oxford, 1999).

Bately, J. M. (ed.), *The Anglo-Saxon Chronicle, MS. A*, The Anglo-Saxon Chronicle: A Collaborative Edition, vol. 3 (Cambridge, 1986).

Bjarni Einarsson (ed.), *Egils saga* (London, 2003).

Bjarni Guðnason (ed.), *Danakonunga sögur*, Íslenzk Fornrit XXXV (Reykjavík, 1982).

Blake, E. O. (ed.), *Liber Eliensis* (London, 1962).

Burgess, Glyn S. and Leslie C. Brook (eds), *The Anglo-Norman Lay of Havelok* (Cambridge, 2015).

Byrhtferth of Ramsey, *The Lives of St Oswald and St Ecgwine*, ed. Michael Lapidge (Oxford, 2009).

Camden, William, *Britain, or a chorographicall description of the most flourishing kingdomes, England, Scotland, and Ireland, and the ilands adioyning, out of the depth of antiquitie*, trans. Philemon Holland (London, 1610).

Campbell, Alistair (ed.), *The Battle of Brunanburh* (London, 1938).

—— (ed.), *Encomium Emmae Reginae*, with an introduction by Simon Keynes, Camden Classic Reprints 4 (Cambridge, 1998).

Clark, Cecily (ed.), *The Peterborough Chronicle 1070–1154* (Oxford, 1970).

Colgrave, Bertram (ed.), *Felix's Life of Saint Guthlac* (Cambridge, 1956).

Colgrave, Bertram and R. A. B. Mynors (eds), *Bede's Ecclesiastical History of the English People* (Oxford, 1991).

Cubbin, G. P. (ed.), *The Anglo-Saxon Chronicle, MS. D*, The Anglo-Saxon Chronicle: A Collaborative Edition, vol. 6 (Cambridge, 1996).

D'Evelyn, Charlotte and Anna J. Mill (eds), *The South English Legendary*, Early English Text Society Original Series 235–6, 244 (London, 1956–9), 3 vols.

Dumville, David and Michael Lapidge (eds), *The Annals of St Neots, with Vita Prima Sancti Neoti*, The Anglo-Saxon Chronicle: A Collaborative Edition, vol. 17 (Cambridge, 1985).

Eadmer of Canterbury, *Lives and Miracles of Saints Oda, Dunstan and Oswald*, ed. Andrew J. Turner and Bernard J. Muir (Oxford, 2006).

Edwards, E. (ed.), *Liber Monasterii de Hyda* (London, 1866).

Elmham, Thomas, *Historia Monasterii S. Augustini Cantuariensis*, ed. Charles Hardwick (London, 1858).

Ewert, Alfred (ed.), *Gui de Warewic: roman du XIIIe siècle* (Paris, 1932–3), 2 vols.

Faulkes, Anthony (trans.), *Hemings þáttr* (Dundee, 2016).

Fellows Jensen, Gillian (ed.), *Hemings þáttr Áslákssonar* (Copenhagen, 1962).

Finch, R. G. (ed.), *Völsunga saga* (London, 1965).

Finlay, Alison (trans.), *Fagrskinna, a Catalogue of the Kings of Norway* (Leiden, 2004).

Finnbogi Guðmundsson (ed.), *Orkneyinga saga*, Íslenzk Fornrit XXXIV (Reykjavík, 1965).

Finnur Jónsson (ed.), *Fagrskinna: Nóregs kononga tal* (Copenhagen, 1902–3).

—— (ed.), *Morkinskinna* (Copenhagen, 1932).

Foote, P. G. (ed.), *Gunnlaugs saga Ormstungu* (London, 1957).

Foster, C. W. and T. Longley (eds), *The Lincolnshire Domesday and the Lindsey Survey* (Horncastle, 1924).

Gade, Kari Ellen (ed.), *Poetry from the Kings' Sagas 2: From c.1035 to c.1300*, Skaldic Poetry of the Scandinavian Middle Ages 2 (Turnhout, 2009), 2 vols.

Gaimar, Geffrei, *Estoire des Engleis: History of the English*, ed. Ian Short (Oxford, 2009).

Geoffrey of Monmouth, *The History of the Kings of Britain*, ed. Michael D. Reeve and Neil Wright (Woodbridge, 2007).

Gertz, M. C. (ed.), *Scriptores Minores Historiæ Danicæ Medii Ævi* (Copenhagen, 1917–18), 2 vols.

Goscelin of Saint-Bertin, *The Hagiography of the Female Saints of Ely*, ed. Rosalind C. Love (Oxford, 2004).

de Gray Birch, Walter (ed.), *The Chronicle of Croyland Abbey by Ingulph* (Wisbech, 1883).

—— (ed.), *Vita Haroldi, The Romance of the Life of Harold, King of England* (London, 1885).

Hardy, T. D. and C. T. Martin (eds), *Lestorie des Engles solum la translacion Maistre Geffrei Gaimar* (London, 1888–9), 2 vols.

Henry, Archdeacon of Huntingdon, *Historia Anglorum*, ed. Diana Greenway (Oxford, 1996).

Herman the Archdeacon and Goscelin of Saint-Bertin, *Miracles of St Edmund*, ed. Tom Licence and Lynda Lockyer (Oxford, 2014).

Hervey, Lord Francis (ed.), *Corolla Sancti Eadmundi* (London, 1907).

Holden, A. J. (ed.), *Le Roman de Waldef* (Cologny-Genève, 1984).

Horstmann, Carl (ed.), *Nova Legenda Anglie* (Oxford, 1901), 2 vols.

Hugh Candidus, *The Chronicle of Hugh Candidus, a Monk of Peterborough*, ed. W. T. Mellows (London, 1949).

Irvine, Susan (ed.), *The Anglo-Saxon Chronicle, MS. E*, The Anglo-Saxon Chronicle: A Collaborative Edition, vol. 7 (Cambridge, 2004).

John of Worcester, *The Chronicle of John of Worcester*, ed. R. R. Darlington, P. McGurk and J. Bray (Oxford, 1995), 3 vols.

Johnson South, Ted, (ed.) *Historia de Sancto Cuthberto: A History of Saint Cuthbert and a Record of his Patrimony* (Cambridge, 2002).

Knighton, Henry, *Chronicon Henrici Knighton vel Cnitthon, Monachi Leycestrensis*, ed. J. R. Lumby (London, 1889), 2 vols.

Kölbing, Eugen (ed.), *The Romance of Sir Beues of Hamtoun*, Early English Text Society Extra Series 46, 48, 65 (London, 1885–6, 1894), 3 vols.

Lydgate, John, *Lives of Ss Edmund and Fremund and the Extra Miracles of St Edmund*, ed. Anthony Bale and A. S. G. Edwards (Heidelberg, 2009).

Madden, Frederick (ed.), *The Ancient English Romance of Havelok the Dane* (London, 1828).

Martin, J. D. (ed.), *The Cartularies and Registers of Peterborough Abbey* (Peterborough, 1978).

Matthew Paris, *Chronica Majora*, ed. H. R. Luard (London, 1872–83), 7 vols.

Michel, Francisque (ed.), *Chroniques anglo-normandes: Recueil d'extraits et d'écrits relatifs à l'histoire de Normandie et d'Angleterre pendant les XIe et XIIe siècles* (Rouen, 1836–40), 3 vols.

Möbius, T. (ed.), *Kormaks saga* (Halle, 1886).

O'Brien O'Keeffe, Katherine (ed.), *The Anglo-Saxon Chronicle, MS. C*, The Anglo-Saxon Chronicle: A Collaborative Edition, vol. 5 (Cambridge, 2001).

Ohlgren, Thomas H. (ed.), *Medieval Outlaws: Ten Tales in Modern English* (Stroud, 1998).

Olsen, Magnus (ed.), *Völsunga saga ok Ragnars saga Loðbrókar* (Copenhagen, 1906–8).

Orderic Vitalis, *The Ecclesiastical History of Orderic Vitalis*, ed. M. Chibnall (Oxford, 1969–80), 6 vols.

Osbern of Canterbury, *Vita S. Elphegi*, in Henry Wharton (ed.), *Anglia Sacra* (London, 1691) vol. 2, pp. 122–42.

—— *Vita Sancti Dunstani*, in William Stubbs (ed.), *Memorials of Saint Dunstan Archbishop of Canterbury* (London, 1874), pp. 69–128.

—— 'Translatio Sancti Ælfegi Cantuariensis archiepiscopi et martiris', trans. Rosemary Morris and Alexander R. Rumble, in Rumble (ed.), *The Reign of Cnut: King of England, Denmark and Norway* (London, 1994), pp. 283–315.

—— *Osbern's Life of Alfege*, trans. Frances Shaw (London, 1999).

Plummer, Charles (ed.), *Two of the Saxon Chronicles Parallel* (Oxford, 1899), 2 vols.

Ralph de Diceto, *The Historical Works of Master Ralph de Diceto, Dean of London*, ed. William Stubbs (London, 1876), 2 vols.

Riley, Henry T. (trans.), *Ingulph's Chronicle of the Abbey of Croyland, with the continuations by Peter of Blois and Anonymous Writers* (London, 1854).

Robert of Gloucester, *The Metrical Chronicle of Robert of Gloucester*, ed. William Aldis Wright (London, 1887), 2 vols.

Robert Mannyng of Brunne, *The Chronicle*, ed. Idelle Sullens (Binghamton, NY, 1996).

Roger of Howden, *Chronica Magistri Rogeri de Houedene*, ed. William Stubbs (London, 1869), 4 vols.

Roger of Wendover, *Chronica, sive Flores Historiarum*, ed. H. O. Coxe (London, 1841–4), 4 vols.

Saxo Grammaticus, *The History of the Danes*, trans. Peter Fisher and ed. Hilda Ellis Davidson (Cambridge, 1979–80), 2 vols.

—— *Gesta Danorum: The History of the Danes*, ed. Karsten Friis-Jensen and Peter Fisher (Oxford, 2015), 2 vols.

Scragg, D. G. (ed.), *The Battle of Maldon* (Manchester, 1981).

Serjeantson, R. M., 'A mediæval legend of St Peter's, Northampton', *Associated Architectural Societies' Reports and Papers* 29 (1907), pp. 113–20.

Shakespeare, William, *Macbeth*, ed. Sandra Clark and Pamela Mason, Arden Shakespeare Third Series (London, 2015).

Skeat, W. W. (ed.), *The Lay of Havelok the Dane*, revised by K. Sisam (Oxford, 1915, repr. 1967).

Smithers, G. V. (ed.), *Havelok* (Oxford, 1987).

Snorri Sturluson, *Heimskringla*, ed. Bjarni Aðalbjarnarson, Íslenzk Fornrit XXVI–XXVIII (Reykjavík, 1941–51), 3 vols.

Swanton, Michael (ed.), *Beowulf* (Manchester, 1997).

—— (trans.), *The Anglo-Saxon Chronicles* (London, 2000).

Symeon of Durham, *Libellus de Exordio atque Procursu istius hoc est Dunhelmensis Ecclesie*, ed. David Rollason (Oxford, 2000).

Thomson, Rodney M., 'Geoffrey of Wells, *De Infantia Sancti Edmundi (BHL 2393)*', *Analecta Bollandiana* 95 (1977), pp. 25–42.

Walter Map, *De nugis curialium*, ed. M. R. James, revised by C. N. L. Brooke and R. A. B. Mynors (Oxford, 1983).

Weiss, Judith (ed.), *Boeve de Haumtone and Gui de Warewic: Two Anglo-Norman Romances* (Tempe, 2008).

Whaley, Diana (ed.), *Poetry from the Kings' Sagas 1: From Mythical Times to c.1035*, Skaldic Poetry of the Scandinavian Middle Ages 1 (Turnhout, 2012), 2 vols.

William of Jumièges, *The Gesta Normannorum Ducum of William of Jumièges, Orderic Vitalis, and Robert of Torigni*, ed. Elisabeth M. C. van Houts (Oxford, 1992–5), 2 vols.

William of Malmesbury, *Gesta Regum Anglorum*, ed. R. A. B. Mynors, R. M. Thomson and M. Winterbottom (Oxford, 1998), 2 vols.

—— *Gesta Pontificum Anglorum*, ed. Michael Winterbottom and R. M. Thomson (Oxford, 2007), 2 vols.

William of Newburgh, *Historia Regum Anglicarum*, in Richard Howlett (ed.), *Chronicles of the Reigns of Stephen, Henry II, and Richard I* (London, 1884–9), 4 vols.

William of Poitiers, *The Gesta Guillelmi of William of Poitiers*, ed. R. H. C. Davis and Marjorie Chibnall (Oxford, 1998).

Winterbottom, Michael (ed.), *Three Lives of English Saints* (Toronto, 1972).

Wise, John and W. Mackreth Noble, *Ramsey Abbey, Its Rise and Fall* (Huntingdon, 1882).

Zupitza, J. (ed.), *The Romance of Guy of Warwick: the second or 15th-century version*, Early English Text Society Extra Series 25, 26 (London, 1875–6; reprinted as one volume, 1966).

—— (ed.), *The Romance of Guy of Warwick, edited from the Auchinleck MS. in the Advocates' Library, Edinburgh and from MS. 107 in Caius College, Cambridge*, Early English Text Society Extra Series 42, 49, 59 (London, 1883–91, reprinted as one volume, 1966).

SECONDARY SOURCES

Abrams, Lesley, 'The Anglo-Saxons and the Christianization of Scandinavia', *Anglo-Saxon England* 24 (1995), pp. 213–49.

—— 'Conversion and assimilation', in Dawn M. Hadley and Julian D. Richards (eds), *Cultures in Contact: Scandinavian Settlement in England in the Ninth and Tenth Centuries* (Turnhout, 2000), pp. 135–53.

—— 'The conversion of the Danelaw', in James Graham-Campbell, Michael Hall, Judith Jesch and David N. Parsons (eds), *Vikings and the Danelaw* (Oxford, 2001), pp. 31–44.

Abrams, Lesley and David N. Parsons, 'Place-names and the history of Scandinavian settlement in England', in J. Hines, A. Lane and M. Redknap (eds), *Land, Sea and Home* (Leeds, 2004), pp. 379–431.

Ailes, Marianne, '*Gui de Warewic* in its manuscript context', in Alison Wiggins and Rosalind Field (eds), *Guy of Warwick: Icon and Ancestor* (Cambridge, 2007), pp. 12–26.

Aird, William M., *St Cuthbert and the Normans: The Church of Durham, 1071–1153* (Woodbridge, 1998).

Allison, K. J., *A History of the County of York East Riding: Volume 1, the City of Kingston Upon Hull* (London, 1969).

Ashdown, Margaret, 'The single combat in certain cycles of English and Scandinavian tradition and romance', *The Modern Language Review* 17 (1922), pp. 113–30.

—— 'An Icelandic account of the survival of Harold Godwinson', in Peter Clemoes (ed.), *The Anglo-Saxons: Studies in Some Aspects of their History and Culture Presented to Bruce Dickins* (London, 1959), pp. 122–36.

Ashe, Laura, *Fiction and History in England, 1066–1200* (Cambridge, 2007).

—— 'Harold Godwineson', in Neil Cartlidge (ed.), *Heroes and Anti-Heroes in Medieval Romance* (Cambridge, 2012), pp. 59–80.

Ashman Rowe, Elizabeth, 'Helpful Danes and pagan Irishmen: saga fantasies of the Viking Age in the British Isles', *Viking and Medieval Scandinavia* 5 (2009), pp. 1–21.

—— '*Ragnars saga loðbrókar, Ragnarssona þáttr*, and the political world of Haukr Erlendsson', in Agneta Ney, Ármann Jakobsson, and Annette Lassen (eds), *Fornaldarsagaerne: Myter og virkelighed* (Copenhagen, 2009), pp. 347–60.

—— *Vikings in the West: The Legend of Ragnarr Loðbrók and His Sons* (Wien, 2012).

Bailey, Richard N., *Viking Age Sculpture in Northern England* (London, 1980).

Bale, Anthony (ed.), *St Edmund, King and Martyr: Changing Images of a Medieval Saint* (Woodbridge, 2009).

Barlow, Frank, *The Godwins: The Rise and Fall of a Noble Dynasty* (London, 2003).

Barrett, W. H., *Tales from the Fens* (London, 1963).

Barron, W. R. J., 'The penalties for treason in medieval life and literature', *Journal of Medieval History* 7 (1981), pp. 187–202.

Barrow, Julia, 'Danish ferocity and abandoned monasteries: the twelfth-century view', in Martin Brett and David A. Woodman (eds), *The Long Twelfth-Century View of the Anglo-Saxon Past* (London and New York, 2015), pp. 77–93.

Bates, David, *William the Conqueror* (New Haven, 2016).

Bates, David and Robert Liddiard (eds), *East Anglia and its North Sea World in the Middle Ages* (Woodbridge, 2015).

Baxter, Ron, 'St Peter, Northampton', *The Corpus of Romanesque Sculpture in Britain and Ireland*. Available at http://www.crsbi.ac.uk/site/248/ (accessed 2 June 2017).

Bell, Alexander, 'Buern Bucecarle in "Gaimar"', *Modern Language Review* 27 (1932), pp. 168–74.

—— 'Gaimar's early "Danish" Kings', *Publications of the Modern Language Association of America* 65 (1950), pp. 601–40.

Bell, Kimberly K. and Julie Nelson Couch (eds), *The Texts and Contexts of Oxford, Bodleian Library, MS Laud Misc. 108: The Shaping of English Vernacular Narrative* (Boston, 2011).

Bibire, P., 'North Sea language contacts in the Early Middle Ages: English and Norse', in T. R. Liszka and L. E. M. Walker (eds), *The North Sea World in the Middle Ages: Studies in the Cultural History of North-Western Europe* (Dublin, 2001), pp. 88–107.

Biddle, Martin, 'Excavations at Winchester 1965: fourth interim report', *The Antiquaries Journal* 46/2 (1966), pp. 308–32.

Biddle, Martin, and Birthe Kjølbye-Biddle, 'Danish royal burials in Winchester: Cnut and his family', in Ryan Lavelle and Simon Roffey (eds), *Danes in Wessex: The Scandinavian Impact on Southern England, c.800–c.1100* (Oxford, 2016), pp. 212–49.

Bjork, Robert E., 'Scandinavian relations', in P. Pulsiano and E. Treharne (eds), *A Companion to Anglo-Saxon Literature* (Oxford, 2001), pp. 388–99.

Blair, John, *Anglo-Saxon Oxfordshire* (Oxford, 1998).

Bolton, Timothy, 'Was the family of Earl Siward and Earl Waltheof a lost line of the ancestors of the Danish royal family?', *Nottingham Medieval Studies* 51 (2007), pp. 41–71.

—— *The Empire of Cnut the Great: Conquest and the Consolidation of Power in Northern Europe in the Early Eleventh Century* (Leiden, 2009).

—— *Cnut the Great* (New Haven, 2017).

Brett, Martin and David A. Woodman (eds), *The Long Twelfth-Century View of the Anglo-Saxon Past* (London, 2016).

Briggs, Katherine M. (ed.), *A Dictionary of British Folk-Tales in the English Language* (London, 1971).

Brink, Stefan, 'Law and legal customs in Viking Age Scandinavia', in Judith Jesch (ed.), *The Scandinavians from the Vendel Period to the Tenth Century: An Ethnographic Perspective* (Woodbridge, 2012), pp. 87–127.

Brooks, Nicholas, *The Early History of the Church of Canterbury: Christ Church from 597 to 1066* (Leicester, 1984).

Bugge, Alexander, 'Havelok and Olaf Tryggvason: a contribution towards the further understanding of the kings' sagas', *Saga-Book of the Viking Society* VI (1910), pp. 257–95.

Bull, Edvard, 'The Cultus of Norwegian Saints in England and Scotland', *Saga-Book of the Viking Society* VIII (1913–14), pp. 135–48.

Cameron, Kenneth and John Insley, *A Dictionary of Lincolnshire Place-Names* (Nottingham, 1998).

Camp, Cynthia Turner, *Anglo-Saxon Saints' Lives as History-Writing in Late Medieval England* (Cambridge, 2015).

Campbell, James, 'Some Twelfth-Century Views of the Anglo-Saxon Past', in *Essays in Anglo-Saxon History* (London, 1986), pp. 209–28.

Clark, Cecily, 'Onomastics', in Richard M. Hogg (ed.), *The Cambridge History of the English Language, Volume 1* (Cambridge, 1992), pp. 452–89.

Colker, M. L., *Trinity College Library, Dublin: Descriptive Catalogue of Medieval and Renaissance Latin Manuscripts* (Aldershot, 1991), 2 vols.

Cooper, Helen, 'When romance comes true', in Neil Cartlidge (ed.), *Boundaries in Medieval Romance* (Woodbridge, 2008), pp. 13–27.

Cooper, Janet (ed.), *The Battle of Maldon: Fiction and Fact* (London, 1993).

Couch, Julie Nelson, 'The vulnerable hero: Havelok and the revision of romance', *Chaucer Review* 42 (2008), pp. 330–52.

Coupland, Simon, 'The rod of God's wrath or the people of God's wrath? The Carolingian theology of the Viking invasions', *Journal of Ecclesiastical History* 42/4 (1991), pp. 535–54.

Cownie, Emma, *Religious Patronage in Anglo-Norman England 1066–1135* (Woodbridge, 1998).

Cox, Barrie, 'Yarboroughs in Lindsey', *Journal of the English Place-Name Society* 28 (1995–6), pp. 50–60.

Crane, Ronald S., 'The vogue of Guy of Warwick from the close of the Middle Ages to the Romantic revival', *Publications of the Modern Language Association of America* 30 (1915), pp. 125–94.

Crane, Susan, *Insular Romance: Politics, Faith and Culture in Anglo-Norman and Middle English Literature* (Berkeley, 1986).

Croxton-Smith, Patricia, 'The site of the Battle of Assandun, 1016', *Saffron Walden Historical Journal* 3 (2002).

Cubitt, C., 'Archbishop Dunstan: a prophet in politics?' in Julia Barrow and Andrew Wareham (eds), *Myth, Rulership, Church and Charters: Essays in Honour of Nicholas Brooks* (Aldershot, 2008), pp. 145–66.

Dalton, Paul, 'The date of Geoffrey Gaimar's *Estoire des Engleis*, the connections of his patrons, and the politics of Stephen's reign', *The Chaucer Review* 42 (2007), pp. 23–47.

Dance, Richard, *Words Derived from Old Norse in Early Middle English: Studies in the Vocabulary of the South-West Midlands Texts* (Tempe, 2003).

—— 'North Sea currents: Old English–Old Norse relations, literary and linguistic', *Literature Compass* 1 (2004), ME 117, pp. 1–10.

Danielli, Mary, 'Initiation ceremonial from Old Norse literature', *Folklore* 56/2 (1945), pp. 229–45.

Davidson, Hilda R. Ellis, 'The hill of the dragon: Anglo-Saxon burial mounds in literature and archaeology', *Folklore* 61/4 (1950), pp. 169–85.

Dehaisnes, Chrétien, *Manuscrits de la bibliothèque de Douai* (Paris, 1878).

Demidoff, Lene, 'The death of Sven Forkbeard – in reality and later tradition', *Medieval Scandinavia* 11 (1978–9), pp. 30–47.

Denholm-Young, N., 'An early thirteenth-century Anglo-Norman MS', *The Bodleian Quarterly Record* 6 (1931), pp. 225–30.

Dickins, Bruce, 'The cult of S. Olave in the British Isles', *Saga-Book of the Viking Society* XII (1937–45), pp. 53–80.

Downham, Clare, *Viking Kings of Britain and Ireland: The Dynasty of Ívarr to A.D. 1014* (Edinburgh, 2007).

Dunn, Charles W., '*Havelok* and Anlaf Cuaran', in J. B. Bessinger and R. P. Creed (eds), *Medieval and Linguistic Studies in Honour of Francis Peabody Magoun, Jr* (London, 1965), pp. 244–9.

Eckardt, Hella, et al., 'The Bartlow Hills in context', *Proceedings of the Cambridge Antiquarian Society* XCVIII (2009), pp. 47–64.

Ellis, Hilda Roderick, *The Road to Hel: A Study of the Conception of the Dead in Old Norse Literature* (New York, 1968).

Fell, Christine, 'Old English *wicing*: a question of semantics', *Proceedings of the British Academy* 72 (1986), pp. 295–316.

Fellows Jensen, Gillian, *Scandinavian Personal Names in Lincolnshire and Yorkshire* (Copenhagen, 1968).

—— 'Scandinavian influence on the place-names of England', in P. S. Ureland and G. Broderick (eds), *Language Contact in the British Isles* (Tübingen, 1991), pp. 337–54.

—— *The Vikings and Their Victims: The Verdict of the Names* (London, 1995).

—— 'The myth of Harold II's survival in the Scandinavian sources', in Gale R. Owen-Crocker (ed.), *King Harold II and the Bayeux Tapestry* (Woodbridge, 2005), pp. 53–64.

Fewster, Carol, *Traditionality and Genre in Middle English Romance* (Cambridge, 1987).

Field, Rosalind, 'Romance as history, history as romance', in Maldwyn Mills, Jennifer Fellows and Carol M. Meale (eds), *Romance in Medieval England* (Cambridge, 1991), pp. 163–73.

—— '*Waldef* and the matter of/with England', in Judith Weiss, Jennifer Fellows and Morgan Dickson (eds), *Medieval Insular Romance: Translation and Innovation* (Cambridge, 2000), pp. 25–39.

—— 'From *Gui* to *Guy*: the fashioning of a popular romance', in Alison Wiggins and Rosalind Field (eds), *Guy of Warwick: Icon and Ancestor* (Cambridge, 2007), pp. 44–60.

Fjalldal, Magnús, *Anglo-Saxon England in Icelandic Medieval Texts* (Toronto, 2005).

Forte, Angelo, Richard Oram and Frederik Pedersen, *Viking Empires* (Cambridge, 2005).

Fox, Adam, *Oral and Literate Culture in England, 1500–1700* (Oxford, 2000).

Frank, Roberta, 'Skaldic verse and the date of *Beowulf*', in Colin Chase (ed.), *The Dating of Beowulf* (Toronto, 1981), pp. 123–39.

—— 'Viking atrocity and skaldic verse: the rite of the blood-eagle', *English Historical Review* 99 (1984), pp. 332–43.

—— 'Anglo-Scandinavian poetic relations', *ANQ* 3:2 (1990), pp. 74–9.

—— 'King Cnut in the verse of his skalds', in Alexander R. Rumble (ed.), *The Reign of Cnut: King of England, Denmark and Norway* (London, 1994), pp. 106–24.

Frankis, John, 'Views of Anglo-Saxon England in post-Conquest vernacular writing', in Herbert Pilch (ed.), *Orality and Literacy in Early Middle English* (Tübingen, 1996), pp. 227–47.

—— 'Sidelights on post-Conquest Canterbury: towards a context for an Old Norse runic charm ("DR" 419)', *Nottingham Medieval Studies* 44 (2000), pp. 1–27.

Freeman, Edward A., *The History of the Norman Conquest of England: Its Causes and Results* (Oxford, 1870–6), 6 vols.

Freeman, Elizabeth, 'Geffrei Gaimar, vernacular historiography, and the assertion of authority', *Studies in Philology* 93 (1996), pp. 188–206.

Fuglesang, Signe Horn, *Some Aspects of the Ringerike Style: A Phase of 11th-Century Scandinavian Art* (Odense, 1980).

Galloway, Andrew, 'Writing history in England', in David Wallace (ed.), *The Cambridge History of Medieval English Literature* (Cambridge, 1999), pp. 255–83.

Garmonsway, G. N., *Canute and his Empire* (London, 1964).

Garmonsway, G. N. and Jacqueline Simpson, *Beowulf and Its Analogues* (London, 1980).

Gazzoli, Paul, 'Anglo-Danish relations in the later eleventh century' (unpublished DPhil thesis, University of Cambridge, 2010).

Gelling, Margaret, *The Place-Names of Berkshire* (Cambridge, 1974).

——— *Signposts to the Past* (Chichester, 1988).

Gelling, Margaret and Ann Cole, *The Landscape of Place-Names* (Stamford, 2000).

Gerchow, Jan, 'Prayers for King Cnut: the liturgical commemoration of a conqueror', in Carola Hicks (ed.), *England in the Eleventh Century: Proceedings of the 1990 Harlaxton Symposium* (Stamford, 1992), pp. 219–38.

Gillett, Edward, *A History of Grimsby* (London, 1970).

Gillingham, John, *The English in the Twelfth Century: Imperialism, National Identity, and Political Values* (Woodbridge, 2000).

Goddard Leach, Henry, *Angevin Britain and Scandinavia* (London, 1921).

Gransden, Antonia, *Legends, Tradition and History in Medieval England* (London, 1992).

Gray, H. St George, 'Notes on "Danes' Skins"', *Saga-Book of the Viking Society* V (1907–8), pp. 218–29.

Grinsell, L. V., *The Rollright Stones and their Folklore* (St Peter Port, 1977).

Gutch, E. and Mabel Peacock, *Examples of Printed Folk-Lore Concerning Lincolnshire*, County Folk-Lore 5 (London, 1908).

Hadley, Dawn M., '"And they proceeded to plough and support themselves": the Scandinavian settlement of England', *Anglo-Norman Studies* 19 (1997), pp. 69–96.

——— '"Cockles amongst the wheat": the Scandinavian settlement of England', in William O. Frazer and Andrew Tyrrell (eds), *Social Identity in Early Medieval Britain* (London and New York, 2000), pp. 111–35.

——— *The Vikings in England: Settlement, Society and Culture* (Manchester, 2006).

Hadley, Dawn M. and Julian D. Richards (eds), *Cultures in Contact: Scandinavian Settlement in England in the Ninth and Tenth Centuries* (Turnhout, 2000).

Halsall, Guy, *Warfare and Society in the Barbarian West, 450–900* (London, 2003).

Hart, Cyril, 'The East Anglian Chronicle', *Journal of Medieval History* 7 (1981), pp. 249–82.

——— *The Danelaw* (London, 1992).

Hayward, J., 'Hereward the outlaw', *Journal of Medieval History* 14 (1988), pp. 293–304.

Hayward, Paul Anthony, 'Sanctity and lordship in twelfth-century England: Saint Albans, Durham, and the cult of Saint Oswine, King and Martyr', *Viator* 30 (1999), pp. 105–44.

—— 'Geoffrey of Wells' *Liber de infantia sancti Edmundi* and the "Anarchy" of King Stephen's reign', in Anthony Bale (ed.), *St Edmund, King and Martyr: Changing Images of a Medieval Saint* (Woodbridge, 2009), pp. 63–86.

Heslop, T. A., 'The production of *de luxe* manuscripts and the patronage of King Cnut and Queen Emma', *Anglo-Saxon England* 19 (1990), pp. 151–95.

Hibbard, Laura A., *Mediæval Romance in England: A Study of the Sources and Analogues of the Non-Cyclic Metrical Romances* (New York, 1960).

Hines, J., 'Scandinavian English: a creole in context', in P. S. Ureland and G. Broderick (eds), *Language Contact in the British Isles* (Tübingen, 1991), pp. 403–27.

Hobson, J., 'National-ethnic narratives in eleventh-century literary representations of Cnut', *Anglo-Saxon England* 43 (2014), pp. 267–95.

Hofmann, Dietrich, *Nordisch-englische Lehnbeziehungen der Wikingerzeit* (Copenhagen, 1955).

Holman, Katherine, *The Northern Conquest: Vikings in Britain and Ireland* (Oxford, 2007).

Holt, J. C., *Robin Hood* (London, 1982).

van Houts, Elisabeth, 'Scandinavian influence in Norman literature of the eleventh century', *Anglo-Norman Studies* 6 (1983), pp. 107–21.

—— 'Genre aspects of the use of oral information in medieval historiography', in B. Frank, T. Haye and D. Tophinke (eds), *Gattungen mittelalterlicher Schriftlichkeit* (Tübingen, 1997), pp. 297–311.

—— 'Hereward and Flanders', *Anglo-Saxon England* 28 (1999), pp. 201–23.

—— *Memory and Gender in Medieval Europe, 900–1200* (Basingstoke, 2009).

Howard, Ian, *Swein Forkbeard's Invasions and the Danish Conquest of England 991–1017* (Woodbridge, 2003).

Huntington, Joanna, 'The taming of the laity: writing Waltheof and rebellion in the twelfth century', *Anglo-Norman Studies* 32 (2010), pp. 79–95.

Hutton, Ronald, *The Stations of the Sun: A History of the Ritual Year in Britain* (Oxford, 1996).

Innes, Matthew, 'Danelaw identities: ethnicity, regionalism and political allegiance', in D. M. Hadley and Julian D. Richards (eds), *Cultures in Contact: Scandinavian Settlement in England in the Ninth and Tenth Centuries* (Turnhout, 2000), pp. 65–88.

James, M. R., *A Descriptive Catalogue of the Manuscripts in the Library of Pembroke College, Cambridge* (Cambridge, 1905).

Jesch, Judith, 'England and *Orkneyinga saga*' in C. Batey, J. Jesch and C. Morris (eds), *The Viking Age in Caithness, Orkney and the North Atlantic* (Edinburgh, 1993), pp. 222–39.

—— 'Knútr in poetry and history', in Michael Dallapiazza et al. (eds), *International Scandinavian and Medieval Studies in Memory of Gerd Wolfgang Weber* (Trieste, 2000), pp. 243–56.

—— 'Skaldic verse in Scandinavian England', in James Graham-Campbell, Michael Hall, Judith Jesch and David N. Parsons (eds), *Vikings and the Danelaw* (Oxford, 2001), pp. 313–25.

—— 'Scandinavians and "cultural paganism" in late Anglo-Saxon England', in Paul Cavill (ed.), *The Christian Tradition in Anglo-Saxon England* (Cambridge, 2004), pp. 55–67.

John, Eric, 'The *Encomium Emmae Reginae*: a riddle and a solution', *Bulletin of the John Rylands University Library of Manchester* 63 (1980), pp. 58–94.

—— 'The Annals of St Neots and the defeat of the Vikings', in R. Evans (ed.), *Lordship and Learning: Studies in Memory of Trevor Aston* (Woodbridge, 2004), pp. 51–62.

Jón Stefansson, 'The oldest known list of Scandinavian names', *Saga-Book of the Viking Society* IV (1905–6), pp. 296–311.

Jones, Gwyn, *Kings, Beasts and Heroes* (London, 1972).

Kabir, Ananya J., 'Forging an oral style? *Havelok* and the fiction of orality', *Studies in Philology* 98 (2001), pp. 18–48.

Kapelle, William E., *The Norman Conquest of the North: The Region and Its Transformation, 1100–1135* (London, 1979).

Keen, Maurice, *The Outlaws of Medieval Legend* (London and New York, 1961, rev. 2000).

Ker, N. R., *Catalogue of Manuscripts Containing Anglo-Saxon* (Oxford, 1957).

Ker, N. R. and A. J. Piper (eds), *Medieval Manuscripts in British Libraries* (Oxford, 1969–2002), 5 vols.

Keynes, Simon, *The Diplomas of King Æthelred 'the Unready' 978–1016: A Study in their Use as Historical Evidence* (Cambridge, 1980).

—— 'Cnut's earls', in Alexander R. Rumble (ed.), *The Reign of Cnut: King of England, Denmark and Norway* (London, 1994), pp. 43–88.

—— 'The Vikings in England, *c*.790–1016', in Peter Sawyer (ed.), *The Oxford Illustrated History of the Vikings* (Oxford, 1997), pp. 48–82.

—— 'The declining reputation of King Æthelred the Unready', in D. A. E. Pelteret (ed.), *Anglo-Saxon History: Basic Readings* (New York, 2000), pp. 157–90.

—— 'Apocalypse then: England A.D. 1000', in Przemysław Urbańczyk (ed.), *Europe Around the Year 1000* (Warsaw, 2001), pp. 247–70.

—— 'The massacre of St Brice's Day (13 November 1002)', in N. Lund (ed.), *Beretning fra seksogtyvende tværfaglige vikingesymposium* (Aarhus, 2007), pp. 32–67.

—— 'The burial of King Æthelred the Unready at St Paul's', in David Roffe (ed.), *The English and Their Legacy, 900–1200: Essays in Honour of Ann Williams* (Woodbridge, 2012), pp. 129–48.

Kjølbye-Biddle, Birthe and R. I. Page, 'A Scandinavian rune-stone from Winchester', *The Antiquaries Journal* 55/2 (1975), pp. 389–94.

Kleinman, Scott, 'The legend of Havelok the Dane and the historiography of East Anglia', *Studies in Philology* 100 (2003), pp. 245–77.

Lavelle, Ryan, *Æthelred II: King of the English, 978–1016* (Stroud, 2002).

Lawson, M. K., 'Archbishop Wulfstan and the homiletic element in the laws of Æthelred II and Cnut', in Alexander R. Rumble (ed.), *The Reign of Cnut: King of England, Denmark and Norway* (London, 1994), pp. 141–64.

—— *Cnut: England's Viking King, 1016–35* (Stroud, 2011).

Lendinara, Patrizia, 'The Battle of Brunanburh in later histories and romances', *Anglia* 117 (1999), pp. 201–35.

Licence, Tom, 'Goscelin of St. Bertin and the Life of St. Eadwold of Cerne', *Journal of Medieval Latin* 16 (2006), pp. 182–207.

—— 'History and hagiography in the late eleventh century: the life and work of Herman the Archdeacon, monk of Bury St Edmunds', *English Historical Review* 124/508 (2009), pp. 516–44.

—— (ed.), *Bury St Edmunds and the Norman Conquest* (Woodbridge, 2014).

Lind, E. H., *Norsk-isländska personbinamn från medeltiden* (Uppsala, 1920–5).

Liuzza, R. M., 'Representation and readership in the Middle English *Havelok*', *Journal of English and Germanic Philology* 93 (1994), pp. 504–19.

Livingston, Michael (ed.), *The Battle of Brunanburh: A Casebook* (Exeter, 2011).

Loomis, Grant, 'The growth of the Saint Edmund legend', *Harvard Studies and Notes in Philology and Literature* 14 (1932), pp. 83–115.

Loyn, H. R., *The Vikings in Britain* (London, 1977).

Lukman, Niels, 'The raven banner and the changing ravens: a Viking miracle from Carolingian court poetry to saga and Arthurian romance', *Classica et Medievalia* 19 (1958), pp. 133–51.

—— 'Ragnarr Lothbrok, Sigifrid, and the saints of Flanders', *Medieval Scandinavia* 9 (1976), pp. 7–50.

Madan, F. and H. H. E. Craster, *A Summary Catalogue of Western Manuscripts in the Bodleian Library at Oxford*, vol. 6 (Oxford, 1924).

Marafioti, Nicole, *The King's Body: Burial and Succession in Late Anglo-Saxon England* (Toronto, 2014).

Margeson, Sue, 'The Völsung legend in medieval art', in Flemming G. Andersen et al. (eds), *Medieval Iconography and Narrative: A Symposium* (Odense, 1980), pp. 183–211.

Mason, Emma, 'Legends of the Beauchamps' ancestors: the use of baronial propaganda in medieval England', *Journal of Medieval History* 10 (1984), pp. 25–40.

—— *The House of Godwine: The History of a Dynasty* (London, 2004).

Mason Bradbury, Nancy, 'The traditional origins of *Havelok the Dane*', *Studies in Philology* 90 (1993), pp. 115–42.

McGuigan, Neil, 'Ælla and the descendants of Ivar: politics and legend in the Viking Age', *Northern History* 52 (2015), pp. 20–34.

McKinnell, John, 'The context of *Völundarkviða*', *Saga-Book of the Viking Society* XXIII (1990–3), pp. 1–27.

—— 'Eddic poetry in Anglo-Scandinavian northern England', in James Graham-Campbell, Michael Hall, Judith Jesch and David N. Parsons (eds), *Vikings and the Danelaw* (Oxford, 2001), pp. 327–44.

—— *Meeting the Other in Norse Myth and Legend* (Cambridge, 2005).

McTurk, Rory, *Studies in Ragnars saga Loðbrókar and its Major Scandinavian Analogues* (Oxford, 1991).

—— *Chaucer and the Norse and Celtic Worlds* (Aldershot, 2005).

Mills, Maldwyn, 'Techniques of translation in the Middle English versions of *Guy of Warwick*', in Roger Ellis (ed.), *The Medieval Translator II* (London, 1991), pp. 209–29.

Morris, Christopher J., *Marriage and Murder in Eleventh-Century Northumbria: A Study of 'De Obsessione Dunelmi'* (York, 1992).

Napier, A. S. and W. H. Stevenson (eds), *The Crawford Collection of Early Charters and Documents now in the Bodleian Library* (Oxford, 1895).

Niedorf, Leonard, '*II Æthelred* and the politics of *The Battle of Maldon*', *Journal of English and Germanic Philology* 111 (2012), pp. 451–73.

O'Donoghue, Heather, *Old Norse-Icelandic Literature: A Short Introduction* (Oxford, 2004).

—— *From Asgard to Valhalla: The Remarkable History of the Norse Myths* (London, 2007).

—— *English Poetry and Old Norse Myth: A History* (Oxford, 2014).

Olrik, Axel, 'Siward Digri of Northumberland: a Viking saga of the Danes in England', *Saga-Book of the Viking Society* VI (1908–9), pp. 212–37.

—— *The Heroic Legends of Denmark*, trans. Lee M. Hollander (New York, 1919).

Olsen, Alexandra H., 'The valkyrie reflex in Havelok the Dane', in Loren C. Gruber (ed.), *Essays on Old, Middle, Modern English and Old Icelandic, in honour of Raymond P. Tripp, Jr.* (Lewiston, NY, 2000), pp. 317–35.

Orchard, Andy, 'Literary background to the *Encomium Emmae Reginae*', *Journal of Medieval Latin* 11 (2001), pp. 157–84.

Page, R. I., '*A Most Vile People': Early English Historians on the Vikings* (London, 1987).

—— *Chronicles of the Vikings: Records, Memorials and Myths* (London, 1995).

Palmer, James, 'Apocalyptic outsiders and their uses in the Early Medieval West', in W. Brandes, F. Schmieder and R. Voß (eds), *Peoples of the Apocalypse: Eschatological Beliefs and Political Scenarios* (Berlin and Boston, 2016), pp. 307–20.

Parker, Eleanor, 'Pilgrim and patron: Cnut in post-Conquest historical writing', *The Medieval Chronicle* 9 (2014), pp. 271–95.

—— 'Siward the dragon-slayer: mythmaking in Anglo-Scandinavian England', *Neophilologus* 98 (2014), pp. 481–93.

—— 'Havelok and the Danes in England: history, legend, and romance', *Review of English Studies* 67 (2016), pp. 428–47.

—— 'So very memorable a matter: Anglo-Danish history and the *Encomium Emmae Reginae*', in Ian Giles et al. (eds), *Beyond Borealism: New Perspectives on the North* (London, 2016), pp. 41–53.

Parker, Joanne, *England's Darling: The Victorian Cult of Alfred the Great* (Manchester, 2007).

Phelpstead, Carl, 'King, martyr and virgin: *Imitatio Christi* in Ælfric's *Life of St Edmund*', in Anthony Bale (ed.), *St Edmund, King and Martyr: Changing Images of a Medieval Saint* (Woodbridge, 2009), pp. 27–44.

Pinner, Rebecca, *The Cult of St Edmund in Medieval East Anglia* (Woodbridge, 2015).

Poole, Russell, 'Skaldic verse and Anglo-Saxon history: some aspects of the period 1009–1016', *Speculum* 62 (1987), pp. 265–98.

—— *Viking Poems on War and Peace: A Study in Skaldic Narrative* (Toronto, 1991).

Pulsiano, Phillip, '"Danish men's words are worse than murder": Viking guile and *The Battle of Maldon*', *Journal of English and German Philology* 96 (1997), pp. 13–25.

Radulescu, Raluca L., 'Genealogy in insular romance', in Raluca L. Radulescu and Edward Donald Kennedy (eds), *Broken Lines: Genealogical Literature in Late-Medieval Britain and France* (Turnhout, 2008), pp. 7–25.

Rand, Kari Anne, *The Index of Middle English Prose, Handlist XVIII: Manuscripts in the Library of Pembroke College, Cambridge, and the Fitzwilliam Museum* (Cambridge, 2006).

Rauer, Christine, *Beowulf and the Dragon: Parallels and Analogues* (Cambridge, 2000).

Reiss, Edmund, '*Havelok the Dane* and Norse mythology', *Modern Language Quarterly* 27 (1966), pp. 115–24.

Richmond, Velma Bourgeois, *The Popularity of Middle English Romance* (Bowling Green, 1975).

—— *The Legend of Guy of Warwick* (New York, 1996).

Ridyard, Susan J., *The Royal Saints of Anglo-Saxon England: A Study of West Saxon and East Anglian Cults* (Cambridge, 1988).

Roach, Levi, *Æthelred the Unready* (New Haven, 2016).

Robinson, Fred C., '*The Tomb of Beowulf*' and Other Essays on Old English (Oxford, 1993).

Rodwell, Warwick, 'The Battle of *Assandun* and its memorial church', in Janet Cooper (ed.), *The Battle of Maldon: Fiction and Fact* (London, 1993), pp. 127–58.

Rollason, David, 'Lists of saints' resting-places in Anglo-Saxon England', *Anglo-Saxon England* 7 (1978), pp. 61–93.

—— *Northumbria, 500–1100: Creation and Destruction of a Kingdom* (Cambridge, 2003).

Rouse, Robert Allen, *The Idea of Anglo-Saxon England in Middle English Romance* (Cambridge, 2005).

Rubenstein, Jay, 'The life and writings of Osbern of Canterbury', in R. Eales and R. Sharpe (eds), *Canterbury and the Norman Conquest: Churches, Saints and Scholars, 1066–1109* (London, 1995), pp. 27–40.

—— 'Liturgy against history: the competing visions of Lanfranc and Eadmer of Canterbury', *Speculum* 74 (1999), pp. 279–309.

Sanmark, Alexandra and Sarah Semple, 'Places of assembly: new discoveries in Sweden and England', *Fornvännen* 103 (2008), pp. 245–59.

Sawyer, Peter H., *The Age of the Vikings* (London, 1971).

—— 'Swein Forkbeard and the historians', in Ian Wood and G. A. Loud (eds), *Church and Chronicle in the Middle Ages: Essays Presented to John Taylor* (London, 1991), pp. 26–40.

Schmidt, Paul Gerhard, 'Biblisches und hagiographisches Kolorit in den *Gesta Herwardi*', in Katherine Walsh and Diana Wood (eds), *The Bible in the ·Medieval World: Essays in Memory of Beryl Smalley* (Oxford, 1985), pp. 85–95.

Scott, Forrest S., 'Earl Waltheof of Northumbria', *Archaeologia Aeliana* 30 (1952), pp. 149–215.

—— 'Valþjófr jarl: an English earl in Icelandic sources', *Saga-Book of the Viking Society* XIV (1953–7), pp. 78–94.

Scragg, Donald (ed.), *The Battle of Maldon AD 991* (Oxford, 1991).

—— *The Return of the Vikings: The Battle of Maldon 991* (Stroud, 2006).

Semple, Sarah, 'A fear of the past: the place of the prehistoric burial mound in the ideology of Middle and Later Anglo-Saxon England', *World Archaeology* 30/1 (1998), pp. 109–26.

—— *Perceptions of the Prehistoric in Anglo-Saxon England: Religion, Ritual, and Rulership in the Landscape* (Oxford, 2013).

Short, Ian, 'Patrons and polyglots: French literature in twelfth-century England', *Anglo-Norman Studies* 14 (1992), pp. 229–49.

Simpson, Jacqueline, *Folklore of Sussex* (Stroud, 2013).

Smith, A. H., 'The early literary relations of England and Scandinavia', *Saga-Book of the Viking Society* XI (1928–36), pp. 215–32.

Smyth, Alfred P., *Scandinavian York and Dublin: The History and Archaeology of Two Related Viking Kingdoms* (Dublin, 1975–9), 2 vols.

—— *Scandinavian Kings in the British Isles 850–880* (Oxford, 1977).

Southern, R. W., *Saint Anselm and his Biographer: A Study of Monastic Life and Thought 1059–c.1130* (Cambridge, 1963).

—— 'Aspects of the European tradition of historical writing: 4, The sense of the past', *Transactions of the Royal Historical Society* 23 (1973), pp. 243–63.

Speed, Diane, 'The construction of the nation in medieval English romance', in Carol M. Meale (ed.), *Readings in Medieval English Romance* (Cambridge, 1994), pp. 135–57.

Spence, John, 'Genealogies of noble families in Anglo-Norman', in Raluca L. Radulescu and Edward Donald Kennedy (eds), *Broken Lines: Genealogical Literature in Late-Medieval Britain and France* (Turnhout, 2008), pp. 63–77.

—— *Reimagining History in Anglo-Norman Prose Chronicles* (Woodbridge, 2013).

Stafford, Pauline, *Queen Emma and Queen Edith: Queenship and Women's Power in Eleventh-Century England* (Oxford, 2001).

Stenton, Frank M., 'The Danes in England', *Proceedings of the British Academy* XIII (Oxford, 1927).

Stitt, J. Michael, *Beowulf and the Bear's Son: Epic, Saga, and Fairytale in Northern Germanic Tradition* (New York & London, 1992).

Storm, Gustav, 'Havelok the Dane and the Norse king Olaf Kuaran', *Englische Studien* III (1880), pp. 533–5.

Swanton, Michael J., "'Dane-skins": excoriation in early England', *Folklore* 87/1 (1976), pp. 21–8.

Taylor, Paul Beekman, *Sharing Story: Medieval Norse–English Literary Relationships* (New York, 1998).

Tengvik, Gösta, *Old English Bynames* (Uppsala, 1938).

Thomas, Hugh, *The English and the Normans: Ethnic Hostility, Assimilation, and Identity 1066–c.1220* (Oxford, 2003).

Townend, Matthew, '*Ella*: an Old English name in Old Norse poetry', *Nomina* 20 (1997), pp. 23–35.

—— 'Contextualizing the *Knútsdrápur*: skaldic praise-poetry at the court of Cnut', *Anglo-Saxon England* 30 (2001), pp. 145–79.

—— *Language and History in Viking Age England: Linguistic Relations between Speakers of Old Norse and Old English* (Turnhout, 2002).

—— 'Whatever happened to York Viking poetry? Memory, tradition and the transmission of skaldic verse', *Saga-Book of the Viking Society* XXVII (2003), pp. 48–90.

—— 'Knútr and the cult of St Óláfr: poetry and patronage in eleventh-century Norway and England', *Viking and Medieval Scandinavia* 1 (2005), pp. 251–79.

—— 'Cnut's poets: an Old Norse literary community in eleventh-century England', in E. M. Tyler (ed.), *Conceptualising Multilingualism in Medieval England, 800–1250* (Turnhout, 2011), pp. 197–215.

—— *Viking Age Yorkshire* (Pickering, 2014).

Tracy, Larissa, *Torture and Brutality in Medieval Literature: Negotiations of National Identity* (Cambridge, 2012).

Trafford, Simon, 'Ethnicity, migration theory, and the historiography of the Scandinavian settlement of England', in Dawn M. Hadley and Julian D. Richards (eds), *Cultures in Contact: Scandinavian Settlement in England in the Ninth and Tenth Centuries* (Turnhout, 2000), pp. 17–39.

Treharne, Elaine M., 'Romanticizing the past in the Middle English *Athelston*', *Review of English Studies* 50 (1999), pp. 1–21.

—— *Living Through Conquest: The Politics of Early English, 1020–1220* (Oxford, 2012).

Turville-Petre, Thorlac, '*Havelok* and the history of the nation', in Carol M. Meale (ed.), *Readings in Medieval English Romance* (Cambridge, 1994), pp. 121–34.

—— *England the Nation: Language, Literature and National Identity, 1290–1340* (Oxford, 1996).

—— 'Representations of the Danelaw in Middle English literature', in James Graham-Campbell, Michael Hall, Judith Jesch and David N. Parsons (eds), *Vikings and the Danelaw* (Oxford, 2001), pp. 345–55.

Tweddle, Dominic, et al. (eds), *Corpus of Anglo-Saxon Stone Sculpture Volume IV: South-East England* (Oxford, 1995).

Tyler, Elizabeth M., 'Fictions of family: The *Encomium Emmae Reginae* and Virgil's *Aeneid*,' *Viator* 36 (2005), pp. 149–79.

—— 'Talking about history in eleventh-century England: the *Encomium Emmae Reginae* and the court of Harthacnut', *Early Medieval Europe* 13 (2005), pp. 359–83.

de Vries, Jan, 'Die Entwicklung der Sage von den Lodbrokssöhnen in den historischen Quellen', *Arkiv för nordisk filologi* 44 (1928), pp. 117–63.

Wareham, Andrew, 'Saint Oswald's family and kin', in Nicholas Brooks and Catherine Cubitt (eds), *St Oswald of Worcester: Life and Influence* (London, 1996), pp. 46–63.

Watkins, Carl, 'The cult of Earl Waltheof at Crowland', *Hagiographica* III (1996), pp. 95–111.

Watts, Donald, *Dictionary of Plant Lore* (Boston, 2007).

Weiss, Judith, 'Thomas and the Earl: literary and historical contexts for the *Romance of Horn*', in Rosalind Field (ed.), *Tradition and Transformation in Medieval Romance* (Woodbridge, 1999), pp. 1–13.

—— 'Insular beginnings: Anglo-Norman romance', in Corinne Saunders (ed.), *A Companion to Romance: From Classical to Contemporary* (Oxford, 2004), pp. 26–44.

—— '*Gui de Warewic* at home and abroad: a hero for Europe', in Alison Wiggins and Rosalind Field (eds), *Guy of Warwick: Icon and Ancestor* (Cambridge, 2007), pp. 1–11.

Westwood, Jennifer, *Albion: A Guide to Legendary Britain* (London, 1987).

—— 'The Rollright Stones, Part 1: The Danes', *3rd Stone* 38 (2000), pp. 6–10.

Westwood, Jennifer and Jacqueline Simpson, *The Lore of the Land: A Guide to England's Legends, from Spring-Heeled Jack to the Witches of Warboys* (London, 2005).

Whistler, C. W., 'Brunanburh and Vinheith in Ingulf's Chronicle and Egil's Saga', *Saga-Book of the Viking Society* VI (1908–9), pp. 59–67.

Whitbread, L., 'St Ragner of Northampton', *Notes and Queries* CXCV (November 1950), pp. 511–12.

Whitelock, Dorothy, 'The conversion of the Eastern Danelaw', *Saga-Book of the Viking Society* XII (1937–45), pp. 159–76.

—— 'Scandinavian personal names in the *Liber Vitae* of Thorney Abbey', *Saga-Book of the Viking Society* XII (1937–45), pp. 127–53.

—— 'The dealings of the kings of England with Northumbria in the tenth and eleventh centuries', in Peter Clemoes (ed.), *The Anglo-Saxons: Studies in Some Aspects of their History and Culture, Presented to Bruce Dickins* (London, 1959), pp. 70–88.

—— 'Fact and fiction in the legend of St Edmund', *Proceedings of the Suffolk Institute of Archaeology* 31 (1969), pp. 217–33.

Wiggins, Alison, 'The manuscripts and texts of the Middle English *Guy of Warwick*', in Alison Wiggins and Rosalind Field (eds), *Guy of Warwick: Icon and Ancestor* (Cambridge, 2007), pp. 61–80.

Williams, Ann, *The English and the Norman Conquest* (Woodbridge, 1995).

—— *Æthelred the Unready: The Ill-Counselled King* (London, 2003).

Williams, John H., 'From "palace" to "town": Northampton and urban origins', *Anglo-Saxon England* 13 (1984), pp. 113–36.

Williams, Howard M. R., 'Placing the dead: investigating the location of wealthy barrow burials in seventh-century England', in Martin Rundkvist (ed.), *Grave Matters: Eight Studies of First Millennium AD Burials in Crimea, England, and Southern Scandinavia* (Oxford, 1999), pp. 57–86.

—— *Death and Memory in Early Medieval Britain* (Cambridge, 2006).

Wilson, David M. and Ole Klindt-Jensen, *Viking Art* (London, 1980).

Wilson, R. M., *The Lost Literature of Medieval England* (London, 1952).

Wood, Michael, 'The making of King Aethelstan's empire: an English Charlemagne?' in Patrick Wormald, Donald Bullough and Roger Collins (eds), *Ideal and Reality in Frankish and Anglo-Saxon Society: Studies Presented to J. M. Wallace-Hadrill* (Oxford, 1983), pp. 250–72.

Woolf, Daniel, 'Of Danes and giants: popular beliefs about the past in early modern England', *Dalhousie Review* 71 (1991), pp. 166–209.

—— *The Social Circulation of the Past: English Historical Culture, 1500–1730* (Oxford, 2003).

Wright, C. E., *The Cultivation of Saga in Anglo-Saxon England* (Edinburgh, 1939).

Yarrow, Simon, *Saints and Their Communities: Miracle Stories in Twelfth-Century England* (Oxford, 2006).

Yorke, Barbara, *Wessex in the Early Middle Ages* (London and New York, 1995).

Zatta, Jane, 'Gaimar's rebels: outlaw heroes and the creation of authority in twelfth-century England', *Essays in Medieval Studies* 16 (1999), pp. 27–40.

INDEX